BEST PLACES®
SEATTLE COOKBOOK

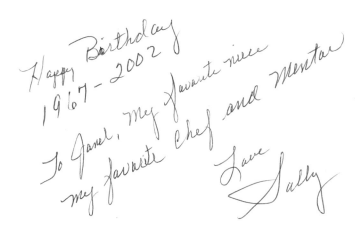

Happy Birthday
1967 - 2002

To Janel, My favorite niece
my favorite chef and Mentor

Love
Sally

BEST PLACES®
SEATTLE COOKBOOK

★

Recipes
from the City's
Outstanding
Restaurants
and Bars

CYNTHIA C. NIMS & KATHY CASEY

SASQUATCH BOOKS
SEATTLE

Printed in Canada
Distributed in Canada by Raincoast Books Ltd.
07 06 05 04 03 02 01   5 4 3 2 1

Cover and interior design: Karen Schober
Cover photograph: Rick Dahms
Interior illustrations: Brian Owada
Composition: Justine Matthies

Library of Congress Cataloging in Publication Data

Nims, Cynthia C.
Best places Seattle cookbook : recipes from the city's outstanding restaurants and bars /
Cynthia Nims and Kathy Casey.
p. cm.
Includes index.
ISBN 1-57061-261-7
1. Cookery, American. 2. Cookery—Washington (State)—Seattle.
3. Restaurants—Washington (State)—Seattle. I. Casey, Kathy. II. Title.

TX715 .N6832 2001
641.59797'772—dc21

Sasquatch Books
615 Second Avenue
Seattle, Washington 98104
(206)467-4300
books@SasquatchBooks.com
www.SasquatchBooks.com

CONTENTS

Recipe List vii

Acknowledgments xi

Introduction xii

General Recipe Notes xv

Appetizers 1

Clams and Mussels 7

Wood Cookery 19

Oysters 30

Artisan-Baked Bread 47

Pacific Rim and Asian Influences 51

Soups, Salads & Sides 53

Dungeness Crab—Are You a Picker or a Piler? 57

Stinging Nettles 67

Herbs—From Backyards to Menus 77

Asparagus—Herald of Spring 83

Farmers' Markets, P-Patches, and Garden Gourmets 87

Wonderful Winter Squash 95

Main Dishes 99

City Grilling 105

Eastern Washington 114

Cherries 123

Salmon 132

Comfort Foods and Sacred Cows 142

Wild Mushrooms 150

Chefs' Secrets 162

Peppers 170

Desserts 177

Northwest Fall Fruits—Pears and Apples 183

Local Cheesemakers 191

Putting Foods Up 200

Beautiful Berries 211

Drinks 221

Cocktails 230

Appendix: Restaurants & Bars 243

Index 251

RECIPE LIST

Appetizers

Ahi Tuna Tartare 24

Artichoke Ramekins .38

Asian Barbecue Beef Triangles with a
    Tropical Fruit Salsa 10

Bahia Mussels 17

Baked Oysters with Beurre Blanc 28

Cataplana Mussels 9

Cedar Plank–Roasted Crab-Stuffed
    Mushrooms 18

Creole Shrimp with Two Salsas 22

Four-Onion Tart 20

Geoduck Batayaki .36

Herb-Infused Olives .3

Jalapeño Mussels 49

Kippered Salmon and Asparagus
    Bread Pudding .46

Muhammara 26

Pan-Fried Mussels on Rosemary Skewers 32

Pan-Seared Steelhead with Black
    Bean Vinaigrette 14

Pâté de Campagne 34

Razor Clams with Brown Butter and
    Salsify Chips 6

Scallop and Shrimp Seviche with Cilantro Oil . . .12

Spicy Vegetable Fritters 16

Squid in Their Own Ink 44

Steamed Clams 39

Tequila-Cured Gravlax Salmon 40

Tuscan White Bean and Rosemary Spread 27

Vietnamese Spring Rolls 50

Walla Walla Onion Pancakes with
    Smoked Trout Rémoulade 4

Wild Mushroom Terrine with Goat Cheese Caillé and
    Berry Vinaigrette 42

Soups, Salads & Sides

Avocado Carpaccio with Radish
    and Herb Salad 76

Caesar for Two 79

Cameo Apple Salad with Treviso, Arugula, Oregon
    Blue Cheese, and Cider Vinaigrette 74

Chilled Cucumber Soup with Smoked
    Sturgeon and Curry Oil 64

Corn Chowder with Dungeness Crab 56

Dungeness Crab with Red Radishes and
    Braeburn Apples 84

Fall Pumpkin and Squash Bisque 69

Fresh Roasted Corn with Lime and Chile 93

Granny Smith Apple Bread Pudding 89

Gratin de Chou-fleur (Cauliflower Gratin) 90

Heirloom Tomato Salad with Rode Esterling
    Potatoes and Tapenade 86

Herb Roasted Chicken and Bread Salad 70

Hungarian Mushroom Soup 62

Kale and Tomato Gratin 97

Local Garden Greens with Asian Pears
    and Five-Spice Glazed Walnuts 72

Nettle Soup 66

Orange and Fennel Salad with Sicilian
    Olives and Pecorino Romano Shavings 75

Red Kuri Squash and Pear Timbales 94

Rice Pulao 98

Roasted Pepper and Grilled Asparagus Salad . .82

Sausage and Lentil Soup 63

Savory Nectarine and Shiso Soup 59

Seafood Chowder 68

Seattle Cioppino .60

Sichuan Green Beans 92

Smoked Turkey, Brown Rice, and Vegetable
  Salad in Creamy Balsamic-Soy Vinaigrette . .80

Swiss Leek, Oat, and Smoked Chicken Soup . . .58

Tom Kah Gai 55

Yakima Cherry, Walla Walla Sweet Onion, and Basil
  Salad with Balsamic Vinaigrette 85

Main Dishes

Alaskan Halibut with Tagliatelle of Vegetables,
  Beurre Blanc, and American Caviar 166

Alder-Barbecued King Salmon with
  Fennel and Mint 101

"Blue Plate Special" Lingcod with Sour Cream,
  Red Onions, and Fresh Dill 159

Bruschetta Steak Sandwiches 108

Coconut Curried Lamb Shanks 128

Crab Cakes with Ancho Chile Mayonnaise . . .102

Cumin-Seared Columbia River Sturgeon 144

Enchiladas en Salsa Suiza 126

Grilled Ahi in Licorice Root "Tea" with
  Braised Red Cabbage 120

Grilled Pork with Pumpkin Poblano Tamales and
  Green Chile Sauce 168

Grilled Salmon with Lentils and Brown Butter
  Balsamic Vinaigrette 112

Kasu Black Cod .174

Lamb Chops with Arugula Pesto 158

Lemongrass Rubbed Filet with Braised Short Ribs
  and Spicy Red Pepper Sauce 146

Malai Kebab 104

Morel Mushroom Ravioli with Chanterelle
  Mushroom Ragout 148

Orcas Rack of Lamb with Spring Pea
  Flan and Morels 172

Orecchiette with Fall Vegetables 118

Paella 156

Pan-Fried Oysters with Jack Daniel's Sauce . . .125

Pan-Seared Alaskan Cod with Green Beans,
  Niçoise Olives, and Smoked Paprika 154

Pan-Seared Duck Breast with Muscadet
  Wine Sauce 116

Plig King Tofu 107

Pork Tenderloin with Bing Cherries and Mint . .122

Roasted Chicken with Caramelized
  Garlic and Sage 143

Salmon con Tamarindo 130

Saucisse de Toulouse 140

Smothered Game Hens 164

Spaghetti con le Sarde (Spaghetti with
  Sardines) 110

Spicy Polenta with Braised Fennel, Olives,
  and Goat Cheese 136

Steak Teriyaki 134

Steamed King Salmon on Hungarian
  Paprika Sauerkraut 153

Thai Basil–Seared Mahimahi with Red
  Curry Lobster Essence 160

Thiebu Djen (Parsley-Stuffed Halibut with
  Vegetables and Rice) 138

Yassa au Poulet (Chicken in Onion-
  Mustard Sauce) 171

Desserts

Apricot, Rose, and Saffron Tart 196

Baked Hawaii 214

Bananas Foster .188

Bing Cherry Cake 185

Chocolate Chai Tea Soufflé Cake 202

Chocolate Hazelnut Kisses 186

Cinnamon Ice Cream 205

Earl Grey Sorbet 213

Flan with Caramelo Drizzle 206

Fresh Blackberry Tart 180

Gateau de Riz Façon Grand-Mère

   (Old-Fashioned Rice Pudding) 208

Hawaiian-Style Coconut Cake 194

Honey-Chèvre Cheesecake with

   Blueberry-Port Sauce 198

Lavender-Honey Ice Cream 193

Lemon Rosemary Biscotti 218

Nectarine Blackberry Crisp 204

Old Chatham Camembert with Pear and

   Dried Cherry Chutney 190

Pear and Rose Hip Sorbet 182

Pinchineta (Almond Tart) 216

Raspberry and Peach Shortcakes with

   Honey Whipped Cream 210

Spoon Cheesecake 179

Drinks

Absolut Mandarin Martini 223

Cadillac Margarita 224

Classic Martini .235

Elsie's Bloody Mary 226

Hawaiian Punch 228

Honey Peach Julep 232

Italian Caramel Apple 234

Mojito 237

The Paradigm Shift 241

The Priestess 227

Rain City Punch 236

Rosemary Lemonade 238

Silver Rocket 229

Strawberry Spice and Everything Nice 225

Ultraviolet Martini 239

Watermelon Kazi 240

Zoë Cocktail 233

ACKNOWLEDGMENTS

First and foremost, I would like to thank
the many Seattle-area chefs, bartenders, and restaurateurs who
not only contributed their recipes and stories, but endured my special
requests and repeat phone calls to help hone this collection to best represent
Seattle's restaurant scene in tasty style. They are the reason that
Seattle has become such a distinctive food city and why a job like mine
is so exhilarating. Kristine Britton jumped right in with both feet to help
collect and test these recipes, for which I'm very grateful. I also must thank
other recipe testers, who include my beautiful sister Barbara Nims, Ed
Silver, Mike Amend, Jeff Ashley, Susan Volland, and Tim and Katherine
Kehrli. Thanks, too, to Kathy Casey for being such a great friend and
cohort, on this project as with so many other things. And finally,
as always, thanks to Bob, who lights my life and
whatever path it takes me down.

—CYNTHIA NIMS

I would like to thank John Casey, most loving
and wonderful husband; Ann Manly for her years of invaluable
assistance with research editing and fact-checking; Joani McGowen
for her prized support in ways too numerous to list; and
Charlotte Rudge, sous chef par excellence.

—KATHY CASEY

INTRODUCTION

Welcome to the city. For some time now, the Northwest region has been getting a lot of attention in cookbooks, but few yet have captured the distinctive essence of dining in the city of Seattle. This cookbook brings together recipes from 65 restaurants in the Seattle area, which together create an interesting snapshot of the contemporary dining scene in the Emerald City. Reflecting the heritage of Northwest cuisine, the recipes are chock full of regional ingredients such as Bing cherries, wild mushrooms, salmon, crab, pears, apples, berries, mussels, you name it. But they go well beyond the traditional regional boundaries to include a vast array of ingredients and cooking styles, representing global influences that have become common in most large cities today.

The 125 recipes that follow were collected from restaurants featured in the 8th edition of the *Best Places Seattle* guidebook, though we slipped in a few more recent openings that are certain to show up in the next edition: Waterfront on Pier 70, Restaurant Zoë in Belltown, Brasa downtown, and Le Pichet near the Pike Place Market, to name a few. These restaurants help represent the city's culinary landscape at its most up-to-date. Woven among the recipes, you'll find essays that help define the building blocks of Seattle's self-styled "cuisine," from ingredients such as oysters, cheese, and fall fruit, to broader themes such as grilling, Asian influences, and the city's lively farmers' markets.

The urban scene of a city like Seattle is one that is diverse, vibrant, and eclectic. This is echoed in recipes such as Yassa au Poulet from the Senegalese restaurant Afrikando, Sichuan Green Beans from Wild Ginger, Squid in Their Own Ink from the Basque taverna Harvest Vine, butter-sautéed Geoduck Batayaki from Nishino, and Salmon con Tamarindo from El Camino.

But much of what draws us out to eat in Seattle is casual, comforting fare from favorite spots around town. You'll find recipes such as Nectarine Blackberry Crisp from Anthony's, Corn Chowder with Dungeness Crab from Macrina Bakery and Café, Alder-Barbecued King Salmon with Fennel and Mint from Ivar's Salmon House, Lemon Rosemary Biscotti from the Still Life in Fremont Coffeehouse, and the deliciously classic Elsie's Bloody Mary from Hattie's Hat—recipes that represent the more homey side of the city's restaurants.

Seattle is a still-growing city. While construction cranes bring more high-rises to downtown, traffic gridlock becomes an everyday thing, and the population continues to swell, the restaurant scene keeps pace by becoming more dynamic and inspiring with each passing year. Chefs and restaurateurs bring to this city increasingly distinctive dining experiences, blending flavors from close to home with those from far and wide. Whether you're a local recreating dishes from your favorite restaurants or a visitor wanting to savor Seattle in your kitchen elsewhere, we hope you'll enjoy this taste of Seattle.

— CYNTHIA NIMS AND KATHY CASEY

General Recipe Notes

Unless otherwise specified in individual recipes:

■ Butter is unsalted.

■ Eggs are large.

■ Onions are yellow.

■ Milk is whole milk; 2% could be used, but don't use skim—the lack of butterfat may have an adverse effect on the results of the recipe.

■ Herbs are fresh; in general, if using a dried herb in place of a fresh herb you will want to use less, because the flavor of the dried herb is more concentrated.

■ Salt is your choice, most chefs prefer kosher and/or sea salt and often use coarsely ground salt rather than fine salt; you'd be surprised the difference in flavor and texture from one salt to the next; use what you have on hand, but you might want to consider adding kosher or sea salt to your cupboard if it's not already there.

■ "Season to taste" doesn't always mean that you will actually be tasting at the time that you season; in general, you know if you prefer foods that are light on salt, or generously peppered; when you're seasoning something that you don't want to taste (as a custard prior to baking), use your seasoning preference as a guideline.

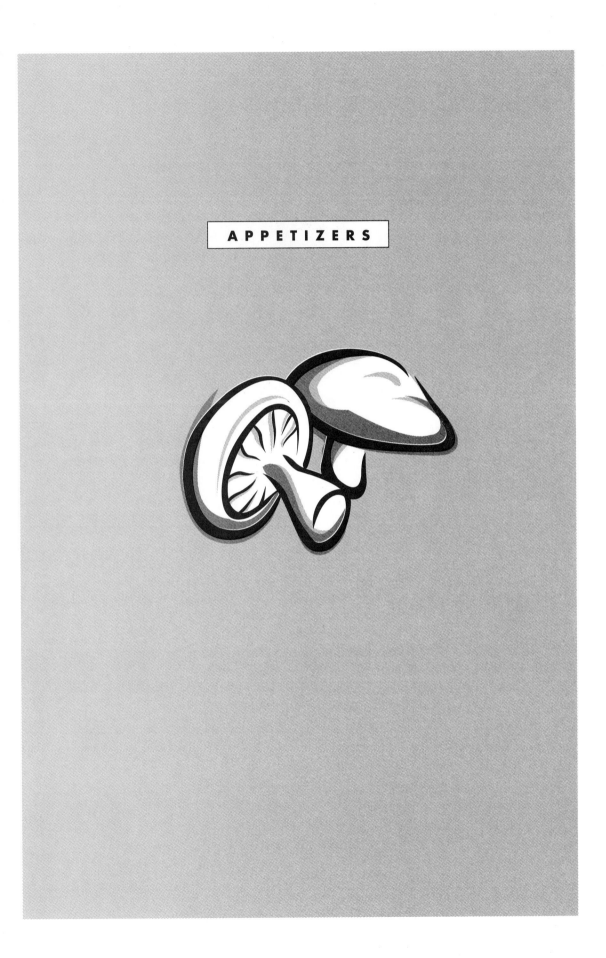

APPETIZERS

Herb-Infused Olives

Boat Street Café

At Boat Street Café, a few of these herbed olives arrive in the dish of olive oil
that accompanies the bread, and a full dish of the olives is available as an appetizer. Serve the
olives with bread (to dip in their marinating oil, which is delicious) or alone. The oil will
turn opaque in the cold of the refrigerator, but it will clear up as it
returns to room temperature before serving.

The olives will have some herbal flavor after 24 hours and more after a few days.
With time, the spiciness from the red pepper flakes develops, too. You could also use
picholine or other good-quality olives, but Niçoise are the best match with this
particular combination of seasonings.

1 ½ cups olive oil	2 teaspoons grated lemon or orange zest
4 cloves garlic, thinly sliced	2 bay leaves
2 tablespoons rosemary leaves	½ teaspoon freshly ground black pepper
1 tablespoon fennel seeds	¼ teaspoon coarse salt
2 teaspoons dried red pepper flakes	1 pound Niçoise olives

HEAT THE OIL in a small saucepan over medium heat until gently warmed, 2 to 3 minutes.
Take the pan from the heat and add the garlic, rosemary, fennel seeds, red pepper flakes, zest,
bay leaves, pepper, and salt; stir until well combined.

PUT THE OLIVES in a medium heatproof bowl and pour the marinade over them. Let sit until
the oil cools to room temperature, then cover the bowl and store in the refrigerator until ready
to serve, at least 1 day. Allow the olives to come back to room temperature before serving.

Makes about 3 cups

Walla Walla Onion Pancakes
with *Smoked Trout Rémoulade*

Chez Shea

Once you've tasted these Walla Walla onion pancakes, you might be tempted to whip them up for breakfast one day. Their touch of sweetness plays beautifully with the rich rémoulade sauce, a freshly made mayonnaise enriched with smoked trout, capers, and shallot. Smoked salmon can be used in place of the smoked trout, if you prefer.

1 head frisée, rinsed, tough outer leaves trimmed, tender leaves separated	¼ cup olive oil
Juice of 1 lemon	1 green onion, white and pale green parts only, cut into julienne strips, for garnish

SMOKED TROUT RÉMOULADE

1 egg yolk	4 ounces smoked trout, skin and bones removed
2 teaspoons freshly squeezed lemon juice	½ shallot, finely chopped
½ teaspoon Dijon mustard	1 tablespoon capers, chopped
½ cup olive oil	Salt and freshly ground black pepper

WALLA WALLA ONION PANCAKES

3 tablespoons unsalted butter, more if needed	¼ teaspoon salt
½ cup finely diced Walla Walla Sweet onion	¾ cup milk
¾ cup all-purpose flour	1 egg
1 teaspoon baking powder	

FOR THE RÉMOULADE, combine the egg yolk, lemon juice, and mustard in a food processor and pulse until smooth and well blended. With the blades running, begin adding the oil, a few drops at a time, until an emulsion begins to form. Continue adding the oil in a thin stream to form a thick mayonnaise. Add the smoked trout, shallot, and capers and pulse once or twice to blend (you want to maintain some chunky texture). Season to taste with salt and pepper, adding more lemon juice, mustard, or capers to taste as well. Transfer the rémoulade to a medium bowl and refrigerate, covered, until ready to serve.

FOR THE PANCAKES, melt 2 tablespoons of the butter in a medium skillet over medium heat. Add the onion and sauté until it just begins to soften but not brown, 3 to 5 minutes. Set aside to cool. Combine the flour, baking powder, and salt in a medium bowl and stir to mix, making a well in the center. In a separate bowl, whisk together the milk and egg. Add this mixture to the well in the dry ingredients and stir gently, gradually drawing flour into the center from the outer edges, just until the batter is blended. Add the cooled onion and all the butter from the skillet and stir to mix.

MELT THE REMAINING 1 TABLESPOON BUTTER over medium heat in a large skillet, preferably nonstick. Spoon about ¼ cup of the batter into the skillet to form each pancake. Do not crowd the pan. Cook until bubbles appear on the surface and pop, 1 to 2 minutes, then turn the pancakes over and continue to cook until browned on the bottom, about 2 minutes longer. Transfer the pancakes to a plate and continue with the remaining batter, adding more butter to the skillet as needed. You should have 8 pancakes. Keep warm.

PUT THE FRISÉE in a large bowl. In a small bowl, combine the lemon juice with a pinch each of salt and pepper. Whisk in the olive oil, then drizzle the dressing over the frisée and toss to coat.

ARRANGE THE DRESSED FRISÉE in the center of individual salad plates. Place 2 pancakes on top or to the side of the frisée. Top each pair of pancakes with a generous dollop of the rémoulade, garnish with the julienned green onion, and serve.

Makes 4 servings

Razor Clams with Brown Butter and Salsify Chips

Etta's Seafood

Properly cooked, razor clams are tender and full of flavor, but they are easy to overcook, which makes them as tough as rubber bands. This method calls for searing the clams very briefly in a super-hot pan, here dressed up with a touch of vinegar to complement their sweetness. Razor clams are time-consuming to shuck and clean, so look for them in their already-cleaned state. You're on your own if you dig the clams yourself.

Salsify, a nutty-flavored root vegetable popular in Europe, isn't particularly exotic but it can nonetheless be quite hard to find. Parsnips are a more-available alternative.

4 razor clams, shucked and cleaned (about 8 ounces shucked clams)	2 tablespoons unsalted butter
1 tablespoon peanut or vegetable oil	2 tablespoons good-quality red wine vinegar
	1 tablespoon minced chives, for garnish

SALSIFY CHIPS

Peanut or vegetable oil, for frying
2 salsify roots or small parsnips
Salt and freshly ground black pepper

FOR THE SALSIFY CHIPS, pour oil to a depth of 3 to 4 inches into a deep, heavy saucepan and heat over medium-high heat to a temperature of 350°F. (The oil should come no more than halfway up the sides of the pan.) While the oil is heating, prepare the salsify.

PEEL THE SALSIFY ROOT with a vegetable peeler. Discard the peel and continue to use the peeler to make long, thin strips of salsify. (If you come to a tough central core, particularly with parsnip, discard the rest.) To test the temperature of the oil, add a strip of salsify; the oil is hot enough if it bubbles gently as the salsify is added. Fry the salsify strips, in batches, until light brown, about 1 minute, turning gently as needed to ensure they fry evenly. Scoop out the chips with a slotted spoon and drain on paper towels; season to taste with salt and pepper. Continue with the remaining salsify, allowing the oil to reheat between batches as needed.

PAT THE RAZOR CLAMS DRY with paper towels and season to taste with salt and pepper. Heat the oil in a large skillet over high heat. When the oil is hot, carefully add the clams to the pan and cook for about 30 seconds, using a pair of tongs to push down on the clams so that they cook evenly. Turn the clams and continue cooking until they are firm and opaque, about

30 seconds longer. Take the skillet from the heat and transfer the clams to a warmed plate along with any juice they released in the skillet.

ADD THE BUTTER to the skillet and return it to medium-high heat. Melt the butter and continue to cook, gently swirling the skillet to prevent burning, until the butter is a golden brown and has a nutty aroma, 2 to 3 minutes. Carefully add the vinegar and any juice from the clams. (Be careful because the vinegar will bubble up and give off vapors that can sting your eyes; turn your head away slightly.) Swirl the pan gently to mix. Remove the butter sauce from the heat and season to taste with salt and pepper. Add the clams and stir to coat them with the sauce.

DIVIDE THE SALSIFY CHIPS between individual warmed plates, and lay 2 clams over each mound of chips. Pour the sauce from the pan over the clams, sprinkle with chives, and serve.

Makes 2 servings

Clams and Mussels

Clam digging has always been a favorite Northwest pastime, with native littlenecks and black-striped Manilas being the most popular steamers. If you live by the shore, then you almost surely have gone clam digging at some time or another.

Clams are a versatile carrier of flavors. Some people prefer them steamed very simply, just the shellfish and the broth, with a little splash of local white wine and a pinch of garlic imparting their flavors to each other. But clams are also delicious in more exotic preparations. Seattle diners have been the beneficiaries of some of the wonderful things Asian cuisines do with shellfish—such as steamed clams with coconut milk, lemongrass, and yellow Thai curry.

The Northwest does have its share of curiously strange shellfish species. The giant geoduck clam is known to get up to 9 pounds, with the preferred harvest weight being 2 pounds. In Puget Sound it lives up to an average of 40 years—with a record age of 135 years—in marine mud at depths of 4 to 6 feet. Named after an Indian word meaning "dig deep," this giant clam is even the mascot of The Evergreen State College. And do these bivalves ever bring big-eyed stares and looks of awe from tourists at Seattle's Pike Place Market, where the clams' long hose-like necks hang over a foot down the sides of iced barrels.

Geoduck meat is often chopped for flavorful chowders, but the Chinese community probably deals with this giant clam the best, slicing it thinly and quickly poaching or stir-frying it with black beans, scallions, and garlic. Slightly crunchy and sweet-tasting, thin, raw slices of this king clam appear on sushi menus as *mirugai*. A mouth-watering, fusion treatment is found at Nishino, where Geoduck Batayaki (page 36) is sautéed in butter with shiitake mushrooms and blanched asparagus and seasoned with soy sauce and sake. ➤

Occasionally, when you're really lucky, you'll see delicate razor clams on Seattle menus. Prepare these simply by dipping them in egg and bread crumbs and lightly sautéing in butter, then finish with a quick squeeze of lemon and freshly chopped parsley. They need nothing else!

In the 1970s mussels were thought of as those weird blue things that grew off rocks and pilings. Considered too much trouble to harvest, these mollusks are now all the rage. Prepared similarly to steamer clams, mussels need to be debearded (the fuzzy part that attaches them to rocks and pilings is pulled off), rinsed, and scrubbed clean. Take your inspiration from the French love of aromatic herbs and earthy roots, and meld the delicate brininess of this shellfish with rich cream, slivers of leek, and fresh tarragon leaves for an extraordinary taste experience. Or steam them simply, like the Cataplana Mussels (page 9) served at Brasa, with a little wine, garlic, and fresh herbs, letting their own fresh flavors come through.

Mussels also pair well with more assertive flavors. In Fandango's appetizer, Bahia Mussels (page 17), they are cooked in a bold purée of pasilla chiles and tomatoes.

A popular feature of steaming mussels and clams is that they are fast, fast, fast—they should be steamed only until their shells pop open and the meat is just plumped. If overcooked, they will be tough. And there's nothing better than sticking a big hunk of crusty, local artisan-baked bread into the rich and garlicky broth to soak up all that goodness.

A big bowl of steamed shellfish makes a great starter for a group meal. It's fun, too, when eating mussels, to use an empty shell as a natural utensil to pick the mussel meat up and pop it into your mouth. But if you have major shellfish lovers there, you'd better be quick.

—KC

Cataplana Mussels

Brasa

The name for this dish is derived from the Portuguese lidded pan in which
it is prepared. A *cataplana* is a two-piece domed metal (often tin-lined copper) casserole
that clips tightly closed for cooking, holding in all the flavorful juices and aromas. At Brasa,
chef Tamara Murphy roasts the mussels in her super-hot wood-fired oven. The pan is opened
at the table and the lid becomes a bowl for discarded shells. An ovenproof skillet with a
tight-fitting lid is a workable substitute.

Chervil is a wonderful herb that can unfortunately be hard to find in stores.
It is easy to grow at home, however, if you have an herb garden or a sunny windowsill.
Its delicate parsleylike leaves have a subtle anise flavor and are a classic component of
fines herbes. If you can't find chervil, increase the parsley to 2 tablespoons.

2 pounds mussels, scrubbed and debearded	1 tablespoon coarsely chopped chives
3 shallots, thinly sliced	1 tablespoon minced chervil
Juice of 2 lemons	1 tablespoon minced tarragon
¼ cup dry white wine	1 tablespoon minced flat-leaf (Italian) parsley
2 tablespoons unsalted butter, cut into pieces	1 teaspoon minced garlic

PREHEAT THE OVEN to 500°F.

PUT THE MUSSELS in the bottom of a medium cataplana. Scatter the shallots over the top,
then drizzle on the lemon juice and white wine. Finally, add the butter, herbs, and garlic, distributing them evenly over the top. Toss the ingredients gently, then clip on the lid.

BAKE UNTIL THE MUSSELS HAVE OPENED, about 15 minutes. Carefully open the lid and
serve right away, discarding any mussels that failed to open. Use the empty half of the cataplana for discarded shells.

Makes 2 to 4 servings

Asian Barbecue Beef Triangles
with a Tropical Fruit Salsa

Roy's

You will need to set aside a few hours to make this recipe, but the results are worth the effort. The flaky, crisp phyllo triangles are stuffed with a richly flavored beef-and-vegetable mixture scented with ginger, hoisin, garlic, and other Asian flavors, and a fresh fruit salsa alongside makes a wonderful complement. The dish is a perfect addition to your next dinner party or elegant cocktail buffet.

The ribs used for the pastry filling are braised for a couple of hours with aromatic vegetables, which leaves a flavorful broth that would be an ideal base for a stew or soup.

3 pounds beef short ribs	3 ounces shiitake mushrooms, wiped clean,
2 quarts beef stock, preferably homemade	stemmed, and finely chopped
1 cup chopped yellow onion	2 heads baby bok choy, trimmed and
½ cup chopped celery	finely chopped
½ cup chopped carrot	¾ cup finely chopped onion, preferably
2 bay leaves	Walla Walla Sweet
1 teaspoon black peppercorns	Salt and freshly ground black pepper
2 tablespoons olive oil	1 package (1 pound) phyllo dough (18 sheets)
1 teaspoon minced garlic	½ cup unsalted butter, melted
1 teaspoon minced or grated ginger	

ASIAN BARBECUE SAUCE

¼ cup hoisin sauce	1½ teaspoons minced green onion
1 tablespoon soy sauce	1 teaspoon minced garlic
1 tablespoon *sambal oelek* or other	1 teaspoon minced or grated ginger
hot chile sauce	1 teaspoon water
1 tablespoon sugar	

TROPICAL FRUIT SALSA

1 tablespoon sesame seeds	2 tablespoons sweet chile sauce
1 ripe mango, peeled, pitted, and finely diced	1 tablespoon seasoned rice wine vinegar
1 ripe papaya, peeled, seeded, and finely diced	1 tablespoon minced cilantro
½ cup finely diced red bell pepper	1 teaspoon sesame oil
½ cup finely diced green bell pepper	

PLACE THE SHORT RIBS in a Dutch oven or other large, deep pot and pour in the beef stock. If necessary, add some water so that the liquid just covers the ribs. Add the yellow onion, celery, carrot, bay leaves, and peppercorns. Bring to a boil over high heat and boil for 5 minutes. Reduce the heat to medium-low and simmer until the meat is very tender, about 1½ hours. As needed, add hot water to the pot to keep the ribs covered while they simmer.

WHILE THE RIBS ARE COOKING, prepare the Asian barbecue sauce. Combine the hoisin sauce, soy sauce, hot chile sauce, sugar, green onion, garlic, and ginger in a small bowl and stir to mix. Add the water and stir to form a smooth consistency; set aside.

FOR THE SALSA, put the sesame seeds in a small, heavy skillet and toast over medium heat, shaking the skillet often, until the seeds are lightly browned and aromatic, 3 to 5 minutes; set aside to cool. Combine the mango, papaya, bell peppers, sweet chile sauce, vinegar, toasted sesame seeds, cilantro, and sesame oil in a medium bowl and stir to mix well. Cover and refrigerate until ready to serve.

WHEN THE RIBS ARE COOKED, use tongs to transfer them to a colander in the sink to drain and cool. Pull the rib meat from the bones and finely dice the meat. (Strain and save the broth for another use, if you like.)

HEAT THE OLIVE OIL in large skillet over medium-high heat. Add the garlic and ginger and sauté until aromatic, about 30 seconds. Add the shiitake mushrooms, baby bok choy, and onion, and sauté until just tender and dry, 3 to 5 minutes. Add the diced beef and the barbecue sauce and stir to mix evenly. Season to taste with salt and pepper and set aside to cool completely.

PREHEAT THE OVEN to 350°F.

SET THE PHYLLO SHEETS on a cutting board, with the long side facing you, and use a large knife to cut the sheets in half crosswise (vertically). Lift off 1 half-sheet and set it on the work surface with the shorter side facing you; lay a kitchen towel over the remaining dough sheets to prevent them from drying out. Lightly brush the half-sheet of phyllo with melted butter. Set 1 tablespoon of the beef filling about 2 inches from the bottom of the strip, in the center. Fold the lower edge up over the filling, then fold each long side inward to the center, overlapping slightly. Fold the filled pocket upward at an angle, then continue folding the filling away from you and at an angle (as you would fold a flag) to form a triangular pillow. Brush the top lightly with melted butter and set the triangle, seam side down, on a baking sheet. Repeat until all the filling and phyllo are used, using a second baking sheet if necessary.

BAKE THE BEEF TRIANGLES until browned and crisp, 12 to 15 minutes. Remove from the oven and transfer the baked triangles to a wire rack to cool. You should have about 36 triangles.

ARRANGE THE TRIANGLES on individual plates or on a serving platter. Add the tropical salsa alongside, for spooning onto the triangles as they are eaten.

Makes 12 servings

Scallop and Shrimp Seviche with Cilantro Oil

Restaurant Zoë

Seviche is often made just with lime juice, but this variation uses
equal parts lime juice and seasoned rice vinegar for a hint of Asian influence.
Keep in mind that even though the seafood will become opaque and firm from the acid of
the marinade, it is never technically cooked. If you have concerns about eating raw shellfish
(pregnant women, children, the elderly, and people with compromised immune systems are
advised not to eat raw seafood), lightly poach the seafood before adding it to the marinade.
You'll have more cilantro oil than needed for this recipe. The extra can be drizzled over
pan-fried shrimp or grilled fish, used in a vinaigrette, or served as a dip for bread.
Or, you can omit the cilantro oil.

Ask for "dry pack" scallops at the fish market. These are scallops that have not
been treated with sodium tripolyphosphate, an additive that keeps them plump by
soaking up excess water, making their flavor less intense.

½ English (seedless) cucumber, peeled and finely diced	8 ounces medium shrimp, peeled, deveined, and coarsely chopped
⅓ cup freshly squeezed lime juice	8 ounces sea scallops, cut horizontally into ¼-inch-thick slices
⅓ cup seasoned rice vinegar	
¼ cup finely diced red onion	1 tablespoon chopped cilantro
¼ teaspoon cayenne pepper	1 tablespoon chopped flat-leaf (Italian) parsley
	Corn chips, for serving

CILANTRO OIL

1 cup canola oil	¼ cup moderately packed flat-leaf (Italian) parsley leaves
¼ cup moderately packed cilantro leaves	¼ teaspoon salt

AVOCADO PURÉE

1 small, ripe avocado	2 tablespoons minced tomato (seeds removed)
2 teaspoons freshly squeezed lemon juice	½ teaspoon minced garlic
2 teaspoons freshly squeezed lime juice	Salt and freshly ground black pepper
2 tablespoons minced red onion	

FOR THE CILANTRO OIL, combine the oil, cilantro, parsley, and salt in a blender and purée until well blended, about 1 minute, scraping down the sides once or twice. Taste the oil for seasoning, adding more salt if needed. Transfer the cilantro oil to a squeeze bottle or small bowl and refrigerate until needed.

COMBINE THE CUCUMBER, lime juice, rice vinegar, onion, and cayenne in a large bowl and stir to mix. Add the shrimp and scallops and toss to mix evenly. Refrigerate for $1\frac{1}{2}$ to 2 hours to allow the flavors to blend, stirring once or twice.

SHORTLY BEFORE SERVING, prepare the avocado purée. Halve, pit, and peel the avocado, then coarsely chop it and put it in a medium bowl. With a potato masher or large whisk, mash the avocado until it is nearly smooth, adding the lemon and lime juices as you work (they help keep the avocado bright green). Stir in the onion, tomato, and garlic with salt and pepper to taste. Refrigerate, covered with plastic wrap, until ready to serve.

TO SERVE, drain off most of the marinating liquid from the seviche. Add the cilantro and the parsley, toss to mix evenly, and taste for seasoning, adding salt and pepper to taste. Arrange the seviche in a circle in the center of individual plates and top the seafood with a generous spoonful of the avocado purée. Drizzle a teaspoon or two of the cilantro oil around the seviche, add a small pile of corn chips to one side, and serve.

Makes 4 to 6 servings

Pan-Seared Steelhead with Black Bean Vinaigrette

Flying Fish

This Asian-inspired appetizer can also be served as a main course, doubling the portion sizes of fish to about six ounces per person. Nori is the name of the deep green, thin sheets of dried seaweed commonly used to wrap sushi rolls. Here, chef-owner Christine Keff juliennes the salty sheets to serve as a garnish, along with deep-fried julienned leek.

Steelhead is a rainbow trout that lives its life more like a salmon than a trout. Rather than spending its time exclusively in fresh water, steelhead swim out to salt water for much of their life, then return to fresh water to spawn. The flesh looks and tastes much like salmon, which makes it a great alternative if you can't find steelhead. Bet you didn't know that steelhead is Washington's official state fish!

4 steelhead fillet pieces (about 3 ounces each), skin and pin bones removed

2 heads baby bok choy

½ English (seedless) cucumber, peeled and thinly sliced

1 small or ½ large fennel bulb, trimmed, cored, and thinly sliced

1 tablespoon julienned pickled ginger

Peanut or canola oil, for frying

1 medium leek, white and pale green parts only, julienned

¼ cup julienned nori (optional)

FIVE-SPICE MARINADE

2 tablespoons sesame oil

½ teaspoon five-spice powder

½ teaspoon sugar

½ teaspoon salt

¼ teaspoon freshly ground black pepper

BLACK BEAN VINAIGRETTE

1 tablespoon Chinese fermented black beans

2 tablespoons minced shallot

2 tablespoons soy sauce

2 tablespoons mirin (sweet Japanese cooking wine)

2 tablespoons freshly squeezed lime juice

2 teaspoons minced or grated ginger

1 teaspoon sesame oil

¼ cup canola oil

¼ cup olive oil

FOR THE MARINADE, combine the sesame oil, five-spice powder, sugar, salt, and pepper in a shallow dish and stir to blend. Add the fish pieces, turning to coat them evenly with the marinade, cover, and refrigerate while preparing the rest of the dish.

FOR THE VINAIGRETTE, put the black beans in a small bowl, add warm water to cover, and set aside to soak for 15 minutes.

MEANWHILE, bring a medium saucepan of lightly salted water to a boil and prepare a medium bowl of ice water. Add the whole baby bok choy to the boiling water and blanch for 30 seconds, then drain well and put the bok choy in the ice water to cool thoroughly. When cold, drain the bok choy and pat dry on paper towels. Cut the bok choy into julienne strips, working crosswise and at a slight angle. Put it in a medium bowl with the cucumber, fennel, and pickled ginger. Set aside.

DRAIN AND RINSE the black beans, and pat them dry on paper towels. Then, to complete the vinaigrette, finely chop the beans and put them in a small bowl with the shallot, soy sauce, mirin, lime juice, ginger, and sesame oil. Whisk to blend, then slowly whisk in the canola and olive oils. Drizzle 1¼ cup of the vinaigrette over the vegetable mixture and toss to mix; set the vegetables and the rest of the vinaigrette aside.

FOR THE LEEK GARNISH, pour the peanut oil to a depth of 2 to 3 inches into a small, deep, heavy saucepan and heat over medium-high heat to 350°F. (The oil should come no more than halfway up the sides of the pan.) To test the temperature of the oil, add a piece of leek; the oil is hot enough if it bubbles gently as the leek is added. Fry the julienned leek, in batches, until light brown, about 1 minute. Scoop out the fried leek with a slotted spoon and drain on paper towels. Continue with the remaining leeks, allowing the oil to reheat between batches as needed.

HEAT 1 TABLESPOON PEANUT OIL in a medium skillet over medium-high heat. When the oil is hot, take the steelhead pieces from the marinade, allowing the excess marinade to drip off, and add them, fleshy side down, to the skillet. Pan-fry the steelhead until nicely browned, 2 to 3 minutes. Turn the fish over and continue cooking until just a bit of pink remains at the center, 2 to 4 minutes longer, depending on the thickness of the fish.

ARRANGE THE VEGETABLES on warmed individual plates and set the steelhead on top. Drizzle the remaining vinaigrette over and around the fish, and top the fish with the fried leeks and julienned nori (if using). Serve immediately.

Makes 4 servings

Spicy Vegetable Fritters

Raga Cuisine of India

This is an addictive recipe that is also quite versatile. The same spiced batter
could coat shrimp, cubed fish, or strips of chicken to serve as a more substantial starter
or part of a main course. The batter will thicken the longer it stands, so it's best to coat the
vegetables and fry them right after it is made. Be sure to have the vegetables already
trimmed and portioned before you begin to mix the batter.

A wide variety of tasty chutneys are available in stores today. Pick a couple of contrasting
ones—perhaps one spicy, one milder—to serve with the fritters. Ajwain is a unique spice,
related to caraway and cumin but with a flavor more reminiscent of thyme. It's available in
Indian markets and specialty spice shops but can also be omitted from the recipe. Gram flour
(not to be confused with graham flour) may also be labeled *besan* or chickpea flour.

2 teaspoons vegetable oil, plus more
for deep-frying
1 cup gram (chickpea) flour
1 teaspoon cumin seeds, lightly crushed
1 teaspoon coriander seeds, lightly crushed
½ teaspoon cayenne pepper
½ teaspoon minced garlic
½ teaspoon salt
¼ teaspoon baking powder

¼ teaspoon ajwain seed, lightly crushed
(optional)
About 1 cup water
1 pound mixed vegetables (such as cauliflower,
zucchini, shiitake mushrooms, onion, and/or
green beans), trimmed and cut into bite-size
pieces
Chutney, for serving

POUR OIL to a depth of 3 to 4 inches into a deep-fryer or a large, heavy saucepan and heat over
medium-high heat to 350°F. (The oil should come no more than halfway up the sides of the pan.)

WHILE THE OIL IS HEATING, prepare the batter. Combine the flour, 2 teaspoons vegetable
oil, cumin, coriander, cayenne, garlic, salt, baking powder, and ajwain (if using) in a medium
bowl. While stirring, gradually pour in enough water to make a batter of coating consistency.

WORKING IN BATCHES, dip the vegetable pieces into the batter, letting the excess drip back
into the bowl, then carefully lower the coated vegetables into the hot oil. Do not crowd the
pan. Fry until golden brown, 2 to 3 minutes. Remove the fritters from the oil with tongs or a
slotted spoon and drain on paper towels. Continue with the remaining vegetables, allowing the
oil to reheat between batches as needed. Arrange the fritters on a warmed platter and serve
immediately with chutney alongside for dipping.

Makes 4 to 6 servings

Bahia Mussels

Fandango

Here, Latin American fusion is explored, with Mexican chiles used in a dish inspired by Brazilian cuisine. Fandango chef-owner Christine Keff uses the *chile pasilla de Oaxaca*, which has a particularly rich flavor, but other pasilla chiles can replace it. Some fresh chiles are mistakenly labeled as pasillas, but true pasillas are always dried (their fresh form is the *chilaca*). They are slender, very deep—nearly black—in color, and carry moderate heat.

5 pasilla chiles	1 can (14 ounces) chopped tomatoes
3 tablespoons lard or vegetable oil	1 can (14 ounces) coconut milk
1 white onion, chopped	Salt and freshly ground black pepper
1 red bell pepper, cored, seeded, and chopped	2 pounds mussels, scrubbed and debearded
2 cloves garlic, chopped	

PULL THE STEM FROM EACH CHILE and scrape out as many seeds as possible. Lightly toast the chiles under the broiler or over a gas flame just until aromatic, but not burned, which will take only a few seconds. Halve the chiles crosswise, put them in a small heatproof bowl, and add boiling water to cover. Let sit for about 20 minutes. Drain the chiles, reserving the liquid. Remove any remaining seeds along with the veins inside each chile. Put the chiles in a blender with half of the soaking liquid and pulse several times to blend. Continuing to pulse, add enough of the remaining liquid to create a purée with the consistency of whipping cream.

HEAT 1 TABLESPOON OF THE LARD in a medium skillet over medium heat. Add the chile purée and cook, stirring with a wooden spoon, until it is slightly thickened, about 5 minutes. A path should remain clear for a second or two when you draw the spoon across the bottom of the skillet. Set aside.

HEAT THE REMAINING 2 TABLESPOONS lard in a large skillet over medium heat. Add the onion, bell pepper, and garlic and cook, stirring, until tender and aromatic but not browned, about 5 minutes. Stir in the tomatoes and coconut milk, followed by the pasilla purée. Reduce the heat to very low and simmer, covered, until the vegetables are very tender, about 1 hour.

WORKING IN BATCHES, purée the tomato mixture in a food processor or blender, then strain through a sieve into a large saucepan. Season to taste with salt and pepper. Add the mussels to the sauce in the pan, cover the pan, and cook over medium-high heat, gently shaking the pan occasionally, until the mussels open, 3 to 5 minutes. Spoon the mussels and their cooking sauce into warmed individual bowls, discarding any mussels that failed to open. Serve at once.

Makes 4 servings

Cedar Plank–Roasted Crab-Stuffed Mushrooms

Palisade

Chef John Howie is a big fan of cedar planks and is regularly preaching the gospel of wood-plank cooking, including during an appearance alongside Martha Stewart on her television show. Cedar planks are widely available in the Northwest at most kitchen stores and many larger grocery stores. You could bake the crab-stuffed mushrooms on a baking sheet instead, but you'll miss out on the subtle woodsy aroma that the mushrooms absorb.

3 tablespoons unsalted butter
¼ cup minced carrot
¼ cup minced celery
1 tablespoon minced shallot
½ cup whipping cream
24 large white mushrooms (about 2 inches in diameter)
Salt and freshly ground black pepper

1 cup Dungeness crabmeat (about 6 ounces), larger pieces broken up
1 tablespoon minced tarragon
2 tablespoons grated Asiago cheese
Juice of ½ lemon
1 tablespoon minced chives, for garnish (optional)

MELT THE BUTTER in a medium skillet over medium-high heat. Add the carrot, celery, and shallot and sauté, stirring constantly, until slightly tender and aromatic, 2 to 3 minutes. Add the cream and reduce by half, 3 to 5 minutes. Set aside to cool.

WHILE THE VEGETABLE MIXTURE IS COOLING, preheat the oven to 375°F. Snap the stems from the mushrooms and discard. Be sure to remove the entire stem, leaving a good cavity for the filling. Wipe the caps clean, then season lightly with salt and pepper. Set aside.

WHEN THE VEGETABLE MIXTURE IS COOL, add the crabmeat, tarragon, and about ¼ teaspoon of pepper; stir until well combined. Fill each mushroom cap with stuffing (about 2 teaspoons), mounding it slightly. Top each stuffed mushroom with a pinch of the Asiago cheese and set the mushrooms on a cedar roasting plank.

BAKE UNTIL THE CHEESE IS SLIGHTLY BROWNED and the filling is heated through, 10 to 15 minutes. Drizzle the lemon juice over the mushrooms and sprinkle with the chives (if using). Serve warm, directly from the plank. Or, if you've used a baking sheet, transfer the mushrooms to a platter for serving.

Makes 6 to 8 servings

Wood Cookery

Wood cookery is a very ancient form of food preparation, and it has certainly come back into style in the past decade. Chefs and restaurateurs are firing up wood-burning ovens to cook crisp, delish pizzas and stoking their grills with local woods. Little and Big Chief smokers have been billowing in neighborhood backyards for years, perfuming anglers' just-caught salmon fillets, marinated in soy and brown sugar-brine.

In the Northwest, apple is the preferred wood for cooking. It imparts a light, fruity smoke to the foods and burns nice and slow. You'll often see out behind local restaurants huge, neatly stacked piles of apple wood logs, trimmed to just the right length and covered for curing before they hit the stoves, ovens, rotisseries, or grills. The name of chef Tamara Murphy's Belltown restaurant, Brasa, literally means "live coals."

Planking is one of the earliest modes of Northwest cooking. Either alder wood or cedar is used for this style of conveying a woodsy flavor. At Palisade restaurant chef John Howie's signature appetizer of Cedar Plank–Roasted Crab-Stuffed Mushrooms (page 18) is ever popular. You can try your hand at planking, too. These days you can purchase ready-to-use planks from sources such as Chinook Planks, which are sold at local kitchen stores, or on line at John Howie's www.plankcooking.com. You place your halibut, salmon, or even halved (cut side down) Russet potatoes directly on the wood, thus imparting a succulent perfume and wonderful, aromatic wild flavor to whatever you are cooking!

—KC

Four-Onion Tart

Madison Park Café

The sweetness of the caramelized onions and the savory character of the Gruyère cheese and herbs provide delicious balance for this tart, which can be served as an appetizer by itself or as a light lunch with a garden salad alongside. Not sure you can find the four onions in this recipe? There are yellow onions, shallots, green onions, and chives, the latter a member of the onion family disguised as an herb.

¼ cup unsalted butter	2 tablespoons sour cream
3 large yellow onions, halved and cut into	Salt and freshly ground black pepper
¼-inch-thick slices	3 tablespoons minced chives
4 shallots, thinly sliced	2 tablespoons minced flat-leaf (Italian) parsley
2 cloves garlic, minced	1 tablespoon minced tarragon
3 tablespoons all-purpose flour	1¼ cups grated Gruyère cheese
1 bunch green onions, white and pale green	½ cup whipping cream
parts only, sliced	Crème fraîche or sour cream, for serving

PASTRY CRUST

1½ cups all-purpose flour	½ teaspoon salt
½ cup unsalted butter, cut into pieces and chilled	5 to 6 tablespoons cold water

FOR THE PASTRY CRUST, combine the flour, butter, and salt in a food processor and pulse just until the mixture has a crumbly texture. Add the water a tablespoon at a time, pulsing a few times after each addition, just until the dough begins to have a smooth texture. (Be careful not to overwork the dough or it will become tough.) Turn the dough onto a lightly floured work surface and form it into a ball. Wrap the dough in plastic and refrigerate for at least 30 minutes.

PREHEAT THE OVEN to 400°F.

ROLL OUT THE CHILLED DOUGH on a lightly floured work surface into a round large enough to line a 10-inch removable-base tart pan. Gently form the dough into the tart pan, pressing it well into the corners and trimming and fluting the edges. Prick the bottom a few times with a fork, then line the pastry with foil and partially fill it with pie weights or dried beans. Bake for 15 minutes. Take the pan from the oven, remove the weights and foil, and continue baking until the pastry is lightly browned on the bottom, 8 to 10 minutes longer. Set the pastry aside to cool. Reduce the oven temperature to 350°F.

MELT THE BUTTER in a large skillet over medium heat. Add the yellow onions, shallots, and garlic and sauté, stirring frequently, until the onions are tender and a deep golden brown, 20 to 30 minutes. Stir in the flour until well mixed, then stir in the green onions and sour cream with salt and pepper to taste. Continue to cook, stirring frequently, until well blended and slightly thickened, about 2 minutes. Take the skillet from the heat, stir in 2 tablespoons of the chives, the parsley, and the tarragon, and allow the mixture to cool to room temperature.

SPREAD THE COOLED ONION MIXTURE on the bottom of the tart shell and scatter the cheese evenly over the onion mixture. Pour the cream evenly over the top.

BAKE THE TART until golden brown, about 20 minutes. Allow the tart to cool for at least 30 minutes before removing the outer rim and cutting to serve. Garnish each slice with a small dollop of crème fraîche and some of the remaining 1 tablespoon chives.

Makes 8 servings

Creole Shrimp with Two Salsas

Bandoleone

Owner Danielle Philippa points out that this recipe was inspired by an Andalusian dish called *gambas al ajillo*, but she has richly embellished the classic preparation. The two sauces have multiple uses, either (or both) would be delicious served with grilled or roasted halibut or salmon. Achiote, also known as annatto seed, is found in kitchens in Latin America and the Caribbean. It has a fragrant, earthy flavor, despite being most commonly used for its vibrant yellow-gold color (it will stain, so take care when working with it). Look for achiote paste in Mexican or Latin American shops or in specialty food stores.

To make the shrimp stock called for in the sauces, simply simmer the shrimp shells in water for about 20 minutes, then strain. For a little extra flavor, add the same aromatics— onion, carrot, celery, bay leaf, thyme—that you'd use for other stocks.

3 tablespoons unsalted butter, melted
20 large shrimp (about 1 ¼ pounds), peeled and deveined
2 tablespoons Creole or Cajun spice mix

SALSA AMARILLA

8-ounce piece butternut squash, seeds discarded	2 tablespoons unsalted butter
1 tablespoon olive oil	⅛ teaspoon ground cinnamon
1 small onion, chopped	⅛ teaspoon freshly grated or ground nutmeg
2 cloves garlic, thinly sliced	⅛ teaspoon ground allspice
¼ cup shrimp stock or water	2 tablespoons brandy
¼ cup half-and-half	Salt and freshly ground black pepper

SALSA ROJA

¼ cup dry sherry	1 tablespoon chopped cilantro
¼ cup shrimp stock or water	1 teaspoon chopped garlic
1 tablespoon achiote paste	¼ cup olive oil

PREHEAT THE OVEN to 350°F. Oil a baking sheet or small baking dish.

FOR THE SALSA AMARILLA, set the squash cut side down on the prepared baking sheet or dish and bake until tender, about 40 minutes. Set aside until cool enough to handle, then remove the peel and chop the flesh. Set aside and leave the oven set at 350°F.

HEAT THE OIL in a medium saucepan over medium heat. Add the onion and garlic and sauté until fragrant and tender, about 5 minutes. Do not let them color or the sauce will be brown instead of vibrant yellow. Add the squash, stock, half-and-half, butter, cinnamon, nutmeg, and allspice. Stir to combine, then cook over medium-low heat until softened and evenly heated, about 10 minutes. Let the sauce cool slightly, then purée it in a blender or food processor and return the purée to the pan. Stir in the brandy and season to taste with salt and pepper. The sauce should be thick enough just to coat the back of a spoon. If it seems too thick, add a little water. Set aside.

FOR THE SALSA ROJA, put the sherry, stock, achiote paste, cilantro, and garlic in a blender and blend until smooth. With the blender running on low speed, add the oil in a thin stream. Season to taste with salt and pepper. Pour the sauce into a small saucepan and set aside.

PUT THE MELTED BUTTER in a shallow baking dish. Add the shrimp, sprinkle them with the Creole spice, and toss to coat evenly. Bake until the shrimp are just opaque through and evenly pink, 7 to 10 minutes.

WHILE THE SHRIMP ARE BAKING, heat the sauces over medium heat. When the shrimp are done, arrange them in the centers of warmed individual plates and accompany them with both sauces. Either spoon a pool of each sauce to each side of the shrimp, or drizzle the sauces over and around the shrimp in a freestyle pattern.

Makes 4 servings

Ahi Tuna Tartare
with Hazelnuts, Shaved Pear Salad, and Cilantro Hollandaise

Avenue One

One of the most popular ways to enjoy raw fish is tartare, a preparation
that offers an endless array of flavor and style variations. This version from chef Charles
Walpole includes some surprises that bring Northwest flavors to the dish, with toasted
hazelnuts added to the tuna mixture and slivers of crisp pear tossed with fresh herbs for a
garnish. The rich hollandaise sauce is another distinctive complement, though the tartare
would also be delicious without it if you prefer a short-cut option. Be sure the pear is
firm enough to hold up to being cut into thin shavings.

8 to 10 hazelnuts	1 tablespoon minced chives
½ pound ahi tuna, cut into ½-inch dice	½ teaspoon chile oil, more to taste (optional)
1 tablespoon minced shallot	Salt and freshly ground black pepper

CILANTRO HOLLANDAISE

1 tablespoon coriander seeds	2 tablespoons water
2 egg yolks	½ cup melted butter
1 tablespoon rice vinegar	1½ teaspoons minced cilantro
2 teaspoons dry white wine	1 teaspoon freshly squeezed lemon juice

PEAR AND HERB SALAD

8 shiso leaves	1 firm, ripe red Bartlett pear
12 sprigs cilantro	1 teaspoon extra virgin olive oil

PREHEAT THE OVEN to 350°F. Scatter the hazelnuts in one baking pan and the coriander
seeds in another. Toast both in the oven, gently shaking the pans once or twice to help them
toast evenly until the seeds are aromatic, 5 to 7 minutes, and the nuts are lightly browned, 8 to
10 minutes. Set the coriander seeds aside. Transfer the nuts directly to the center of a lightly
dampened kitchen towel, wrap the towel up around the nuts, and rub them around vigorously
(but carefully, since they're hot) to remove as much of their skin as possible. Let the nuts cool
completely, then chop them finely and set aside.

FOR THE TARTARE, toss the tuna, shallot, chives, and hazelnuts in a medium bowl. Drizzle
the chile oil over, if using, and season to taste with salt and pepper. Keep the mixture chilled
while you make the hollandaise.

FOR THE HOLLANDAISE, put the egg yolks in a medium nonreactive heatproof bowl. Combine the coriander seeds, vinegar, and wine in a small saucepan and simmer over medium heat until almost no liquid remains. Add the water to the pan, and swirl to blend with the reduction before straining it into the bowl with the egg yolks, whisking to mix. Put the bowl over (not in) a pan of simmering water and whisk constantly until the mixture thickens, about 5 minutes. (Be careful not to overheat the yolks or they will cook into eggy bits; if necessary, take the bowl from the heat and whisk vigorously to help cool before continuing.)

REMOVE THE BOWL from the heat and, whisking constantly, slowly drizzle in the butter until well blended. Add the cilantro and lemon juice with salt and pepper to taste. Keep the hollandaise warm over the pan of warm water (off the heat).

COMBINE THE SHISO LEAVES and cilantro sprigs in a medium bowl. (You can tear some of the larger leaves, if you like, but the chef uses them whole.) Cut the pear in half. Using a swivel peeler and beginning with a cut edge, make long shavings of the pear, working from the stem to blossom end and cutting around the core. Combine the pear with the shiso and cilantro. Drizzle the olive oil over, season to taste with salt and pepper, and toss gently.

FOR EACH SERVING, gently press one-quarter of the tartare into a lightly oiled ½-cup ramekin and unmold the tartare in the center of the plate. Or simply spoon the tartare onto the plate and press gently into a tidy circle. Drape the pear salad over the top and drizzle a couple of tablespoons of the cilantro hollandaise around the tartare. Serve immediately.

Makes 4 servings

Muhammara

Carmelita

Warmed pita or other flatbread is the ideal accompaniment for this distinctive purée
that's based on roasted red peppers and toasted walnuts, with a good dose of spicy heat. For
a cocktail party or buffet spread, the muhammara could be served with a variety of other
Middle Eastern dips such as hummus, tzatziki, and baba ghanouj.

The pomegranate molasses used in this recipe is a thick, deeply flavored, tangy-sweet
ingredient available in Middle Eastern stores and specialty food markets. There really isn't a
substitute, but if you're unable to find pomegranate molasses, you can simply leave it out of
this recipe. Results will be different, but still tasty.

2 large red bell peppers (about 1 pound)	½ teaspoon ground cumin
⅓ cup walnut pieces	½ teaspoon dried red pepper flakes
2 tablespoons bread crumbs	½ teaspoon ground cayenne pepper
2 tablespoons freshly squeezed lemon juice	Salt
2 to 3 tablespoons pomegranate molasses	Pita or other flatbread, warmed, for serving
1 tablespoon extra virgin olive oil	

ROAST THE RED PEPPERS over a gas flame or under the broiler until the skin blackens,
turning occasionally to roast evenly, 5 to 10 minutes total. Put the peppers in a plastic bag,
securely seal it, and set aside to cool.

WHILE THE PEPPERS ARE COOLING, preheat the oven to 350°F. Scatter the walnuts in a
baking pan and toast in the oven until lightly browned and aromatic, 5 to 7 minutes, gently
shaking the pan once or twice to help the nuts toast evenly. Set aside to cool completely.

WHEN THE PEPPERS ARE COOL enough to handle, peel away and discard the skin.
Remove the core and seeds and coarsely chop the peppers.

COMBINE THE CHOPPED PEPPERS, cooled nuts, and bread crumbs in a blender or food
processor and pulse to form a thick purée. Add the lemon juice and pomegranate molasses,
pulse to blend, then drizzle in the olive oil with the blades running. Add the cumin, pepper
flakes, and cayenne, then season to taste with salt. Refrigerate, covered, until ready to serve,
passing the warmed bread alongside for dipping into the muhammara.

Makes 4 to 6 servings

Tuscan White Bean and Rosemary Spread

Macrina Bakery and Café

"This spread is delicious on many of Macrina's rustic breads," notes owner
Leslie Mackie, although you can serve it with toasted baguette slices or crisp cracker
bread as well. The aromatic spread makes a great snack for the cocktail hour, perhaps with
some roasted nuts and interesting olives alongside. The dried beans should soak overnight
before cooking, but if you're in a big hurry, you can cover them generously with boiling
water and let them sit for an hour or so before continuing as directed.

2 cups dried cannellini or Great Northern beans	¼ cup extra virgin olive oil
½ cup diced onion	1 bay leaf
2 tablespoons chopped garlic	1 teaspoon salt
2 teaspoons chopped rosemary	Salt and freshly ground black pepper
1 teaspoon chopped thyme	1 loaf country-style bread, cut in thick slices

PUT THE DRIED BEANS in a large bowl and add cold water to cover by at least 2 inches. Let
soak overnight.

THE NEXT DAY, preheat the oven to 300°F. Combine the onion, garlic, rosemary, and thyme
on a piece of foil and drizzle with the olive oil. Fold up the edges of the foil to cover the vegetables. Roast until the onions are very tender, about 45 minutes.

DRAIN THE SOAKED BEANS and put them in a saucepan with fresh cold water to cover by
2 inches. Add the bay leaf and salt and bring to a boil. Reduce the heat to medium and simmer
until the beans are tender but not falling apart, about 45 minutes. The beans should simmer
gently, uncovered; boiling will burst the skins and make them mushy. Add more hot water as
needed to keep the beans completely covered. Drain the beans, reserving ¼ cup of the cooking
liquid; discard the bay leaf.

PUT THE BEANS in the bowl of a stand mixer fitted with the paddle attachment. Add the
roasted vegetables and reserved cooking liquid, and mix until the spread has a soft but slightly
chunky texture. You can use a potato masher instead, if you prefer. Season the spread to taste
with salt and pepper. Spoon it into a serving dish and let cool to room temperature. Serve at
room temperature accompanied with the bread. If you make the spread in advance, store it
covered in the refrigerator and let it come to room temperature before serving.

Makes about 4 cups (about 8 servings)

Baked Oysters with Beurre Blanc

Anthony's HomePort

This takeoff on oysters Rockefeller calls for a similar bed of spinach for the
freshly shucked oysters, but finishes with a sprinkle of fresh tomato and a zippy gremolata,
an Italian flourish of parsley, lemon zest, and garlic. At Anthony's, the appetizer
is served with garlic toast.

A large piece of aluminum foil can replace the rock salt used for steadying
the oysters on the baking sheet: Cut a piece about twice as long as the baking sheet and
roughly crumple it up to fit on the sheet. When you nestle the shells into the
crumpled foil, they should sit still.

1 small plum (roma) tomato
About 3 cups rock salt
12 medium Pacific oysters in the shell, scrubbed

SPINACH SAUTÉ

1 tablespoon olive oil
1 teaspoon minced shallot
¾ pound spinach, rinsed, dried, and tough stems
trimmed (about 5 cups loosely packed)

1 to 2 teaspoons anise liqueur such as Pernod
Salt and freshly ground black pepper

GREMOLATA

1 tablespoon minced flat-leaf (Italian) parsley
½ teaspoon grated lemon zest
¼ teaspoon minced garlic

BEURRE BLANC

2 tablespoons dry white wine
2 teaspoons minced shallot
½ teaspoon freshly squeezed lemon juice

1 tablespoon whipping cream
½ cup unsalted butter, cut into pieces and chilled

BRING A SMALL SAUCEPAN OF WATER TO A BOIL and prepare a small bowl of ice water. With the tip of a sharp knife, score an X on the bottom of the tomato. Add the tomato to the boiling water and blanch until the skin begins to split, 20 to 30 seconds. Scoop the tomato out with a slotted spoon and put it in the ice water for quick cooling. When cool, drain the tomato, then peel away and discard the skin. Quarter the tomato lengthwise, scoop out and discard the seeds, and finely chop the tomato. Set aside.

FOR THE SPINACH, heat the olive oil in a medium skillet over medium-high heat. Add the shallot and sauté until aromatic and tender, about 1 minute. Add the spinach and liqueur and season with salt and pepper to taste. Sauté until the spinach is wilted and bright green, about 1 to 2 minutes. This process goes quickly; take care to avoid overcooking the spinach. Drain the spinach in a colander set in the sink and let cool.

FOR THE GREMOLATA, combine the parsley, lemon zest, and garlic in a small bowl. Season with salt and pepper to taste, and stir to mix evenly. Set aside.

FOR THE BEURRE BLANC, combine the wine, shallot, and lemon juice in a small saucepan over medium-high heat. Bring the mixture to a boil and reduce the liquid by half, 2 to 3 minutes. Add the cream and reduce the heat to low. Whisk in the butter, bit by bit, careful that the butter melts creamily without becoming oily. Move the pan off the heat as needed to avoid overheating. Season the beurre blanc to taste with salt and set aside in a warm spot, or over a pan of barely simmering water, until ready to use. Do not overheat the sauce, or it will separate.

PREHEAT THE OVEN to 375°F. Prepare a bed of the rock salt on a rimmed baking sheet or shallow baking dish.

SHUCK THE OYSTERS, prying off the top shell and removing the oyster from the bottom shell. Put the oysters in a bowl and set the cupped bottom shells on the prepared baking sheet. Press on the cooled spinach in the colander with the back of a spoon to remove excess liquid, then line the bottom shells with the spinach, dividing it evenly. Put an oyster on top of each spinach bed. Sprinkle the tomato evenly over the oysters, spoon about 2 teaspoons of the beurre blanc over each, and then sprinkle evenly with the gremolata.

BAKE UNTIL HOT AND PLUMP, 3 to 5 minutes. Serve immediately.

Makes 2 to 3 servings

Oysters

The unpolluted waters of the Pacific Northwest are a key factor in growing superior oysters. Oysters filter feed about 100 gallons of water a day. Since they gain their unique flavor characteristics from the water they are grown in, clean water is essential to their freshness and flavor.

Pacific Northwest seafood guru Jon Rowley says, "You can tell it's oyster time in Seattle when the skies turn oyster gray, which is generally around the first of November." Thus, oysters are best eaten during the cold months when the waters are chilly, usually December through March.

Pacific oysters came to the Northwest waters by accident; it is assumed that they came here on the bottom of Japanese trade ships. This oyster loved the pristine waters and, after 150 years of commercial oyster harvesting, in the early 1990s the Pacific coast region became Number 1 in national oyster production.

The native, small Olympia oyster has had some hard times. Between the 1930s and '40s it became very scarce due to pulp mill pollution; finally in the late '50s, the Shelton pulp mill closed down. Olympia oysters are back again now, thanks to many oyster growers' dedication, hard work, and a receptive market. These tiny, tasty bivalves are great for a first-time raw slurper and ever so coveted by local restaurants and their diners.

Puget Sound area oysters range in size from the little Olympias to extra-large Pacifics, which sometimes get as big as tennis shoes. In between are the Kumomoto, a local favorite, and European flats. The smaller oysters are preferred for half-shell service, though seasoned oyster slurpers don't mind an occasional big one.

The larger Pacifics are often seen breaded and pan-fried and served up with tartar sauce or as morning fare mingled in a Hangtown Fry. On Asian menus in the International District, extra-large Pacifics are also the oysters of choice for quickly grilling in the shell and splashing with a scallion-chile sauce.

Oyster purists say there is no better way to eat raw oysters than unadorned and accompanied only by a crisp white wine, a loaf of bread, and maybe a squirt of lemon. But for first-time slurpers this can be a bit scary. So, sometimes, a little extra something is needed, such as mignonette sauce, a classical French preparation of red wine vinegar, black pepper, and shallots, or the more traditional, and sometimes maligned, cocktail sauce.

When these local bivalves are cooked, they are usually prepared simply. Simmered in heavy cream and topped with a pat of butter and a sprinkle of parsley, they emerge on Seattle waterfront fishhouse menus as traditional oyster stew. In addition to offering a large variety of local, fresh oysters on the half-shell, Elliott's Oyster House serves Pan-Fried Oysters with Jack Daniel's Sauce (page 125).

And if you're craving some pristine raw oysters mixed with a great deal of local fun—and washed down by a number of award-winning "oyster wines"—then head to the Oyster Olympics sponsored by Anthony's Restaurant on Shilshole Bay. This annual oyster orgy is held in March and is an oyster lover's paradise. While downing oysters on the half shell, you can watch twenty restaurant teams compete in oyster-shucking and wine and oyster identification. Plenty of local notables get into the act, too. Singer/songwriter Duffy Bishop may sing her slightly bawdy "Ode to the Noble Oyster," and local media personality Patti Payne has often had folks swaying and clapping along to the "Bivalve Blues." Then comes the moment when local celebrities make total fools of themselves (for a good cause of course) slurping ten oysters out of the half-shell, with no hands allowed! All proceeds from the event go to the educational and cleanup programs of the Puget Soundkeepers, a nonprofit organization that helps keep our local oysters tasting so good.

—KC

Pan-Fried Mussels on Rosemary Skewers

The Herbfarm

Chef Jerry Traunfeld is a true master in the art of cooking with herbs.
Since becoming chef at The Herbfarm in 1990, he has experimented with virtually
every herb he could get his hands on. This recipe gives rosemary the chance to serve a
functional purpose—its sturdy stems are used as skewers for the plump mussels—in addition
to adding flavor and aroma. One skewer per person might be good for a cocktail party,
while two or three each for a first course would be ideal.

The chef's method for making the aïoli, a wonderfully garlicky mayonnaise,
is to do it by hand. Making mayonnaise this way offers a great sense of accomplishment,
but it does take a bit of coordination to add the oil in a slow, steady stream while whisking
constantly. You can also prepare the aïoli in a food processor, blending the garlic-salt paste
with the egg yolks, lemon juice, and hot pepper sauce and, with the blades running,
adding the oil in a steady stream. The aïoli can be made up to two days in advance,
but it is at its best when served freshly made.

2 pounds large mussels (30 to 40), scrubbed and debearded	1 cup all-purpose flour
½ cup dry white wine	1 teaspoon salt
10 thick, woody rosemary sprigs, about 4 inches long	½ teaspoon freshly ground black pepper
	Olive oil, for frying

AÏOLI

2 cloves garlic	2 tablespoons freshly squeezed lemon juice
½ teaspoon salt	Dash hot pepper sauce
2 egg yolks	1 cup extra virgin olive oil

FOR THE AÏOLI, finely chop the garlic and, while it is still on the cutting board, sprinkle the salt over it. Work the garlic and salt into a paste by alternately pressing it with the side of the knife and then chopping it finer. Scrape up the garlic paste and put it in a medium bowl. Anchor the bowl on the counter by setting it on top of a damp towel. Add the egg yolks, lemon juice, and hot pepper sauce and whisk to blend evenly with the garlic. Pour the olive oil into a spouted measuring cup or pitcher. While whisking constantly, begin to add the oil, first drop by drop, then in a very slow trickle. The mixture will begin to emulsify (thicken) after about ¼ cup is added. Continue to whisk in the rest of the oil in a slow stream. Check the aïoli for seasoning, adding more salt or hot pepper sauce to taste. Store, covered, in the refrigerator until ready to serve.

PUT THE MUSSELS in a pot large enough so that the mussels fill it only halfway. Pour in the wine, cover the pot, and set it over high heat. Cook the mussels, occasionally gently shaking the pan, until they are all open, and then for an additional minute, 3 to 5 minutes total. Drain the mussels into a colander (you can reserve the liquor for a chowder or another use), discarding any mussels that failed to open. Spread the mussels out on a baking sheet and refrigerate until chilled, then remove the meats from the shells.

CUT THE BOTTOM of the rosemary sprigs at a sharp angle so they can easily pierce the mussels. Strip the leaves off the lower three-quarters of each stem, leaving a tuft of leaves at the top. Spear 3 or 4 mussels lengthwise onto each skewer.

MIX THE FLOUR with the salt and pepper on a large plate. Heat olive oil to a depth of ¼ inch in a large, heavy skillet over medium heat. Dredge a few skewers in the seasoned flour, patting off the excess flour. Carefully lower the skewers into the hot oil. (Cover the pan with a splatter screen or a loose piece of foil, to protect yourself if the skewers spit or pop.) Cook the mussels, turning once, until lightly browned on both sides, 1 to 2 minutes per side. Drain the skewers on paper towels and repeat with the remaining skewers.

SEASON THE SKEWERS lightly with salt and pepper, then arrange them on a platter. Serve hot, with the aïoli alongside for dipping.

Makes 10 skewers

Pâté de Campagne

Campagne

This pâté has been a signature at Campagne for years. It is a traditional country-style French pâté, based simply on seasoned ground meat rather than any fancy flourishes. The flavor is rich and delicious and perfect. The best accompaniments are the classics: sliced baguette, tangy Dijon mustard, and cornichons (small pickles).

Note that you need to start the pâté at least two days before you plan to serve it, although its flavor will be more fully developed if you give it an extra day or two in the fridge before serving. It needs to be weighted down in the refrigerator, to ensure its dense, firm texture. If you have a second terrine mold or loaf pan, nest it on top of the pâté and fill it with heavy cans of food. Otherwise, set a clean piece of wood (or something similarly sturdy) directly on the pâté and then top it with cans. Cover the clean wood well with foil and/or plastic wrap before using.

1 pound boneless pork butt, cut into cubes	8 ounces fatty bacon, thinly sliced
¾ pound pork fat, cut into cubes	Bread, mustard, and cornichons, for serving
1 pound chicken livers, veins removed, coarsely chopped	

MARINADE

3 tablespoons port	2 teaspoons salt
2 tablespoons brandy	1 teaspoon freshly grated or ground nutmeg
2 tablespoons dry sherry	1 teaspoon freshly ground black pepper
1½ tablespoons minced garlic	¼ teaspoon sugar
1½ tablespoons minced flat-leaf (Italian) parsley	Pinch ground cloves
1 tablespoon minced thyme	

FOR THE MARINADE, combine the port, brandy, sherry, garlic, parsley, thyme, salt, nutmeg, pepper, sugar, and cloves in a large nonreactive bowl.

FINELY GRIND THE PORK and pork fat twice through a meat grinder. Add the ground meat to the marinade along with the chicken livers and stir to blend evenly. Cover the bowl with plastic wrap and refrigerate overnight.

THE NEXT DAY, fry about 1 tablespoon of the pâté mixture in a small skillet until cooked through. Taste for seasoning, adjusting the rest of the pâté mixture if needed.

PREHEAT THE OVEN to 350°F.

LINE A 12- BY 3- BY 2½-INCH TERRINE MOLD or a 9- by 4- by 2½-inch loaf pan with the bacon, overlapping the slices in the bottom of the pan and allowing about a 2-inch overhang of bacon all around the rim. Spoon the pâté mixture into the pan, pressing down well with the back of the spoon to avoid any air pockets, and fold the ends of the bacon slices over to cover the top.

COVER THE TERRINE MOLD with its lid, or the loaf pan with a double thickness of foil, folding and sealing the ends securely. Put the pâté in a baking dish and fill the dish halfway with boiling water. Bake the pâté until the internal temperature is 145°F, about 1 hour. If you don't have a thermometer, insert a metal skewer into the center of the terrine, leave it for about 15 seconds, and then remove it; the skewer should be very hot to the touch.

REMOVE THE PÂTÉ MOLD from the baking pan, carefully pour out the water, and return the pâté to the baking pan. Let cool. Remove the lid or foil from the pâté and weight it down with a few large cans (see recipe introduction). Refrigerate the pâté overnight or up to 2 days before serving.

INVERT THE PÂTÉ onto a cutting board and carefully lift off the mold. Cut the pâté into thin slices and arrange on a serving platter, with a basket of bread and bowls of mustard and cornichons alongside.

Makes 10 to 12 servings

Geoduck Batayaki

Nishino

If you think geoduck is nothing but an oversized and terribly tough clam,
you haven't tasted it cooked by chef Tatsu Nishino in this delicious Japanese style,
which calls for sautéing it in butter. Granted, the neck (or siphon) of a geoduck—the part
that's perpetually sticking out of the shell—is very tough and is best ground and delegated
to the chowder pot or a spicy pasta sauce. But the belly meat inside the shell is quite tender,
although it is important not to overcook it, or it will become tough. This is a
rich dish, so the portion sizes are appropriately small.

You may occasionally find cleaned geoduck clams in Asian
seafood markets or other top fish shops, but generally you will have to tackle the
whole geoduck yourself. It seems a bit daunting, but the procedure is actually rather simple.
Slide a sharp flexible knife along the inside of the shell edge to cut the muscles that attach the
flesh to the shell. Pull the shell away from the clam and cut away and discard the viscera,
then rinse the meat well under cold running water. You will now have the long neck attached
to a slipper-shaped belly. Dip the clam meat in very hot water for a few seconds and then
dip it in ice water. The dark skin from the neck and exterior of the body should now
be easy to peel away. Discard it and then separate the belly from the neck at the
point where they meet. Save the neck meat, if you like, for another use.

8 ounces asparagus, trimmed and cut into 2-inch pieces	4 shiitake mushrooms, wiped clean, stemmed, and thinly sliced
1 geoduck belly (about 8 ounces)	2 tablespoons soy sauce
Salt and freshly ground black pepper	1 tablespoon sake
¼ cup all-purpose flour	4 lemon wedges
2 tablespoons unsalted butter	

BRING A SMALL PAN of lightly salted water to a boil and prepare a medium bowl of ice water. When the water boils, add the asparagus pieces and parboil until bright green and just beginning to turn tender, 2 to 3 minutes. Drain well, plunge immediately in the ice water, and set aside until fully chilled. When cool, drain well and pat dry on paper towels.

CUT THE GEODUCK BELLY into slices about ½ inch thick and season with salt and pepper. Put the flour on a plate. Working with a few slices at a time, add the geoduck slices to the flour and toss gently to coat evenly. Pat the pieces to remove excess flour and set them aside on another plate. Repeat with the remaining slices.

MELT THE BUTTER in a large skillet over medium-high heat. Add the geoduck slices and cook, turning once, until just tender-firm and lightly browned, about 1 minute per side. Add the shiitake mushrooms and asparagus and sauté for 1 minute longer. Stir in the soy sauce and sake and continue cooking until the mushrooms are tender, 1 to 2 minutes longer. Spoon the geoduck, vegetables, and sauce onto small warmed individual plates, add a wedge of lemon to each, and serve right away.

Makes 4 servings

Artichoke Ramekins

Santa Fe Café

Toasted baguette slices that have been brushed with garlic butter accompany this
popular appetizer at Santa Fe Café, but any good-quality bread (toasted is best) or crackers
can be served. The ramekins can be baked a day in advance and reheated in a low oven
before serving. To save time, use a good-quality prepared green chile rather than
roasting your own, although the final flavor will be best if you use fresh chiles.

The artichoke mixture can be baked in a single 3-cup baking dish rather than individual
ramekins, though you will need to increase the cooking time to about 25 minutes.

3 Anaheim or poblano chiles (about 8 ounces total)	½ cup mayonnaise
1 can (14 ounces) whole artichoke hearts in water, drained	½ red bell pepper, cored, seeded, and diced
1½ cups grated kasseri cheese (about 6 ounces)	1 tablespoon minced garlic
	Few pinches ground cayenne pepper or paprika

ROAST THE CHILES over a gas flame or under the broiler, turning occasionally to roast
evenly, until the skin blisters and blackens, 5 to 10 minutes total. Put the chiles in a plastic bag,
securely seal it, and set aside to cool. When cool enough to handle, peel away and discard the
skin. Remove the core and seeds, finely chop the chiles, and put them in a medium bowl.

PREHEAT THE OVEN to 350°F. Lightly oil six ½-cup ramekins.

SET ASIDE 1 artichoke heart for garnish, then coarsely chop the remainder. Add the chopped
artichoke hearts, cheese, mayonnaise, bell pepper, and garlic to the bowl with the chiles and stir
to mix well. Fill the ramekins with the artichoke mixture and set them on a baking sheet.

BAKE until the mixture is bubbly and the tops are lightly browned, 15 to 20 minutes. Remove
the ramekins from the oven and lightly sprinkle the tops with the cayenne. Cut the reserved
artichoke heart into 6 wedges, and put a wedge on each of the ramekins for garnish. Serve
immediately.

Makes 6 servings

Steamed Clams

Ivar's Salmon House

Although it's tempting to serve melted butter alongside steamed clams, in this recipe there's a good dose of butter added to the cooking liquid, so its richness is already woven into the dish. Do have bread available, of course, to capture the delicious broth that collects at the bottom of the bowl. A one-pound serving of clams per person might sound excessive, but by the time you eat your way through all those shells, you haven't consumed enough meat to ruin a good appetite. Smaller appetites can start with four pounds instead of six.

3 tablespoons olive oil	1 cup dry white wine
2 tablespoons chopped garlic	½ cup unsalted butter, cut into pieces
4 to 6 pounds Manila clams, scrubbed	1 tablespoon chopped dill

IN A POT large enough to hold all the clams generously, heat the oil over medium-high heat. Add the garlic and sauté, stirring, until aromatic, about 30 seconds. Add the clams and cook for 1 minute, then add the wine, butter, and dill. Cover the pot and cook, gently shaking the pot a few times, until most of the clams have opened, 8 to 10 minutes. (After about 5 minutes, when the clams have begun to open, you can scoop out opened clams with a slotted spoon and transfer them to serving bowls.) Discard any clams that failed to open and scoop the rest into the serving bowls, spooning the cooking liquids over but leaving any grit behind in the bottom of the pan. Serve at once.

Makes 6 servings

Tequila-Cured Gravlax Salmon

Fullers

Gravlax isn't a recipe that you make to serve just four people. It's the kind of dish you prepare for a festive holiday buffet or any special occasion at which you'll be feeding a crowd. Chef Tom Black's recipe begins with a dry brine of only brown sugar and salt for one day, before continuing the curing process with the more flavorful tequila-citrus-herb brine. He serves the gravlax with a refreshing accompaniment of raita, an Indian-inspired concoction of yogurt, cucumber, mint, and cumin.

The salt "cooks" the flesh of the salmon, altering its texture and drawing out excess water, leaving the salmon firm and silky. But the salmon isn't technically cooked and shouldn't be eaten by pregnant women, children, the elderly, or anyone with immune deficiencies. For a recipe such as this, use a whole salmon fillet that has not been previously frozen.

3 cups packed brown sugar	2 tablespoons coarsely chopped mint
1½ cups kosher salt	2 tablespoons coarsely chopped dill
1 whole salmon fillet, skin on and pin bones	2 tablespoons coarsely chopped basil
removed (2 to 2½ pounds)	2 teaspoons coriander seeds, crushed
Grated zest of ½ orange	⅓ cup tequila
Grated zest of 1 lemon	

RAITA SALAD

1 tablespoon olive oil	2 tablespoons minced mint
¼ red onion, minced	1 teaspoon freshly squeezed lemon juice
1 clove garlic, minced	1 teaspoon grated orange zest
1 teaspoon minced or grated ginger	½ teaspoon minced dill
½ teaspoon ground cumin	½ teaspoon hot pepper sauce
1 English (seedless) cucumber, peeled and cut	1 cup plain yogurt
into small dice	Salt and freshly ground black pepper
1 plum (roma) tomato, cored, seeded, and cut	
into small dice	

COMBINE THE BROWN SUGAR and salt in a small bowl to form the brine, and stir to mix. Line a large nonreactive dish with plastic wrap and scatter about half of the brine on the plastic in roughly the shape of the salmon fillet. Lay the salmon, flesh side down, on the brine and draw up the plastic wrap to enclose the fish, taking care that some of the brine is coating all the exposed flesh around the edges. Lay a smaller dish or a chopping board directly on the salmon fillet and weight it down with a few heavy cans. Refrigerate for 24 hours.

THE NEXT DAY, combine the remaining sugar-salt mixture with the orange and lemon zest, mint, dill, basil, and coriander seeds. Stir in the tequila.

TAKE THE SALMON from the first brine, discarding the plastic and wiping out the dish. Lightly rinse the salmon fillet and thoroughly pat dry with paper towels. Reline the dish with plastic wrap and spread the second brine as for the first, again laying the salmon on top, flesh side down. Wrap and weight as before, refrigerating the salmon for at least 24 hours longer. When done curing, the fish will have intensified in color and the texture will feel much firmer to the touch.

SHORTLY BEFORE SERVING, prepare the raita. Heat the olive oil in a small skillet over medium heat. Add the onion, garlic, and ginger and sauté, stirring often, until just tender but not browned, 3 to 5 minutes. Sprinkle the cumin over the top and set aside to cool completely.

IN A LARGE BOWL, combine the cucumber, tomato, mint, lemon juice, orange zest, dill, and hot pepper sauce. Stir to mix, then add the yogurt and the cooled onion mixture, stirring to blend evenly. Season to taste with salt and pepper and refrigerate, covered, until ready to serve.

WIPE EXCESS BRINE from the surface of the fish and lay it on a cutting board or on a large serving platter. To cut slices, use the sharpest and thinnest-bladed knife you have. Cut long, thin slices from the salmon, beginning at the tail end and working with the knife blade at a sharp angle, nearly horizontal. Pass the raita separately.

Makes 16 to 20 servings

Wild Mushroom Terrine
with Goat Cheese Caillé and Berry Vinaigrette

Rover's

An easy but classy start to any meal, this mushroom terrine can be served with a salad of roasted beets tossed with the same berry vinaigrette. You can embellish the terrine, too, with a tuft of tender greens. If fresh wild mushrooms aren't available, use a variety of cultivated mushrooms, such as cremini, shiitake, and button—although the flavor of the final terrine will be a little less elegant. Add an ounce or so of dried wild mushrooms (reconstituted) to improve the flavor, if you like, but don't count on dried mushrooms for the bulk in this terrine (see Wild Mushrooms, page 150).

Chef-owner Thierry Rautureau generally uses a slender half-moon mold, available at specialty cookware stores, for this terrine. But a wide variety of terrines and other molds are available these days. You need one that has a volume of about three cups, preferably more slender than stocky. Or, you can double the recipe and form it in a classic terrine mold (or even a loaf pan), perfect for an elegant buffet.

Quillisascut Cheese Farm in Rice, Washington, produces some of the region's best goat cheeses, of which the caillé (fresh curds, prior to the stage when they would be formed into a mold) is one special variety used by chef Rautureau. The caillé isn't available on the retail level, but any good-quality fresh goat cheese is an ideal substitute.

6 tablespoons unsalted butter	6 ounces cèpe mushrooms (also known as boletus
2 tablespoons minced shallot	or porcini), wiped clean, trimmed,
½ teaspoon minced garlic	and thinly sliced
6 ounces chanterelle mushrooms, wiped clean,	6 ounces oyster mushrooms, wiped clean,
trimmed, and thinly sliced	trimmed, and thinly sliced
Salt and freshly ground white pepper	2 tablespoons minced chives
	4 ounces Quillisascut goat cheese caillé or fresh
	goat cheese log, crumbled

BERRY VINAIGRETTE

⅓ cup extra virgin olive oil
3 tablespoons wild berry vinegar or raspberry vinegar

MELT 2 TABLESPOONS OF THE BUTTER in a large skillet over medium-high heat until it is fully melted and turns a light hazelnut brown. While the butter is heating, stir together the shallot and garlic in a small bowl. Add the chanterelle mushrooms to the hot butter and cook, stirring often, until they begin to soften, about 1 minute. Stir in one-third of the shallot-garlic mixture, season lightly with salt and pepper, and continue cooking until the mushrooms are fully tender, 1 to 2 minutes longer. Put the chanterelles in a large bowl and repeat with the cèpes and then with the oyster mushrooms, using the remaining butter and shallot-garlic mixture and adding the sautéed mushrooms to the bowl with the chanterelles. It is important that the mushrooms cook quickly over relatively high heat, so that they become tender without giving off their flavorful juices. (At the same time, it's important that the mushrooms be fully cooked, so don't be tempted to take any short cuts in the cooking.) The mushrooms should cook in a single layer in the skillet, so you may need to cook each type of mushroom in more than one batch.

STIR THE CHIVES into the sautéed mushrooms. Add the goat cheese and stir until evenly mixed. The cheese should soften and blend smoothly with the mushrooms.

LINE A 3-CUP TERRINE with parchment paper or plastic wrap. Spoon the mushroom-cheese mixture into the terrine, pressing down on the top with the back of a spoon to pack it in well. Cover the terrine with plastic wrap and refrigerate until set, at least 3 hours. (You can also form the mixture into a cylinder about 2 inches across and 8 inches long and wrap securely in a double layer of plastic wrap. Twist the ends firmly to ensure that the cylinder is solidly packed, then tap the ends against the counter to square them off a bit.)

FOR THE BERRY VINAIGRETTE, whisk together the olive oil and vinegar with salt and pepper to taste. Set aside.

UNMOLD THE MUSHROOM TERRINE onto a cutting board and discard the paper or plastic. Cut the terrine into 12 or 18 slices (depending on the size and shape of your terrine) and arrange 2 or 3 slices on each plate, slightly overlapping them. Drizzle the berry vinaigrette over and around and serve.

Makes 6 servings

Squid in Their Own Ink

Harvest Vine

Squid in their own ink is an age-old recipe from the Basque region,
the home of chef-owner Joseph Jiménez de Jiménez. It's an ideal tapas-style dish,
to serve with an assortment of other small plates for dinner, or with olives and roasted
almonds as an appetizer before dinner. Squid ink is available in small packets in specialty
food stores. A little goes a long way in flavoring and coloring this sauce. Tomato *frito* is a
concentrated sauté of tomato and onion (and sometimes red bell pepper). It is sold in shops
specializing in Spanish ingredients and in some gourmet stores (try the Spanish Table in
downtown Seattle). If you cannot locate it, whip up some for yourself, cooking chopped
fresh tomato with onion in good olive oil until the mixture becomes thick.

¼ cup plus 2 tablespoons olive oil	1¼ cups dry white wine
1 large onion, sliced	1 tablespoon sweet smoked paprika
1 red bell pepper, cored, seeded, and sliced	(pimentón de La Vera)
1 green bell pepper, cored, seeded, and sliced	1 teaspoon squid ink
½ cup tomato *frito*	¼ cup brandy
1 tablespoon minced garlic	1 tablespoon cornstarch, dissolved in
1 tablespoon minced flat-leaf (Italian) parsley	2 tablespoons water
1½ teaspoons salt	1 teaspoon sugar
2 bay leaves	2 pounds cleaned squid
2 cups fish stock, preferably homemade	Country-style bread, for serving

HEAT ¼ CUP OF THE OIL in a large sauté pan or skillet over medium heat. Add the onion
and bell peppers and sauté, stirring often, until the vegetables begin to soften but aren't
browned, 8 to 10 minutes. Stir in the tomato *frito*, garlic, half the parsley, salt, and bay leaves.
Continue to sauté, stirring, for about 10 minutes. Add the fish stock, ¾ cup of the wine, half
the *pimentón*, and the squid ink. Simmer for 10 minutes, then stir in the brandy, cornstarch,
and sugar. Cook, stirring, until the sauce is thickened, a few minutes. Remove the bay leaves,
then pass the sauce through the fine disc of a food mill or purée with an immersion blender or
in batches in a blender or food processor. Put the sauce in a large ovenproof saucepan and set
aside. Wipe out the sauté pan and set aside.

PREHEAT THE OVEN to 325°F.

CUT THE SQUID BODIES crosswise into rings ¾ inch wide. Cut large tentacles in half or quarters. Heat the remaining 2 tablespoons oil in the sauté pan over high heat. When hot, add the squid and sauté, stirring constantly, until just evenly opaque. Season the squid with salt, then add the squid to the sauce. Stir in the remaining ½ cup white wine with the remaining *pimentón* and parsley.

BRING THE SAUCE TO A BOIL over high heat, then cover the pan and bake until the squid is very tender, about 2 hours. Spoon the squid and sauce into small, shallow dishes and serve, passing the bread for sopping up any sauce lingering in the dish.

Makes 6 to 8 servings

Kippered Salmon and Asparagus Bread Pudding

Macrina Bakery and Café

This savory bread pudding comes from Leslie Mackie, owner of Belltown's beloved Macrina Bakery and Café. She serves it at lunch with a simple salad. It would also be delicious served as part of a brunch or as a side dish at dinner, perhaps with grilled salmon. Kippered salmon is another term for hot-smoked salmon.

For this recipe, the cooks at Macrina use their Giuseppe bread, a dense country-style loaf that weighs in at about 1¼ pounds. You can use other similar-styled bread of the same size. This recipe can be doubled and baked in a 9- by 13-inch baking dish.

1 loaf day-old country-style bread (about 1¼ pounds)	¼ cup grated fontina cheese
¼ cup unsalted butter, melted, more if needed	¼ cup grated romano cheese
¾ pound asparagus, trimmed and cut into 3-inch pieces	1 cup flaked kippered (hot-smoked) salmon, skin and bones discarded (about 4 ounces)
2 cups milk	3 tablespoons chopped mixed herbs (chives, flat-leaf [Italian] parsley, chervil, and/or tarragon)
3 eggs	
Salt and freshly ground black pepper	

PREHEAT THE OVEN to 325°F. Butter a 9-inch square baking dish that is at least 3 inches deep.

CUT THE CRUST from the bread, and then cut the bread into ½-inch-thick slices that are about 3 inches wide. Brush both sides of each slice with the melted butter and set aside.

BRING A LARGE SAUCEPAN of lightly salted water to a boil and prepare a large bowl of ice water. Add the asparagus pieces to the boiling water and parboil until bright green and just beginning to turn tender, about 2 to 3 minutes. Drain the asparagus and put it in the ice water to cool thoroughly. When cool, drain well and pat dry on paper towels. Set aside.

IN A MEDIUM BOWL, whisk together the milk and eggs until well combined. Season to taste with salt and pepper and set aside. In a small bowl, combine the fontina and romano cheeses and toss to mix.

COVER THE BOTTOM of the prepared baking dish with a layer of bread slices, using about half of the slices and slightly overlapping them for even coverage. Top the bread with three-quarters of the salmon, three-quarters of the asparagus, three-quarters of the grated cheese, and one-half of the herbs, distributing each ingredient evenly. Arrange the remaining bread slices on top, again overlapping them slightly. Sprinkle the bread with the remaining salmon, asparagus, herbs, and cheese. Slowly pour the custard mixture over the layered bread and push the bread slices down gently to absorb the custard better. Butter one side of a piece of foil large enough to cover the dish, then cover it, placing the foil buttered side down. Put the dish in a larger, deeper baking pan. Add boiling water to the pan to reach halfway up the sides of the bread pudding dish.

BAKE UNTIL THE CUSTARD IS FIRM (poke a knife deep into the pudding, pull the blade to one side, and peek in to see that there's no liquid custard remaining), about 1¼ hours. Remove the foil and continue baking to brown the top, 10 to 15 minutes longer. Let cool slightly before cutting the bread pudding into squares to serve.

Makes 6 to 8 servings

Artisan-Baked Bread

Once upon a time, Seattle was speckled with first-rate neighborhood bakeries. Then came the days of "sliced bread," alias, Wonder bread land, there was a near total demise of these fragrant gathering places. All the supermarkets offered was bleached, white, too-soft, too-squishy, too-conditioned, too-taste-less so-called bread whose main value was an almost infinite shelf life.

Well, thank goodness this city was one of the places to lead the way to the gradual return of Daily Bread—that is, bread baked fresh each morning, intended to be eaten that day.

Sourdough, customarily made simply with wheat flour, water and wild yeast, has always been a tradition in the West. But in the 1960s and '70s its popularity rebounded with the natural food movement, making for some tart and tasty baked goods and pancakes. Sometimes you hear tales of folks with sourdough starters that date back for many years.

The Little Bread Co., part of the hippie natural food revival but now gone, was one of the first Seattle bakeries that bulked their products up with whole grains and flavor. Then, in 1972, Gwen Bassetti began turning out her distinctive, slow-rising, rustic loaves at Grand Central Baking Co. Today, there's an array of such bakeries—from one-shop, in-store sales places to larger operations that produce for restaurants and for markets across the city.

Artisan-baked breads now can be found in nearly every Seattle neighborhood and on nearly every restaurant table. The challenge is in deciding which one to use—Como bread from Grand Central, Potato or Giuseppe bread from Macrina, Ciabatta or Rosemary Diamante from Essential, or another of the large variety of Seattle's hearty, hand-crafted breads. ➤

Any of these great breads are excellent spread with Carmelita's Muhammara (page 26). Leslie Mackie suggests using any of Macrina's hearty rustic breads to smear with her Tuscan White Bean and Rosemary Spread (page 27)—a yummy alternative to butter.

La Panzanella Flat Bread (Croccantini) is an experience in itself. It makes an unsurpassed base for spreads and toppings of all sorts. Break the big planks into appetizer-sized pieces to serve.

To use up day-old artisan breads, which generally have no preservatives prolonging their lives, an Italian-style bread salad—such as Union Square Grill's Herb Roasted Chicken and Bread Salad (page 70)—is excellent. Or just toss toasted bread cubes with flavorful roasted or grilled summer vegetables, garden-fresh tomatoes, and nutty arugula. Let these ingredients play against the sharp contrast of a few salty capers and Kalamata olives, and pull everything together with a basil and balsamic vinaigrette.

Bread puddings and strata provide other delicious means to consume bread that's just a little bit stale but way too good for the birds. Macrina Bakery and Café's Kippered Salmon and Asparagus Bread Pudding (page 46) is a terrific style of breakfast bake—just right for a brunch celebration when served with slices of crisp bacon and goblets of sparkling mimosas. Or try mixing up Avenue One's savory Granny Smith Apple Bread Pudding (page 89) as the perfect accompaniment to roast chicken or pork.

In fact, there are myriad uses for dry bread, including croutons, stuffings, gratin toppings, and what the French call *pain perdu* or "lost bread," which Americans know as French toast. You can make some absolutely to-die-for French toast with leftover slices of Grand Central's Como loaf.

With so many great breads available today, finding one you love isn't a chore—it's deciding which one of these toothsome Northwest loaves you want to serve tonight!

—KC

Jalapeño Mussels

Elliott's Oyster House

Don't forget the bread for sopping up the cooking juices from these steamed mussels, here made zippy with jalapeño and a splash of tequila. If you like a good punch of heat, use two chiles rather than only one. Sherry adds a distinctive flavor to the cooking liquids, but without it the tequila and jalapeño flavors come through more fully—it's your choice. A margarita seems ideal for sipping alongside (see Cadillac Margarita, page 224).

½ cup clam juice	1 jalapeño chile, cored, seeded, and diced
¼ cup whipping cream	2 teaspoons minced garlic
2 tablespoons dry sherry (optional)	1½ pounds mussels, scrubbed and debearded
2 tablespoons unsalted butter	2 lime wedges
2 tablespoons tequila	2 teaspoons minced cilantro

COMBINE THE CLAM JUICE, cream, sherry, butter, tequila, jalapeño, and garlic in a large saucepan. Stir to mix, then add the mussels. Cover the pan, set it over high heat, and cook, gently shaking the pan occasionally, until the mussels have opened, 5 to 7 minutes.

SCOOP THE MUSSELS into individual shallow bowls, discarding any mussels that failed to open. Spoon the cooking juices over, garnish each bowl with a lime wedge, and sprinkle with the cilantro. Serve right away, with an extra bowl on the table for the discarded shells.

Makes 2 servings

Vietnamese Spring Rolls

Yarrow Bay Beach Café

The combination of crisp vegetables, sweet shrimp and crab, aromatic herbs, and rich chorizo—all freshly rolled and deep-fried—makes these spring rolls particularly delicious. Chef Cameon Orel serves the spring rolls with sweet Thai chile sauce, a bottled product that is a complex blend of sweet, sour, and hot flavors. Look for good-quality chorizo that isn't too fatty and strongly flavored, or it might overpower the other ingredients.

1 ounce cellophane noodles	½ cup Dungeness crabmeat (about 3 ounces)
1 tablespoon vegetable oil, plus more for deep-frying	¼ cup finely julienned basil
	¼ cup finely julienned mint
8 ounces chorizo sausage, casings removed	¼ cup julienned shiitake mushroom
6 ounces medium shrimp, peeled, deveined, and minced	1 tablespoon Vietnamese or Thai fish sauce (*nuoc nam* or *nam pla*)
2 tablespoons minced shallot	½ teaspoon sugar
1 teaspoon minced garlic	Salt and freshly ground black pepper
3 cups shredded Napa cabbage	16 egg roll wrappers (most of a 1-pound
½ medium carrot, cut into julienne strips	package)

PUT THE CELLOPHANE NOODLES in a medium bowl and add hot water to cover. Let soak until pliable, about 5 minutes, then drain well and use kitchen shears to cut them into 2-inch lengths. Set aside.

HEAT THE 1 TABLESPOON OIL in a large skillet over medium-high heat. Add the chorizo and sauté, breaking the sausage into small pieces with a wooden spoon, until beginning to brown, 3 to 5 minutes. (If the sausage has given off a lot of fat, spoon off all but a tablespoon or so before continuing.) Add the shrimp, shallot, and garlic and sauté until the sausage is just cooked through and the shrimp is pink and firm, about 2 minutes longer. Transfer the mixture to a large bowl and set aside to cool.

ADD THE CELLOPHANE NOODLES to the cooled sausage mixture along with the cabbage, carrot, crabmeat, basil, mint, mushroom, fish sauce, sugar, and salt and pepper to taste. Stir until well combined.

TO FORM THE SPRING ROLLS, lay 1 egg roll wrapper on the work surface with one corner facing you. Put a scant ⅓ cup of the filling in the center of the wrapper and form it into a horizontal strip about 1 inch wide and 3 inches long. Brush the edges of the wrapper lightly with water, then fold each of the side corners in over the filling. Fold the lower corner up, then roll the filling upward to enclose it fully in the wrapper, pressing the final corner well to seal securely and form a neat package. (You're basically folding it up as you would a burrito.) Repeat this process with the remaining filling and wrappers.

POUR OIL to a depth of 2 to 3 inches into a deep-fryer or large, heavy saucepan and heat to about 375°F. (The oil should come no more than halfway up the sides of the pan.) Add 2 or 3 spring rolls and deep-fry, turning as needed, until golden brown, 3 to 4 minutes. Remove with tongs or a wire skimmer and drain on paper towels. Continue with the remaining spring rolls, allowing the oil to reheat between batches as needed.

TO SERVE, cut each spring roll in half on the diagonal, arrange on individual plates, and serve.

Makes 8 servings

Pacific Rim and Asian Influences

What makes Seattle chefs so crazy about Pacific Rim ingredients? Is it the obscurity of what you're really supposed to do with them that explains the appeal? Is it their exotic, bold, and subtle flavors?

Kasu or sake lees—(the word *kasu* means "remnants" in Japanese)—is one such ingredient. Mixed with sugar and sake, it makes a marinade that flavors as well as preserves fish. Kasu preparations have been served in Seattle for about the last 50 years. In the 1980s kasu cod was introduced onto a non-Asian menu by chef Tom Douglas at the now defunct Café Sport. Served up with seaweed salad, kasu cod became a feature of fusion cuisine. This dish is now a staple on many Northwest menus, including Ray's Boathouse and Waterfront (page 174). A sweet rich fish such as black cod or sablefish is usually the fish of choice.

The Asian influence in Seattle's cookery isn't just Chinese or Japanese anymore. It's Korean kim chee nestled up next to steamed salmon, or Filipino chicken adobo, or the fish sauce that's splashed in the fresh Vietnamese Spring Rolls served at Yarrow Bay Beach Café (page 50), or kaffir lime leaves and coconut perfuming that bowl of Thai curry.

Rick and Ann Yoder's Wild Ginger has become a local icon for great Asian food served up with a flair—from its signature crispy duck to the addictive Sichuan Green Beans (page 92). At Christine Keff's Flying Fish there is a definite Pac Rim slant to the menu. Sea scallops show up with Thai curry and fish gets a tangy, salty splash in Pan-Seared Steelhead with Black Bean Vinaigrette (page 14) On almost every Northwest menu you'll see and taste a sprinkling of the Orient.

—KC

SOUPS, SALADS & SIDES

Tom Kah Gai

Bahn Thai

This is one of the best-known and most-loved of all Thai soups. It is aromatic with ginger, coconut milk, and kaffir lime and has a flavor that offers a distinctive balance of sweet (sugar), salty (fish sauce), sour (lime juice), and spicy (chile paste) tastes. The soup is intended to be "medium-hot," as it is served at Bahn Thai, but alter the amount of chile sauce to your taste.

If you're unable to find kaffir lime leaves, use strips of lime zest instead, although you'll miss the uniquely fragrant character of the real thing. The other Thai ingredients are commonly available in well-stocked groceries and specialty food shops.

4 cups chicken stock, preferably homemade	2 teaspoons Thai fish sauce *(nam pla)*
2 stalks lemongrass, trimmed and cut on the diagonal into ½-inch pieces	2 teaspoons freshly squeezed lime juice
4 kaffir lime leaves	1 teaspoon *sambal oelek* or other hot chile sauce
6 slices galangal or ginger	½ teaspoon salt
¾ pound boneless, skinless chicken breast, cut into ½-inch cubes	½ teaspoon sugar
2 cups unsweetened coconut milk	2 to 3 teaspoons chopped green onion, for garnish
1 cup sliced mushrooms	2 to 3 teaspoons chopped cilantro, for garnish

COMBINE THE CHICKEN STOCK, lemongrass, lime leaves, and galangal in a medium saucepan and bring to a boil over high heat. Reduce the heat to medium and simmer for 5 minutes. Add the chicken and simmer, stirring occasionally, until it is just cooked through, about 5 minutes. (Don't boil the chicken, or it will become tough.) Stir in the coconut milk, mushrooms, fish sauce, lime juice, chile sauce, salt, and sugar, and simmer until the mushrooms are tender and the flavors are well blended, about 5 minutes longer. Taste the soup for seasoning, adjusting to taste with lime juice, salt, sugar, and/or chile paste.

LADLE THE SOUP into individual warmed bowls, sprinkle with the green onion and cilantro, and serve. Tell your guests to pick out the galangal, lime leaf, and lemongrass as they're eating.

Makes 4 to 6 servings

Corn Chowder with Dungeness Crab

Macrina Bakery and Café

Macrina, the famous bakery-café in Seattle's Belltown neighborhood,
becomes a wonderful urban lunch counter at midday. This soup is an ideal example
of the simple, satisfying noontime fare. The base of the soup is a corn stock made from
simmering the corn cobs with onion and some of the kernels. Sweet and briny crabmeat is
the perfect addition to the corn chowder, which is garnished with a cilantro salsa
seasoned with lime and roasted jalapeño.

1 tablespoon olive oil	3 ears corn, shucked and broken in half
½ medium yellow onion, sliced	⅓ cup half-and-half
4 cups water	¾ cup Dungeness crabmeat (about 5 ounces)
Salt and freshly ground black pepper	

SPICY CILANTRO SALSA

1 jalapeño chile	¼ cup diced red onion
2 plum (roma) tomatoes, cut into medium dice	Juice of 1 lime
⅓ cup chopped cilantro	1 clove garlic, minced

HEAT THE OIL in a large saucepan over medium heat. Add the yellow onion and cook, stirring often, until tender and translucent, about 5 minutes. Stir in the water and ¼ teaspoon salt, then add the ears of corn. Bring to a boil over high heat and cook just until the corn is tender, 3 to 4 minutes. Take the pan from the heat, use tongs to remove the ears, allowing excess water to drip back into the pan, then set the corn aside on a plate to cool for about 5 minutes. Cut the kernels from the cobs and return half of the kernels and all of the cobs to the pan. Bring the mixture to a boil, reduce the heat to medium-low, and simmer, covered, for 30 minutes.

WHILE THE SOUP IS SIMMERING, make the salsa. Roast the jalapeño over a gas flame or under the broiler, turning occasionally to roast evenly, until the skin blisters and blackens, about 5 minutes total. Put the chile in a plastic bag, securely seal it, and set aside to cool. When cool enough to handle, peel away and discard the skin. Remove the core and seeds and mince the jalapeño. Combine it with the tomatoes, cilantro, red onion, lime juice, and garlic in a medium bowl. Stir to mix well and season to taste with salt. Set aside.

TAKE THE COBS from the soup base and discard. Purée the soup, in batches, in a food processor or blender and return the soup to the pan. Add the half-and-half and remaining corn kernels and bring just to a boil. Stir in the crabmeat and season to taste with salt and pepper.

LADLE THE SOUP into warmed individual bowls, spoon some of the spicy cilantro salsa into the center of each, and serve.

Makes 4 servings

Dungeness Crab—Are You a Picker or a Piler?

Named for the Washington town on the Strait of Juan de Fuca, the Dungeness crab is found all the way from Alaska to lower California. Its scientific name is *Cancer magister,* the big crab, and it's one of the most popular West Coast crab species marketed commercially.

Sweet Dungeness crab has always been a seaside treat. The best way to enjoy it in truly Northwest style is to cook it live right on the beach in a pot of boiling seawater. Cook the crab for about 15 minutes, cool in cold water, then pull off the back shell and featherlike gills while rinsing the crab clean. Then sit down right there in the sand and start cracking while breathing in the fresh sea air. Dip the luscious meat in melted butter or squeeze a little lemon on it. Accompany it with a fresh green salad and hot garlic bread, and wash it all down with a glass of cold, crisp Northwest Semillon. All of a sudden you haven't a care in the world, but just to sit and crack crab.

If you're a crab lover, you've probably noticed that some crab eaters are pickers and some are pilers. The former pick and eat as they go while the latter make a pile of shelled crab, not even tasting a single morsel till they have a good-sized mound. Someday, no doubt, someone will do a study on this peculiarity.

Since the Northwest's sweet Dungeness are most bountiful during the winter, it's a good time to eat crab in another favorite form—crab cakes. Crab cakes are an American tradition. From Chesapeake Bay to Puget Sound, each region has its version. Seattleites and area chefs are opinionated about their crab cakes, sometimes even downright crabby! Some swear by Old Bay Seasoning as their secret ingredient, others say milk-soaked bread crumbs or mayonnaise does the trick for moistness. But few will argue that high-quality crab, preferably fresh rather than frozen—and lots of it—is the best secret ingredient of all.

Locally you will find crab cakes in a multitude of styles, with accompaniments ranging from traditional tartar sauce to sweet roasted pepper coulis, to the Crab Cakes with Ancho Chile Mayonnaise at Ray's Boathouse (page 102).

Fresh and right out of the shell may still be a favorite way to eat this prized Northwest creature, but no one turns it down any way they can get it! From Macrina Bakery and Cafe's Corn Chowder with Dungeness Crab (page 56), to Nell's salad of Dungeness Crab with Red Radishes and Braeburn Apples (page 84), all are deliciously majestic!

—KC

Swiss Leek, Oat, and Smoked Chicken Soup

Kaspar's

Yes, this does sound like an unusual soup, but give it a try and you'll be hooked. The oats contribute body and nutty texture, and the smoked chicken delivers a nice aroma and flavor. This soup could also pass as a main course, with a big, crisp green salad alongside.

2 tablespoons vegetable oil	2 quarts chicken stock, preferably homemade
½ onion, chopped	1½ cups regular rolled oats (not quick-cooking)
2 medium leeks, white and pale green parts only, thinly sliced	2 boneless smoked chicken breasts (about ¾ pound total), finely diced
1 teaspoon chopped thyme	½ cup whipping cream
1 clove garlic, minced	Salt and freshly ground black pepper

HEAT THE OIL in a large saucepan over medium heat. Add the onion and sauté until tender and translucent, 5 to 7 minutes. Add the leeks, thyme, and garlic and sauté until the leeks are fragrant and tender, 3 to 5 minutes. Add the chicken stock and oats and bring to a boil over medium-high heat. Reduce the heat to low and simmer until the oats are tender and the soup has thickened slightly, about 15 minutes.

STIR IN THE CHICKEN and cream and bring to a boil over medium-high heat. Take the pan from the heat and taste for seasoning, adding more salt or pepper if needed. (Note that the smoked chicken will be salty, so you may not need to add salt.) Ladle the soup into warmed bowls and serve immediately.

Makes 6 to 8 servings

Savory Nectarine and Shiso Soup

Le Gourmand

"Nectarines and shiso is a wonderful flavor combination," says Le Gourmand chef-owner Bruce Naftaly. "It is very characteristic of my cooking, combining ingredients and herbs in unusual ways." He notes that the unique soup can be served hot or chilled.

A staple in Japanese cooking, shiso is a bright green leaf with distinctive jagged edges that is often used as a garnish on sushi or sashimi plates. A cousin of both mint and basil, it has a fresh, herbal flavor all its own. The herb sometimes goes by the name perilla, but it is most commonly called shiso in the Seattle area. Chef Naftaly likes to leave the seeds in the Thai chile for this recipe, which contribute extra spicy heat to the otherwise subtly flavored soup.

1 tablespoon olive oil	1 pound ripe nectarines, peeled, quartered,
¾ cup coarsely chopped onion	and pitted
1 large shallot, minced	½ cup loosely packed fresh shiso leaves
2 cloves garlic, coarsely chopped	(about 15 leaves)
½ Thai chile, cored and chopped	2½ cups chicken stock, preferably homemade
1 bay leaf	Salt
1 sprig thyme	

HEAT THE OLIVE OIL in a medium saucepan over medium heat. Add the onion, shallot, garlic, and chile and sauté until tender and aromatic, 5 to 7 minutes. Stir in the bay leaf and thyme. Add the nectarines, shiso, and chicken stock and cook, covered, until the nectarines are soft, 10 to 15 minutes, depending on their ripeness.

TAKE THE PAN from the heat and let cool for a few minutes. Discard the bay leaf and thyme sprig and purée the soup with an immersion blender. (Alternatively, purée the soup, in batches, in a food processor or blender.) Strain the soup through a fine sieve set over a bowl, pressing to remove as much of the flavorful soup as possible, then return the soup to the saucepan.

REHEAT THE SOUP GENTLY, then season to taste with salt, and serve hot, or chill thoroughly to serve cold.

Makes 4 to 6 servings

Seattle Cioppino

Anthony's Pier 66

Cioppino can be made using a variety of fresh fish and shellfish, although Dungeness crab is a classic part of the mix. Other good additions include squid, lobster, scallops, or king crab.

Have your fishmonger clean and portion the Dungeness crab for you. You can use canned tomatoes for the sauce, especially when fresh aren't at their best and most flavorful. You can also simplify the grocery list by reducing the number of seafoods, using just mussels or clams rather than both, or choosing just one type of fish.

1 cooked Dungeness crab (about 2 pounds), cleaned and cracked	¾ pound halibut, lingcod, or other firm white fish fillet, skin and pin bones removed, cut into 1-inch cubes
1½ pounds Manila clams, scrubbed	8 ounces salmon fillet, skin and pin bones removed, cut into 1-inch cubes
1½ pounds mussels, scrubbed and debearded	8 to 12 spot prawns or other large shrimp, peeled and deveined

CIOPPINO SAUCE

2 tablespoons olive oil	Salt and freshly ground black pepper
1 cup minced onion	1¼ pounds plum (roma) tomatoes, cored and diced
1 tablespoon minced garlic	2 cups clam juice
¼ cup chopped basil	1½ cups dry white wine
2 tablespoons minced flat-leaf (Italian) parsley	1 can (6 ounces) tomato paste
2 tablespoons minced marjoram	
1½ teaspoons crushed fennel seeds	

FOR THE SAUCE, heat the oil in a large pot over medium-high heat. Add the onion and garlic and sauté until tender and translucent, 3 to 5 minutes. Add the basil, parsley, marjoram, and fennel seeds with salt and pepper to taste. Stir and cook for 1 minute, then add the tomatoes, clam juice, wine, and tomato paste. Bring to a boil over high heat, then reduce the heat to medium and simmer, uncovered, until the sauce is well flavored and the tomatoes are quite soft, about 45 minutes.

ADD THE CRAB, clams, and mussels—in that order—to the sauce. Cover the pot, bring to a boil over high heat, and boil just until the clams and mussels are beginning to open, 2 to 3 minutes. Scatter the halibut, salmon, and shrimp over the top, reduce the heat to medium, cover, and continue to cook until the fish and shrimp are just cooked through and the shellfish have opened, about 5 minutes longer.

SPOON THE SEAFOOD into large shallow soup bowls, distributing the different types evenly and discarding any clams or mussels that failed to open. Spoon the sauce over the seafood and serve, setting out a large bowl on the table for the discarded shells.

Makes 4 to 6 servings

Hungarian Mushroom Soup

Yarrow Bay Beach Café

You can add more lemon juice and/or sour cream to taste, depending on how tangy and rich you'd like the soup. For the best result, use good-quality Hungarian paprika. If you've had a dusty can of paprika on your spice shelf for an unknown amount of time, this is the time to restock.

6 tablespoons unsalted butter	2 tablespoons soy sauce
1 medium onion, chopped	5 cups chicken stock, preferably homemade
Salt and freshly ground black pepper	½ cup all-purpose flour
¾ pound white mushrooms, wiped clean, trimmed, and sliced	1¼ cups whipping cream
	¼ cup freshly squeezed lemon juice
2 tablespoons chopped garlic	¼ cup chopped flat-leaf (Italian) parsley
2 tablespoons minced dill	¼ teaspoon hot pepper sauce
2 tablespoons sweet Hungarian paprika	½ cup sour cream

MELT 2 TABLESPOONS of the butter in a medium saucepan over medium heat. Add the onion with salt and pepper to taste and sauté until tender and translucent, about 5 minutes. Add the mushrooms, garlic, dill, paprika, and soy sauce, and stir to mix evenly. Add 2 cups of the chicken stock, bring just to a boil, then reduce the heat to medium-low and simmer, uncovered, for 10 to 15 minutes. Take the pan from the heat and set aside.

MELT THE REMAINING 4 tablespoons butter in a large saucepan or soup pot over medium heat. Add the flour and cook, stirring constantly, until the flour is bubbly and has a slightly nutty aroma but is not browned, 2 to 3 minutes. Stir in the cream and cook, stirring frequently, until thickened, 8 to 10 minutes. Gently stir in the mushroom mixture followed by the lemon juice, parsley, hot pepper sauce, and the remaining 3 cups chicken stock. Cook over medium heat, stirring often, until heated through and well blended.

TAKE THE SOUP from the heat and stir in the sour cream. Taste the soup for seasoning, adding more salt and pepper to taste. Ladle into warmed soup bowls and serve.

Makes 8 servings

Sausage and Lentil Soup

Cucina! Cucina!

This is the perfect hearty, warming winter soup, aromatic with mustard and rich with sausage and lentils. If you like spice, feel free to use spicy sausages. The addition of cream certainly embellishes the soup's richness, but you could omit the cream if you prefer.

1 tablespoon unsalted butter	1½ cups dried lentils
1 tablespoon extra virgin olive oil	6 cups chicken stock, preferably homemade
4 links Italian sausage (about 1 pound total)	1 cup whipping cream
½ cup finely chopped onion	1 to 2 tablespoons Dijon mustard
½ cup finely chopped carrot	1 tablespoon red wine vinegar
¼ cup finely chopped leek, white and pale green parts only	1½ cups firmly packed, coarsely chopped spinach
¼ cup finely chopped celery	Freshly grated Parmesan cheese
Salt and freshly ground black pepper	

HEAT THE BUTTER and olive oil in a medium saucepan over medium heat. Add the sausage and cook until evenly browned on all sides and cooked through, 8 to 10 minutes. Transfer the sausages to paper towels and set aside to cool, reserving 2 tablespoons of the cooking fat in the pan.

ADD THE ONION, carrot, leek, and celery to the saucepan and cook over medium-high heat until the vegetables are tender, about 5 minutes. Season to taste with salt and pepper, then stir in the lentils. Add the chicken stock and bring to a boil, stirring occasionally to prevent the lentils from sticking to the bottom of the pan. Reduce the heat to low and simmer, uncovered, until the lentils are tender, about 40 minutes.

CUT THE SAUSAGES into ¼-inch-thick slices. When the lentils are tender, add the sausages, cream, mustard, vinegar, and all but ¼ cup of the spinach. Stir until well combined, bring just to a boil, then reduce the heat to low and simmer, uncovered, for 5 minutes longer. Taste the soup for seasoning, adding more mustard, salt, or pepper to taste.

LADLE THE SOUP into warmed bowls, sprinkle some of the remaining spinach over each serving, and finish with a sprinkling of Parmesan cheese before serving.

Makes 6 to 8 servings

Chilled Cucumber Soup
with Smoked Sturgeon and Curry Oil

Rover's

In many recipes, blenders and food processors are considered to be interchangeable, but here it is important to use a blender to attain the proper smooth, even texture. You can make the soup base a few hours in advance and chill it, but give it one last whirl in the blender just before serving. English cucumbers are technically seedless, but it's still a good idea to scoop out the soft, watery center where the seeds would have been.

Cold-smoked sturgeon, which is not as widely available as cold-smoked salmon, is a great treat and worth seeking out. Salmon makes a great substitute, however. The curry oil yields more than is needed for this recipe, but the extra will keep indefinitely in the refrigerator. Chef-owner Thierry Rautureau suggests using it to baste a whole chicken before and during roasting, in a vinaigrette with soy and ginger, or for sautéing fish.

3 large English (seedless) cucumbers	1 tablespoon finely shredded tarragon
4 large, thin slices cold-smoked sturgeon or salmon (about 4 ounces)	Salt and freshly ground white pepper

CURRY OIL

½ teaspoon yellow mustard seeds	2 teaspoons curry powder
½ teaspoon fennel seeds	½ cup peanut or canola oil

FOR THE CURRY OIL, combine the mustard and fennel seeds in a small skillet and toast over medium heat, stirring often, until the seeds begin to brown and are aromatic, about 5 minutes. Transfer the seeds to the top of a double boiler or to a small heatproof bowl, then stir in the curry powder followed by the oil. Set the oil mixture over a pan of simmering, not boiling, water and heat until the oil is hot and begins to foam around the edges of the bowl, about 5 minutes. Carefully take the spice oil from the water bath and let cool completely, which may take a couple of hours. Don't stir the oil as it cools; you want the spices to settle to the bottom of the bowl, leaving the flavored oil clear. Skim off any spices that insist on floating. When the oil is fully cooled, slowly pour it into a clean squeeze bottle or another small bowl, leaving the spices behind in the bottom of the first bowl. Discard the spices.

PEEL THE CUCUMBERS, halve them lengthwise, and scoop out and discard the soft center (see introduction). Cut the cucumbers into 1-inch chunks and refrigerate until fully chilled, at least 1 hour.

SHORTLY BEFORE SERVING, make rosettes of the smoked sturgeon. Cut 1 slice in half or thirds crosswise to make strips about 1½ inches wide. Place the strips end to end, overlapping them slightly, so you have one long, narrow strip. Loosely roll up the connected strips, then set the roll upright on a small plate, fanning out the outer edges slightly to create a rosettelike effect. Repeat with the remaining slices to make 4 rosettes in all.

PUT 3 OR 4 PIECES of the chilled cucumber in the blender and pulse a few times to chop finely, then purée until smooth, scraping down the sides as needed. Continue adding 1 or 2 pieces at a time and puréeing until very smooth and all of the cucumber has been puréed. Add the tarragon with salt and pepper to taste, then pulse a few more times to blend thoroughly. (Depending on the size of your blender, you may need to purée the cucumber in 2 batches, stirring them together at the end.)

LADLE THE SOUP into chilled shallow soup bowls. Set a rosette of smoked sturgeon in the center and drizzle about ½ teaspoon of the curry oil over each soup. Serve right away.

Makes 4 servings

Nettle Soup

Le Gourmand

Here's your chance to get back at those pesky stinging nettles that can wreak havoc on a nice walk in the woods. Bruce Naftaly, chef-owner of Ballard's glorious Le Gourmand restaurant, has become famous for his nettle soup, which he calls the "first soup of spring," when the nettle leaves are deliciously tender.

Nettles lose their sting once they're cooked, but not a second before. Take care when harvesting and handling them (see Nettles, page 67) to avoid their prickly sting.

4 cups chicken stock, preferably homemade
1 small Yellow Finn or Yukon Gold potato, peeled and diced
½ small celery root, peeled and diced

4 ounces young, tender nettle leaves
Freshly grated or ground nutmeg
Salt and freshly ground black pepper

PUT THE CHICKEN STOCK in a medium saucepan. Add the potato and celery root and bring just to a boil. Reduce the heat to medium-low and simmer, covered, until the vegetables are tender, about 15 minutes. Add the nettles, using tongs to avoid being stung. Cover and simmer until tender, about 10 minutes. Take the pan from the heat and let cool for a few minutes.

PURÉE THE SOUP with an immersion blender. (Alternatively, purée the soup in batches in a food processor or blender and return the soup to the pan.) Reheat the soup over medium heat, season to taste with nutmeg, salt, and pepper, and serve in warmed bowls.

Makes 4 servings

Stinging Nettles

Remember those Scout nature walks and summer day camps at the city park? In Seattle they were often held at Carkeek Park, where forest, swamp, and beach interconnect. Now, what was the first thing they drilled into you head? Look out for nettles! They sting!

In spite of the prickly plant's sting, nettles have been gathered as a tasty and nutritious food for hundreds of years the world over. Stinging nettles *(Urtica dioica)* are best picked in the spring, when the most desirable young leaves and shoots are appearing and before the plants flower. Take a pair of scissors, a pair of good gardening gloves, and a basket for your pickings. Look on country roadsides, trails, stream banks, and at the edges of woods. Pick whole shoots and tops of young, pale green leaves, cutting them with scissors and laying them tidily in your basket. If you happen to get stung, just rub on a little alcohol, toothpaste, or some juice from the nettles themselves.

Nettles are most commonly cooked like spinach, and the cooking process eliminates the sting. Allow 30 or so young nettle tops per person. Wearing rubber gloves, wash the nettles and immediately place them in a large saucepan with a half-teaspoon minced garlic and a teaspoon butter per serving. Cover tightly and steam until tender, 5 to 10 minutes, over medium heat. Season to taste with salt and freshly ground black pepper. Or try substituting nettles in your favorite creamed spinach recipe.

Soup is another great way to enjoy a nettle harvest. Chef Bruce Naftaly, owner-chef of Le Gourmand and one of Seattle's Northwest cuisine pioneers, has made Nettle Soup (page 66) since his restaurant first opened in 1985. And now, if you are inclined to get out and forage about for wild foods, you can make it at home, too.

—KC

Seafood Chowder

Palisade

This rich chowder is a great way to start any meal.
Here, chef John Howie uses crabmeat and shrimp, but you could also use
cubed halibut (or other firm fish fillet), bay scallops, and/or lobster pieces. For a decadent
finish, top each bowl with a splash of sherry just before serving.

3 spears asparagus, trimmed and cut on the diagonal into 1-inch pieces
¼ cup diced red potato
4 tablespoons unsalted butter
¼ cup diced onion
¼ cup diced green bell pepper
¼ cup diced red bell pepper
¼ cup diced yellow bell pepper
¼ cup all-purpose flour
2 cups half-and-half

1 cup clam juice or fish stock
¼ cup dry sherry
4 ounces Dungeness crabmeat
4 ounces bay shrimp or other small cooked shrimp
¼ cup corn kernels (fresh or thawed frozen)
½ teaspoon chopped thyme
Salt and freshly ground white pepper
2 teaspoons minced chives, for garnish

BRING A SMALL SAUCEPAN of lightly salted water to a boil and fill a small bowl with ice water. Add the asparagus pieces to the boiling water and blanch for 1 minute. With a slotted spoon, transfer the asparagus pieces to the ice water until cool, then drain well and set aside. Return the water to a boil, add the diced potato, and cook until just tender, 5 to 7 minutes. Drain well and set aside.

MELT THE BUTTER in a large saucepan over medium heat. Add the onion and sauté until tender and translucent, 3 to 5 minutes. Add the bell peppers and cook until nearly tender, 2 to 3 minutes longer. Add the flour and cook, stirring constantly, until it evenly coats the vegetables but is not browned, 2 to 3 minutes. Slowly add the half-and-half, clam juice, and sherry while stirring constantly. Bring the mixture just to a boil over high heat, then lower the heat to medium and simmer, stirring constantly, until the chowder has thickened, about 5 minutes. Stir in the crab, shrimp, corn, potato, asparagus, and thyme with salt and pepper to taste. Continue stirring until well mixed and all the ingredients are heated through, about 5 minutes longer.

LADLE THE CHOWDER into warmed bowls, garnish with the chives, and serve.

Makes 4 servings

Fall Pumpkin and Squash Bisque

Andre's Eurasian Bistro

A great garnish for this richly colored **autumn soup would be** roasted
pumpkin seeds (see Wonderful Winter Squash, page 95). For extra flavor, toss the seeds in a
bit of melted butter and curry powder before roasting. To simplify the recipe, use only one
squash variety rather than using both acorn and butternut.

¼ cup unsalted butter	1 cup chopped carrot
1 medium onion, diced	½ teaspoon curry powder
1 tablespoon all-purpose flour	¼ teaspoon five-spice powder
½ cup dry white wine	¼ teaspoon ground cinnamon
2 cups pumpkin purée (fresh or canned)	¼ teaspoon paprika
1 cup peeled, seeded, and chopped acorn squash	¼ teaspoon freshly grated or ground nutmeg
	6 cups chicken stock, preferably homemade
1 cup peeled, seeded, and chopped butternut squash	½ cup canned tomato sauce
	Salt and freshly ground black pepper
1 cup peeled and chopped yam	1 cup whipping cream

MELT THE BUTTER in a large, heavy saucepan over medium-high heat. Add the onion and
sauté until tender and translucent, 3 to 5 minutes. Add the flour and stir to mix evenly, about 1
minute. Stir in the wine and cook for 1 to 2 minutes, then add the pumpkin, squashes, yam, and
carrot. Stir in the curry powder, five-spice powder, cinnamon, paprika, and nutmeg, followed by
the chicken stock and tomato sauce. Bring to a boil over high heat, reduce the heat to medium-
low, and simmer, uncovered, until the vegetables are very tender, about 45 minutes. Take the
saucepan from the heat, season to taste with salt and pepper, and let cool for 10 minutes.

PURÉE THE SOUP with an immersion blender until it is fairly smooth but still has texture.
(Alternatively, purée the soup, in batches, in a food processor or blender, or pass it through a
food mill, then return the soup to the pan.) Taste for seasoning, and adjust with salt and
pepper. Stir in the cream and bring to a simmer over medium-high heat.

LADLE INTO WARMED SOUP BOWLS and serve immediately.

Makes 8 servings

Herb Roasted Chicken and Bread Salad

Union Square Grill

This recipe has two parts, each of which could stand alone deliciously: tasty roasted chicken with a wonderful marinade, and a hearty bread salad embellished with peppery arugula. Together they make a generous main-course salad. You could use four chicken breasts (preferably bone-in) instead of the whole cut-up chicken if you prefer. Note that the chicken should marinate overnight before roasting, so plan ahead

A 3-pound chicken, cut up (2 each leg/thigh portions and breasts)	1 cup chicken stock, preferably homemade
	2 tablespoons red wine (optional)
1 tablespoon olive oil	1 tablespoon balsamic vinegar

HERB MARINADE

½ cup olive oil	1½ teaspoons minced rosemary
3 tablespoons minced basil	1 teaspoon minced thyme
2 tablespoons freshly squeezed orange juice	1 teaspoon grated orange zest
2 tablespoons minced garlic	½ teaspoon salt
1 tablespoon grated lemon zest	½ teaspoon freshly ground black pepper

BREAD SALAD

3 tablespoons pine nuts	6 tablespoons chopped green onions
3 tablespoons currants	2 tablespoons julienned garlic
1 teaspoon red wine vinegar	8 ounces crusty bread, cut into 1-inch cubes (about 6 cups)
½ cup plus 1 tablespoon olive oil	
2 tablespoons champagne or white wine vinegar	1 bunch arugula (about 4 ounces), rinsed, trimmed, and large leaves torn in half
Salt and freshly ground black pepper	

IN A LARGE SHALLOW BOWL, combine the herb marinade ingredients and stir to mix. Add the chicken pieces, turning to coat each evenly in the marinade, cover with plastic wrap, and marinate in the refrigerator for 24 hours.

SHORTLY BEFORE COOKING the chicken, preheat the oven to 375°F.

FOR THE BREAD SALAD, scatter the pine nuts in a baking pan and toast in the oven until lightly browned and aromatic, 3 to 5 minutes, gently shaking the pan once or twice to help the nuts toast evenly. Set aside to cool; leave the oven set at 375°F and oil a 1½-quart baking dish.

PUT THE CURRANTS in a small dish and add the red wine vinegar with just enough warm water to cover (about 1 tablespoon). Let soak until plump, about 10 minutes, then drain and set aside. In a small bowl, combine ½ cup of the olive oil and the champagne vinegar with salt and pepper to taste. Whisk to mix and set aside. In a small skillet, heat the remaining tablespoon of olive oil over medium heat, add the green onions and garlic, and sauté until tender and aromatic, 1 to 2 minutes.

IN A LARGE BOWL, combine the bread cubes, pine nuts, currants, vinaigrette, green onions, and garlic. Toss to mix and spoon the bread salad into the prepared baking dish. Let sit for 30 minutes, then bake until the bread cubes just begin to crisp around the edges, 10 to 15 minutes. Cover with foil to keep warm and set aside while baking the chicken.

HEAT THE TABLESPOON OF OLIVE OIL in a large ovenproof skillet over medium-high heat. Take the chicken pieces from the marinade and wipe off most of the marinade (bits of garlic and citrus zest will tend to burn in the skillet if left on the chicken). Sauté the chicken until golden brown on all sides, about 6 to 8 minutes total. Depending on the size of the skillet you're using, you may need to do this in batches. Transfer the chicken to a baking dish. In a small bowl combine the chicken stock, red wine (if using), and balsamic vinegar, and pour this over the chicken. Bake until the chicken is just cooked through, 15 to 20 minutes.

SET ASIDE 4 sprigs of the arugula for garnish and toss the rest with the bread salad. Spoon the bread salad on warmed plates, top with the chicken pieces, garnish with the reserved arugula sprigs, and serve.

Makes 4 servings

Local Garden Greens
with Asian Pears and Five-Spice Glazed Walnuts

The Painted Table

Asian pears have a firmer, crisper flesh when ripe than the more common European varieties do. Also, the Asian varieties are rounder and look more like an apple than a pear. They make a great addition to this salad, offering a crisp texture and a sweet flavor that is echoed in the glazed walnuts. Chef Tim Kelley uses a mixture of whatever fresh seasonal greens are at their best. The list here is just a starting point; you can use any tender green that you like.

1 cup walnut halves	1 Asian pear
⅓ cup honey	Edible flowers (such as pansies, nasturtiums,
1 teaspoon five-spice powder	johnny jump-ups, and/or violets), for garnish
8 ounces mixed seasonal greens (such as red oak, mizuna, tatsoi, baby spinach, curly endive, arugula and/or lamb's lettuce), rinsed, dried, and large leaves torn into pieces	

ANJOU PEAR DRESSING

2 tablespoons Anjou pear juice (see page 73)	2 tablespoons light olive oil
2 tablespoons champagne vinegar	1 teaspoon poppy seeds
¼ cup canola oil	Salt and freshly ground black pepper

FOR THE DRESSING, whisk together the pear juice and vinegar, then whisk in the canola oil, olive oil, and poppy seeds with salt and pepper to taste. Set aside.

PREHEAT THE OVEN to 350°F. Scatter the walnuts in a baking pan and toast, gently shaking the pan once or twice to help the nuts toast evenly, until lightly browned and aromatic, 5 to 7 minutes. While the nuts are toasting, heat the honey to a simmer in a small saucepan over medium-high heat, 2 to 3 minutes. Stir in the five-spice powder and take the pan from the heat. After the walnuts are toasted, add them to the honey mixture and stir gently to coat evenly. Spread the nuts on a piece of foil or waxed paper to cool.

PUT THE GREENS in a large bowl. Halve, core, and thinly slice the Asian pear, then add it to the bowl with the glazed walnuts. Whisk the pear dressing to reblend it, then drizzle the dressing over the greens and toss to mix evenly.

ARRANGE THE SALAD on individual plates, distributing the nuts and pear slices evenly, then top with edible flowers. Serve right away.

Makes 4 servings

Pear Juice

Start with a good, ripe Anjou pear, peeled and cored. If you have a juicer, simply juice the pear according to manufacturer's instructions. Or, purée about half of the pear in a food processor until smooth, then pass through a fine strainer to remove most of the fibrous flesh.

Cameo Apple Salad
with Treviso, Arugula, Oregon Blue Cheese, and Cider Vinaigrette

Palace Kitchen

With so few ingredients, this salad depends on the quality of flavor carried by each one: tender arugula, rich blue cheese, crisp Treviso, and a great tasting apple. Duskie Estes, chef of Palace Kitchen, prefers Cameo apples for this salad, but when they're not available she turns to Braeburn, Akane, or Sweet 16. Use whatever apple tastes best to you. Treviso is a variety of radicchio with narrow, deep red leaves that form a tight, long, tapered head. It looks like a cross between radicchio and Belgian endive, which are from the same family of chicories.

½ head Treviso or other radicchio, rinsed, cored, and dried

2 bunches arugula (about 4 ounces each), rinsed, trimmed, and dried

1 Cameo apple

6 to 8 ounces Oregon blue cheese or other blue cheese, crumbled

VINAIGRETTE

½ cup hard apple cider

1 teaspoon minced shallot

1½ tablespoons sherry vinegar

3 tablespoons olive oil

Salt and freshly ground black pepper

FOR THE VINAIGRETTE, combine the apple cider and shallot in a small saucepan over medium-high heat. Bring to a boil and reduce the mixture by half, then take the pan from the heat and set aside to cool. Whisk together the apple cider reduction and sherry vinegar in a small bowl. Slowly whisk in the olive oil. Season to taste with salt and pepper and set aside.

SEPARATE THE LEAVES of the Treviso, tear them into pieces, and put them in a large bowl with the arugula. (You should have about 10 cups loosely packed salad greens.) Core the apple, cut it into thin slices, and add them to the bowl. Whisk the vinaigrette to reblend, pour it over the salad, and toss to mix evenly. Taste the salad for seasoning, adding more salt or pepper to taste. Divide the salad among chilled plates, sprinkle the blue cheese over the top, and serve.

Makes 4 servings

Orange and Fennel Salad
with Sicilian Olives and Pecorino Romano Shavings

La Medusa

Sherri Serino and Lisa Becklund, chefs and co-owners of La Medusa, note that this is a great opportunity to use "your absolutely favorite olive oil." The mild flavors of the salad allow the fruitiness of top-quality olive oil to come through. Valencia oranges are preferred here because of their juicy, sweet flavor, but navel oranges can be used as well. You'll have some of the Pecorino Romano cheese left over after shaving off the thin slivers used as a garnish, but you'll be glad you do when you make that next batch of pasta for dinner.

2 Valencia or navel oranges	Salt and freshly ground black pepper
1 large fennel bulb	8 leaves Bibb lettuce, rinsed and dried
½ cup julienned red onion	12 Sicilian olives or other good green olives,
2 tablespoons extra virgin olive oil,	pitted
plus more for serving	2-ounce piece Pecorino Romano cheese

GRATE THE ZEST from the oranges and set the zest aside in a large bowl. Cut both ends from 1 of the oranges, just to the flesh. Set the orange upright on a cutting board and use a sharp knife to cut away all of the peel and pith, following the curve of the fruit. Try not to cut away too much of the flesh with the peel. Working over the bowl of zest to catch the juice, hold the peeled orange in your hand and slide the knife blade down one side of a section, cutting it from the membrane. Cut down the other side of the same section and let it fall into the bowl. (Pick out and discard any seeds as you go.) Repeat for the remaining sections, folding back the flaps of the membrane like the pages of a book as you work. Squeeze the juice from the membrane core into the bowl. Repeat with the second orange.

TRIM THE ROOT END and stalks of the fennel bulb, reserving some of the fronds. Cut the bulb lengthwise in half and cut out the tough core. Cut the fennel lengthwise into julienne strips. Mince enough of the fennel fronds to measure 1 tablespoon. Add the fennel, fennel fronds, and onion to the oranges and toss gently. Drizzle the 2 tablespoons olive oil over the mixture and season to taste with salt and pepper.

ARRANGE THE BIBB LETTUCE on chilled salad plates, using 2 leaves for each plate. Spoon the orange and fennel mixture over the bed of lettuce leaves and garnish each salad with 3 olives. Using a cheese shaver or a vegetable peeler, shave slivers of cheese over the salads. Drizzle a bit more olive oil over all and serve.

Makes 4 servings

Avocado Carpaccio with Radish and Herb Salad

Carmelita

Here, the peppery crunch of radishes is a delicious contrast to the silky richness of avocado, not to mention an appealing color contrast. Embellished with zippy horseradish cream and crispy fried shallots, this salad is a wonderful way to wake up the palate at the start of a meal. A combination of different radish types, such as French Breakfast, Purple, or Icicle, will yield a range of colors and flavors, but regular red radishes also work well here.

Vegetable oil, for frying
3 shallots, thinly sliced
¼ cup rice flour or all-purpose flour
3 ripe but firm avocados
Juice of 2 lemons
3 tablespoons extra virgin olive oil
1 bunch radishes, stemmed and thinly sliced

1 cup lightly packed mixed herb leaves
(flat-leaf [Italian] parsley, tarragon, chervil, chives, lemon balm, sweet cicely, and/or salad burnet)
1 tablespoon grated lemon zest

HORSERADISH CREAM

½ cup crème fraîche or sour cream
3 tablespoons grated fresh horseradish

2 tablespoons half-and-half or milk
Salt and freshly ground black pepper

FOR THE HORSERADISH CREAM, combine the crème fraîche, horseradish, and half-and-half in a small bowl. Stir to blend evenly, then season to taste with salt and pepper; set aside.

POUR OIL to a depth of about 2 inches into a small, heavy saucepan and heat over medium-high heat to 350°F. While the oil is heating, separate the shallot slices into rings and put them in a medium bowl. Add the flour and a generous pinch each of salt and pepper. Toss gently to coat the shallot rings evenly. To test the temperature of the oil, add 1 shallot ring: the oil is hot enough if it sizzles as the shallot is added. Working in batches, shake excess flour from the shallot rings and carefully add them to the hot oil. Fry until golden and crispy, 1 to 2 minutes. Scoop out the fried shallot with a slotted spoon and drain on paper towels. Continue with the remaining shallots, allowing the oil to reheat between batches as needed. Season the shallots with salt and set aside.

HALVE, PIT, AND PEEL THE AVOCADOS. Set each half, cut side down, on the cutting board and thinly slice lengthwise. Press gently on the sliced halves to fan them out and transfer each half to the center of a large plate. Spread the slices out a bit more to cover most of the base of the plate, carpaccio style, then gently brush the slices with some of the lemon juice.

DRIZZLE 1 TABLESPOON of the olive oil over the avocado halves and season to taste with salt and pepper. Spoon the horseradish cream around the edge of each serving of avocado.

IN A MEDIUM BOWL, combine the radish slices and herbs. Add the rest of the lemon juice, the lemon zest, the remaining 2 tablespoons olive oil, and salt and pepper to taste. Toss gently to mix and divide the radish salad among the plates, gently mounding it in the center of the avocado. Sprinkle the shallot rings over and around the radish salad and serve.

Makes 6 servings

Herbs—From Backyards to Menus

So many people grow beautiful and exotic herbs but have no idea what to do with them. Sure, a few varieties tied together with a strand of chive make an attractive plate garnish, and some pretty little sprigs of Italian parsley are decorative on roasted chicken, but what about cooking with them—the pineapple and fruit sages of the world, lemon verbena, coconut geranium, chervil, salad burnet, and anise hyssop?

Well, have no more herbal fear. Whether you're an herb-curious cook growing a couple of patio pots of lemon thyme, sexy lavender, and tricolor sage or a true exotic herb plant junkie with every available inch between the plants in your perennial flower bed tucked with rose geranium, curry plant, lemon balm, and Thai basil—the prolific tips and wisdom from Seattle chefs will vanquish the qualms of all you herb gardeners.

Have you seen "herb salad" mentioned on Seattle restaurant menus and wondered what it is? Well, it's simple. Herb salad consists of "picked" leaves of an assortment of nicely flavored herbs, usually a mix of a few stronger herbs tossed with a lot of milder ones. The proportions might be something like this: ¼ cup Italian parsley leaves, ¼ cup chervil leaves, 2 tablespoons thinly sliced chives, 2 tablespoons tarragon leaves, 2 tablespoons torn lemon balm leaves—all of them washed and patted dry, then tossed together. It's a nice embellishment to pouf on top of a simple pasta, grilled fish, or salad, like the Avocado Carpaccio with Radish and Herb Salad (page 76) served at Carmelita, the superpopular vegetarian restaurant in Phinney Ridge.

Mixing several milder, well-known herbs in an herb salad with one unfamiliar variety is a good way to expand your herbal repertoire. And herb salads can be used to display a beauty such as variegated marjoram, which tastes pretty much like its plain green cousin but is much showier.

Also, use your imagination to come up with new applications of common herbs. Almost everyone has had rosemary in spaghetti sauce. Now how about trying the Lemon Rosemary Biscotti recipe (page 218) from Still Life in Fremont →

or Café Flora's Rosemary Lemonade (page 238)? The woody stems developed by some perennial herb plants can even serve as skewers, as in the The Herbfarm's Pan-Fried Mussels on Rosemary Skewers (page 32).

Have you always wanted to investigate edible flowers? Painted Table's Local Garden Greens with Asian Pears and Five-Spice Glazed Walnuts (page 72) would be a good place to start. And the Lavender-Honey Ice Cream recipe from Cassis (page 193) provides a fine illustration of the use of dried herb blossoms.

One creative way to become acquainted with herbs you don't really know what to do with is to pick a leaf, close your eyes, and take a nibble. Now consult your taste memory and dream up "What would this go with?"

Another really good, and more obvious, tip is in what the herb is called. Usually it actually tastes like its name. Take, for instance, lemon verbena. It packs a totally awesome lemon punch in a simple vinaigrette. Similarly, lemon thyme and lime basil are varieties where a familiar herb flavor also carries citrusy notes. Thai basil, one more of the many basil varieties, is often described as having a spicier fragrance than sweet basil. The Thai Basil–Seared Mahimahi with Red Curry Lobster Essence (page 160) served at Roy's takes full advantage of these aromatic characteristics.

Often the name of a seemingly inscrutable herb reveals its culinary attributes, as with rose geranium. Chef Jerry Traunfeld, developer of many great recipes and exciting uses for a plethora of herbs, shared his recipe for Apricot, Rose, and Saffron Tart (page 196). It's absolutely as exotic as you'd expect from this acclaimed chef of The Herbfarm.

—KC

Caesar for Two

Union Square Grill

At Union Square Grill, this salad is served with tableside flourish, assembled and tossed under the scrutiny of diners. Raw egg is a classic element of Caesar salad, but if you have any concerns about eating raw egg (not recommended for pregnant women, children, the elderly, or anyone with immune deficiencies), use ¼ cup pasteurized egg its place.

1 small head romaine lettuce, rinsed, trimmed, and dried	2 teaspoons red wine vinegar
	⅓ cup freshly grated Parmesan cheese
⅓ cup extra virgin olive oil	Salt and freshly ground black pepper

CROUTONS

2 or 3 slices French bread, ½ inch thick
2 teaspoons extra virgin olive oil

DRESSING

1 egg	¾ teaspoon minced garlic
1 teaspoon Worcestershire sauce	¼ teaspoon dry mustard
¾ teaspoon minced anchovy	

PREHEAT THE OVEN to 400° F.

FOR THE CROUTONS, lightly brush both sides of each bread slice with olive oil and arrange them on a baking sheet. Bake until lightly browned, 6 to 8 minutes. Cut the bread into ¾-inch squares and set aside.

FOR THE DRESSING, combine the egg, Worcestershire sauce, anchovy, garlic, and mustard in a small bowl. Mix with a fork until well blended; set aside.

FOR THE SALAD, cut the romaine leaves into 1-inch pieces and put them in a salad bowl. Drizzle the oil and vinegar over and toss until the leaves are shiny and evenly coated. Pour the dressing over the romaine and add the croutons and half of the Parmesan. Toss until evenly coated, adding salt and pepper to taste. Divide the salad and croutons between individual chilled plates and sprinkle with the remaining Parmesan.

Makes 2 servings

Smoked Turkey, Brown Rice, and Vegetable Salad
in Creamy Soy-Balsamic Dressing

Still Life in Fremont Coffeehouse

This salad packs a whole lot of healthfulness into one big bowl, just the kind of good-for-you food that the Still Life is known for.

2½ cups water	1 red bell pepper, cored, seeded, and
1 cup long-grain brown rice	thinly sliced
½ cup pecan pieces	1 cup shredded or diced smoked turkey
4 ounces green beans, trimmed and cut into	(about 6 ounces)
2-inch pieces	½ cup thinly sliced yellow squash
1 cup thinly sliced carrot	½ cup frozen peas, thawed
1 cup finely shredded red cabbage	½ cup minced flat-leaf (Italian) parsley

CREAMY SOY-BALSAMIC DRESSING

¼ cup balsamic vinegar	¾ teaspoon minced rosemary
¼ cup mayonnaise	½ teaspoon yellow mustard seeds
2 tablespoons olive oil	2 ounces mushrooms, wiped clean, trimmed, and
1½ teaspoons minced garlic	coarsely chopped
1½ teaspoons soy sauce	Salt and freshly ground black pepper

FOR THE SOY-BALSAMIC DRESSING, combine the vinegar, mayonnaise, oil, garlic, soy sauce, rosemary, and mustard seeds in a large bowl. Stir to mix evenly, then stir in the mushrooms and season to taste with salt and pepper. (Note that the soy sauce adds saltiness to this dressing, so you may not need to add more salt.) Set aside to marinate at room temperature while preparing the rest of the salad.

BRING THE WATER with a generous pinch of salt just to a boil in a medium saucepan. Stir in the rice, then cover and cook over low heat until all the water has been absorbed, about 45 minutes. Take the pan from the heat and let sit, still covered, for 10 minutes, then stir the rice with a fork to separate the grains. Set aside to cool completely.

PREHEAT THE OVEN to 350°F. Scatter the pecan pieces in a baking pan and toast in the oven, gently shaking the pan once or twice to help the nuts toast evenly, until lightly browned and aromatic, 5 to 7 minutes. Set aside to cool.

BRING A MEDIUM SAUCEPAN of lightly salted water to a boil and fill a medium bowl with ice water. When the water boils, add the green beans and parboil until they are slightly tender but still bright green, 2 to 3 minutes. With a slotted spoon, transfer the green beans to the ice water and let cool. Return the water to a boil, add the carrot, and simmer until they are just barely tender, 2 to 3 minutes. Drain the carrots and put them in the ice water to cool. When the vegetables are cooled completely, drain them well and spread them on paper towels to dry.

ADD THE COOLED RICE, pecans, green beans, carrot, cabbage, red bell pepper, turkey, squash, peas, and parsley to the bowl with the dressing and mushrooms. Stir gently to combine, then taste the salad for seasoning, adding more salt and pepper if needed. Serve right away, or refrigerate until ready to serve.

Makes 6 servings

Roasted Pepper and Grilled Asparagus Salad

The Hunt Club

This easy salad produces elegant results, both in flavor and in presentation. The plump grilled asparagus is paired with red and yellow roasted peppers on a bed of vibrant greens surrounded by a rich reduction of balsamic vinegar. There's a common misconception that the thinnest spears of asparagus are the best, when in fact the fatter spears hold up better to cooking and have great flavor and texture.

1 yellow bell pepper	½ cup balsamic vinegar
1 red bell pepper	1 head frisée, rinsed, tough outer leaves
16 spears asparagus	trimmed, tender leaves separated, and dried
4 tablespoons extra virgin olive oil	1 bunch watercress, rinsed, tough stems trimmed,
Salt and freshly ground black pepper	and dried
¼ cup pine nuts	

ROAST THE BELL PEPPERS over a gas flame or under the broiler, turning occasionally to roast evenly, until the skin blisters and blackens, 5 to 10 minutes total. Put the peppers in a plastic bag, securely seal it, and set aside to cool. When cool enough to handle, peel away and discard the skin. Remove the cores and seeds and cut the peppers into quarters lengthwise. Set aside.

PREHEAT AN OUTDOOR GRILL or the broiler. Snap the tough ends from the asparagus and toss the spears in 2 tablespoons of the oil, coating them completely. Season to taste with salt and pepper. Cook the asparagus on the hot grill or under the broiler, turning occasionally, until just tender but with a bit of crunch, 4 to 6 minutes, depending on the thickness of the spears. Set aside to cool.

PREHEAT THE OVEN to 350°F. Scatter the pine nuts in a baking pan and toast, gently shaking the pan once or twice to help the nuts toast evenly, until lightly browned and aromatic, 5 to 7 minutes. Set aside to cool. In a small saucepan, bring the vinegar to a boil over medium-high heat and boil to reduce by about three-quarters (to a thin glaze), 5 to 7 minutes.

TO ASSEMBLE THE SALADS, arrange a mixture of frisée and watercress on salad plates. Lay 1 piece of yellow bell pepper on the greens and top with 2 asparagus spears, crossing one on top of the other. Cover with 1 piece of red bell pepper, then 2 more asparagus spears. Drizzle the balsamic glaze and the remaining 2 tablespoons oil over and around the salads, then dust lightly with salt and pepper to taste. Sprinkle with the toasted pine nuts and serve.

Makes 4 servings

Asparagus—Herald of Spring

One of the heralds of springtime in the Pacific Northwest is when green asparagus starts to pop up. This delicious, short-season wonder comes bursting into Seattle markets about mid-April and is usually seen on local menus until early July.

The vegetable is extensively grown in home gardens and has widely escaped cultivation to naturalize over large parts of the state as well. Commercial production of local asparagus is centered in the Walla Walla valley of southeastern Washington. There the deep, rich soil and mild climate produce a crop of tender spears with closed, compact tips.

Sometimes called "grass," local asparagus is best eaten just-picked and quickly cooked, only minutes from the earth. Now this is a taste treat!

Most restaurants steam their asparagus to just-tender perfection, but roasting or grilling is another preparation that enhances this vegetable's sweetness. The Hunt Club serves this seasonal favorite in its Roasted Pepper and Grilled Asparagus Salad (page 82), tossed up with frisée and balsamic vinaigrette. Fat spring asparagus has even appeared on local menus as "asparagus fries"—coated in tempura batter and briefly fried, it's delicious dipped in a citrusy soy dipping sauce.

When preparing asparagus there's no need to guess where to cut the stalk; it "knows" where it's tough. If you hold one end in each hand and bend it, the tougher end snaps right off at the perfect point . . . then just trim for neatness if you must.

Although a lot of people say they prefer the skinny, wispy asparagus spears, many Seattle chefs don't think those have the big flavor our larger Northwest stalks have. The fatties—say, finger-size around—are much better tasting.

Asparagus has been a mainstay at fine restaurants forever, from the garnish in a Bloody Mary to the side dish at almost every grand steakhouse, slathered in hollandaise. And, really, who doesn't love that little splurge?

—KC

Dungeness Crab with Red Radishes and Braeburn Apples

Nell's

At Nell's, chef-owner Philip Mihalski uses a ring mold to shape this delicately flavored crab mixture in a tidy circle and serves it with a tuft of arugula on top. You can do the same if a more formal presentation is desired, or you can offer the simplified dish suggested here. Chef Mihalski often finishes the salad with a squeeze of flavored oil—such as parsley—around the outer edge.

8 ounces Dungeness crabmeat
¼ cup peeled and diced Braeburn apple
2 tablespoons julienned red radish
2 tablespoons mayonnaise
2 teaspoons freshly squeezed lemon juice

Salt and freshly ground black pepper
½ bunch arugula (about 2 ounces), rinsed, trimmed, and dried
Extra virgin olive oil, for drizzling

COMBINE THE CRABMEAT, apple, radish, mayonnaise, and lemon juice in a medium bowl. Toss to mix evenly, then season to taste with salt and pepper.

ARRANGE THE ARUGULA in the centers of chilled salad plates. Mound the crabmeat mixture in the center, drizzle some oil around the outer edge of the salad, and serve.

Makes 4 servings

Yakima Cherry, Walla Walla Sweet Onion, and Basil Salad
with Balsamic Vinaigrette

Cassis

Chef Charlie Durham was inspired to create this unusual salad because the three
main ingredients flourish at about the same time each summer: cherries from the Yakima
Valley, sweet onions from Walla Walla, and aromatic basil from the herb garden. He typically
uses Bing cherries, as their juicy sweetness and deep red color are perfect
complements to the onion and basil.

⅓ cup olive oil	3 cups tender whole basil leaves, loosely packed
3 tablespoons balsamic vinegar	2 cups pitted cherries (about ¾ pound)
1 teaspoon minced shallot	2 cups thinly sliced Walla Walla Sweet onion,
Salt and freshly ground black pepper	rings separated

WHISK TOGETHER THE OIL, vinegar, and shallot with salt and pepper to taste in a small
bowl. Set aside.

COMBINE THE BASIL, cherries, and onions in a salad bowl or other large bowl. Drizzle the
vinaigrette over and toss to coat evenly. Arrange the salad on individual plates, distributing the
ingredients evenly, and serve.

Makes 4 servings

Heirloom Tomato Salad
with Rode Esterling Potatoes and Tapenade

Campagne

When heirloom tomatoes abound in late summer, it's hard not to buy
some of each kind available. Why hold back? Here, a blend of sizes, shapes, and colors
forms an ideal kaleidoscope for both the eye and the palate.

The anchovies used by chef Daisley Gordon at Campagne are exquisite
and meaty—not salty—fillets from Spain, where they're called *boquerones*. The fish are
caught in the Bay of Biscay, rinsed in brine, and packed in Spanish olive oil and white wine
vinegar. Don't substitute those "everyday" anchovies, which will overwhelm this salad. If you
can't find the *boquerones* (try Spanish Table, Whole Foods, and some PCC stores in the
Seattle area), it's best to go without and enjoy the salad as is, already a delight.

8 ounces organic Rode Esterling or other small, yellow-fleshed potatoes	¼ cup pitted Niçoise olives, very finely chopped
Salt and freshly cracked or ground black pepper	1 clove garlic, minced
4 tablespoons extra virgin olive oil	1 teaspoon chopped capers
1 tablespoon plus 1 teaspoon chopped flat-leaf (Italian) parsley	1½ pounds mixed heirloom tomatoes
1 teaspoon freshly squeezed lemon juice	8 to 12 imported Spanish white anchovies in vinegar *(boquerones)*

PUT THE POTATOES in a small saucepan and cover with cold water. Add a pinch of salt and
bring to a boil over medium-high heat. Reduce the heat to medium-low and simmer until the
potatoes are just tender, about 10 minutes. To test, insert the blade of a small, sharp knife into
the center of a few potatoes; it should release easily when they are cooked.

USING A SLOTTED SPOON, transfer the potatoes to a plate and let cool slightly. Remove the
tender, thin skin from the potatoes by rubbing with a roughly textured kitchen towel or paper
towel. Cut the potatoes into halves or quarters, depending on their size, and put them in a
small bowl. Add 1 tablespoon of the oil, 1 tablespoon of the parsley, and the lemon juice. Toss
gently to mix and set aside.

FOR THE TAPENADE, combine the olives, garlic, capers, and the remaining 1 teaspoon
parsley in a small bowl. Add the remaining 3 tablespoons oil, whisk to mix, and season to taste
with salt and pepper. Set aside.

CORE ANY LARGE TOMATOES and cut them into ¼-inch-thick slices. Stem smaller tomatoes and cut them into wedges or halves depending on their size. Arrange the tomatoes in the centers of chilled salad plates, varying the varieties on each, and sprinkle with salt. Put the potatoes along one side of the tomatoes and drape the anchovies over them. Spoon a few teaspoons of tapenade around the tomatoes and serve.

Makes 4 servings

Farmers' Markets, P-Patches, and Garden Gourmets

The Pike Place Market is the very heartbeat of Seattle. Established in 1907, it has been bringing the farmers directly to the residents ever since and is the oldest continuously operated market in the country, abounding with local honeys, dairy products, fruits, vegetables, grains, meats, and fish.

Now, thanks to Chris Curtis, the woman who is the "queen of farmers' markets," the University District, West Seattle, and Columbia City all have their own farmers' markets. She has put relentless energy into supporting local agriculture. And the rumor is that other neighborhood farmers' markets are in the wings.

At these markets locals clamor for heirloom tomatoes, fava beans, organic carrots, and unsprayed raspberries. The list of excellent, dedicated small farms continues to grow. From the now veteran Willy Greens to Full Circle Farms to the Indochinese Farming Project, they have brought new variety to our tables and influenced our eating habits. Urbanites now routinely dine on Asian greens, like edible pea vines, baby bok choy, or gai lan (Chinese broccoli) as well as frisée, rainbow chard, or garlic shoots.

Seattle Tilth is a network comprised of a diverse group of people dedicated to the practice and promotion of organic gardening and farming, urban ecology, composting, and creation of sustainable urban and rural communities. At their spring plant sale Tilth offers up to 40 varieties of tomatoes, some of which are planted in their demonstration garden. In early fall at the annual Tilth Organic Harvest Fair, they usually include an event dubbed the Great Tomato Taste Off, where more than 20 varieties grown by Master Gardeners, P-Patch growers, and backyard gardeners are sampled. There are yellow pear and yellow plum, teeny tiny Red Currants the size of peas, Lemon Boy (the color of its name), Green Zebra, and red-and-yellow-striped Tigerella, nicknamed Mr. Stripy. You might also taste Gregori's Altai; adapted for a short growing season, it was brought over from the Altai Mountains in central Asia.

The City of Seattle Department of Neighborhoods coordinates the P-Patch Program, which allows organic gardening only. Operated in conjunction with the nonprofit Friends of P-Patch, the program provides community garden space for→

Seattle residents. Some 1,900 plots serve more than 4,600 urban gardeners on 12 acres of land—spread out among 54 P-Patches. Special programs serve low-income, disabled, youth, and non-English-speaking populations, too.

The Interbay P-Patch has attracted quite a bit of attention for its Celebrity Composting Program. Now, really, in what other city would there be celebrity composters? Well-known Seattleites are invited to the garden on Saturdays for the "compost social." The dignitaries and notables turn a bin of compost, and in turn they get the compost bin named after them. Afterward, everyone gathers round for some homemade soup and Ciro bread.

Longtime Seattle journalist Emmett Watson once wrote in his column: "The best compost in this city, if not the world, is found down at the Interbay P-Patch. Interbay P-Patchers say that if you plant a carrot in their compost, the results are spectacular. They say this planted carrot will shoot up in record time, almost like a rocket off Ivar's fireworks barge on the Fourth of July. Talk to almost any P-Patcher and he or she will tell you there is more effective therapy to be found in a P-Patch than you will find in a bushel of psychiatrists."

P-Patch gardeners supply seven to ten tons of fresh organic vegetables to Seattle food banks each year.

For all the challenge of the short growing season, Seattleites—from back-yard gardeners to patio container gourmets to P-Patch tillers—love their gardens. And for anyone who doesn't have a green thumb, farmers' markets are wonderful sources for fresh local produce.

—KC

Granny Smith Apple Bread Pudding

Avenue One

This savory take on bread pudding is reminiscent of the bread stuffing served at holiday dinners, with onions, sage, thyme, and tart apples flavoring the mix. It makes an ideal accompaniment to sautéed pork, grilled rack of lamb, or roasted chicken.

3 cups milk	1½ cups peeled and chopped Granny Smith
4 cups cubed day-old bread (about	apple (about 1 large apple)
½-inch cubes)	2 teaspoons minced thyme
1 tablespoon olive oil	1 teaspoon minced sage
½ medium onion, preferably Walla Walla Sweet,	3 egg yolks, lightly beaten
finely chopped	¾ teaspoon salt
1½ teaspoons minced garlic	¼ teaspoon freshly ground black pepper

PREHEAT THE OVEN to 375°F. Lightly oil eight ¾-cup ramekins or other small baking dishes.

HEAT THE MILK in a medium saucepan over medium-high heat just until it comes to a boil. While the milk is heating, put the bread cubes in a large heatproof bowl. Pour the hot milk over the bread, stir to mix, and set aside to soak for 20 minutes, stirring occasionally.

MEANWHILE, heat the oil in a large skillet over medium heat. Add the onion and garlic and sauté until tender and aromatic, 3 to 5 minutes. Stir in the apple, thyme, and sage, then reduce the heat to medium-low. Continue cooking until the apple begins to soften, about 2 minutes longer. Take the skillet from the heat and let cool.

ADD THE COOLED APPLE MIXTURE to the soaked bread cubes along with the egg yolks, salt, and pepper. Stir to evenly blend. Spoon the bread pudding mixture into the prepared dishes. Set them in a large baking pan and pour boiling water into the pan to come about halfway up the sides of the ramekins.

BAKE until a knife inserted into the center of a pudding comes out clean, 40 to 50 minutes. Take the ramekins from the water bath and let sit for a few minutes, then run a knife around the inside rim of the ramekins and unmold the puddings onto individual plates. Serve at once.

Makes 8 servings

Gratin de Chou-fleur
(Cauliflower Gratin)

Le Pichet

Chef Jim Drohman serves this gratin as the bed for his house-made garlic sausages (Saucisse de Toulouse, page 140), but it's an addictive side dish you'll want to serve with roasted chicken, pan-fried steak, or any home-style meat. It's just the thing for a cold winter (or chilly Seattle spring or fall) night.

The head of cauliflower is steamed whole before it is cut into florets and covered with sauce and cheese. You'll need a big, deep pan and something to hold the cauliflower just above the level of the steaming water. A folding collapsible steaming basket is perfect, but you could simply use a small can (like a tuna fish can) with both ends removed to serve as a perch for the cauliflower.

1 medium head cauliflower (about 1 1/4 pounds)	2 tablespoons all-purpose flour
1 cup dry white wine	2 cups milk
1 cup water	1/4 teaspoon freshly grated or ground nutmeg
2 cloves garlic, lightly crushed	Salt and freshly ground white pepper
1 bay leaf, preferably fresh	1 cup grated Gruyère cheese
2 tablespoons unsalted butter	

TRIM THE GREEN OUTSIDE LEAVES and any discolored spots from the cauliflower, and cut off the stem flat with the base. In a pot large enough to hold the whole head of cauliflower, bring the wine and water to a simmer over medium-high heat. Add the garlic and bay leaf followed by a steaming basket. Set the cauliflower over the steaming water, cover the pan, reduce the heat to medium-low, and steam the cauliflower until it is tender when pierced with a paring knife, 30 to 40 minutes. (Keep an eye on the water level in the pot, adding more if needed so it doesn't boil dry.) Take the cauliflower from the pan and set aside on a plate to cool.

WHILE THE CAULIFLOWER IS STEAMING, melt the butter in a small saucepan over medium heat until it is foamy. Reduce the heat to medium-low and add the flour, whisking constantly until the paste has a light toasty aroma and is pale golden, 3 to 4 minutes. Slowly whisk in the milk, then increase the heat to medium-high and bring the mixture to a boil, whisking constantly. Reduce the heat to low and simmer, whisking often, until the sauce has the consistency of thick cream, about 5 minutes. Take the pan from the heat and whisk in the nutmeg with salt and pepper to taste; set aside.

PREHEAT THE OVEN to 400°F. Butter a 9-inch square baking dish or a small gratin dish just large enough to hold the cauliflower florets.

REMOVE THE CORE from the cooled cauliflower. Cut the cauliflower into medium florets and arrange them in a single, snug layer in the prepared baking dish. Season to taste with salt and pepper, then sprinkle with half of the cheese. Pour the sauce over the cauliflower, making sure all the florets are coated, and sprinkle the remaining cheese over the top.

BAKE THE GRATIN until it is bubbly and golden brown on top, 15 to 20 minutes. Let sit for a few minutes to cool slightly before serving.

Makes 4 to 6 servings

Sichuan Green Beans

Wild Ginger

At Wild Ginger, the green beans are first deep-fried and then stir-fried with the remaining ingredients, using two separate woks. If you have only one wok, use a saucepan for deep-frying. Simpler yet, stir-fry the green beans in the wok until they begin to turn brown and blister, then continue as directed. The double-whammy technique of deep-frying and stir-frying produces the best, most flavorful results, however.

Note that the green beans must be fully dry before adding them to the hot oil for frying. If any water is clinging to the beans, they'll sputter violently when added to the oil. You'll want to rinse the preserved vegetable under cold running water before using, to wash away excess salt. Sichuan preserved vegetable is available in Asian markets and on well-stocked grocery shelves.

Peanut or canola oil, for frying	1 pound tender green beans, trimmed and
2 tablespoons soy sauce	thoroughly dried
2 teaspoons rice wine vinegar	2 tablespoons minced lean pork
1 teaspoon sesame oil	1 tablespoon minced Sichuan preserved vegetable
1 teaspoon sugar	1 teaspoon dried red pepper flakes

POUR THE OIL to a depth of 2 to 3 inches into a large, deep, heavy saucepan and heat over medium-high heat to 400°F (the oil should come no more than halfway up the sides of the pan).

WHILE THE OIL IS HEATING, whisk together the soy sauce, vinegar, sesame oil, and sugar in a small bowl. Stir until the sugar is dissolved and set aside.

WHEN THE OIL IS HOT, fry the green beans, in small batches, until lightly browned and blistered, 1 to 1½ minutes. Using a slotted spoon, transfer the beans to paper towels to drain. Allow the oil to reheat as needed between batches.

HEAT A WOK over high heat until very hot, then add 1 tablespoon oil (it will begin smoking right away). Add the pork, preserved vegetable, and red pepper flakes and stir-fry for 10 seconds. The pepper flakes will give off peppery fumes, so be prepared with an exhaust fan or nearby open window. Add the soy sauce mixture and heat, stirring, for about 15 seconds, being careful not to burn the sugar. Add the green beans and toss until most of the liquid is reduced and absorbed by the beans, about 30 seconds.

TRANSFER THE BEANS to a warmed platter and serve.

Makes 4 to 6 servings

Fresh Roasted Corn with Lime and Chile

Anthony's HomePort

There is nothing complicated about this recipe, but when it comes to summer's sweet corn, the simpler the better. A quick brush of chile butter and a squeeze of lime juice serve as great complements to the sweet corn.

You'll want to buy ears that are fully covered in husks, since the husks remain on— keeping the kernels tender and moist—during grilling.

6 ears corn, in their husks	Salt
6 tablespoons unsalted butter	1 lime, cut into 6 wedges
¾ teaspoon chile powder	

PREHEAT an outdoor grill.

REMOVE ANY LOOSE OUTER HUSKS from the corn, then gently pull the remaining husks down toward the base of the cob, but do not remove them. Remove and discard the silk, then smooth the husks back into place, fully covering the corn kernels. Tie the husks in place, once at the tip and once in the middle, with strips of the discarded husks or with kitchen twine that has been soaked in water.

WHEN THE GRILL IS HOT, dip the ears of corn in cold water and shake off the excess. Set the corn on the heated grill, and turn the ears every 2 minutes or so until the husks are evenly browned, 10 to 12 minutes total. (Don't worry if the husks char in places—the kernels inside are well protected.) Take the corn from the grill and set aside to cool slightly.

MEANWHILE, melt the butter in a small saucepan over medium heat (or in a heatproof dish on the grill). Take the butter from the heat and stir in the chile powder. When the ears of corn are just cool enough to handle, remove and discard the husks. Brush the kernels with the chile butter, season to taste with salt, and then squeeze and rub a lime wedge over each ear. Serve right away.

Makes 6 servings

Red Kuri Squash and Pear Timbales

Bandoleone

Owner Danielle Philippa suggests serving this sweet-savory custard with grilled fish or with braised greens for a vegetarian entrée. *Kuri* means "chestnut" in Japanese, a hint that this winter squash has a flavor reminiscent of its earthy namesake. It is available primarily during the fall. The rest of the year (or whenever you can't find Red Kuri squash), use butternut squash in its place, although the flavor will be less intriguing.

Dried bread crumbs, for dusting the ramekins	1 onion, thinly sliced
8 ounces Red Kuri squash, peeled, seeded, and diced	1 large Bartlett or Anjou pear, peeled, cored, and diced
8 ounces yam, peeled and diced (about 1 medium yam)	¼ cup dry white wine
½ teaspoon salt	¼ cup whipping cream
3 tablespoons unsalted butter	2 eggs, lightly beaten
	Freshly ground white pepper

PREHEAT THE OVEN to 325°F. Butter four 1-cup ramekins and dust them with the bread crumbs, shaking out the excess.

COMBINE THE SQUASH, yam, and salt in a medium saucepan and add cold water to cover. Bring to a boil over high heat, then reduce the heat to low and simmer, uncovered, until tender, about 20 minutes. Drain the squash and yam, put them in a large bowl, and mash roughly with a large whisk or a potato masher. Set aside.

MELT 2 TABLESPOONS of the butter in a medium skillet over medium heat. Add the onion, stir to coat lightly in the butter, and lay a piece of foil loosely over the skillet. Reduce the heat to medium-low and cook the onion, stirring occasionally, until very tender and caramelized to a light brown, about 30 minutes. Transfer the onion to the squash mixture and set aside. Melt the remaining 1 tablespoon butter in the same skillet over medium heat. Add the pear and sauté for 2 to 3 minutes. Add the wine, cover, reduce the heat to low, and simmer until the pear is tender, about 3 minutes longer, depending on its ripeness.

COMBINE THE SQUASH, yam, onion, pear, and cream in a blender and purée until smooth. Return the mixture to the bowl, then whisk in the eggs until well blended. Season to taste with salt and pepper.

LADLE THE SQUASH MIXTURE into the prepared ramekins. Set them in a baking pan and pour boiling water into the pan to come about halfway up the sides of the ramekins. Bake until the custard pulls away from the sides of the ramekin, 40 to 50 minutes. Take the ramekins from the water and let sit for about 15 minutes, then invert them onto individual plates to serve.

Makes 4 servings

Wonderful Winter Squash

Danish, golden or white acorns, Sweet Mama, Butternut, baby pumpkins, Turban, Hubbard, or Golden Hubbard squash—in fall the farmers' market tables overflow with mountains of the colorful, hard-shelled squash types commonly known as winter squash. They are rich in complex carbohydrates and good sources of fiber, and the deep orange–fleshed varieties such as acorn and buttercup are carotene powerhouses. Very low in calories, fat, and sodium, they are best harvested after the first cold snap, which enhances their sugar content.

When pumpkins and squash come to mind, many of us want to cook up something good, decorate the table with pressed autumn leaves, and toast some pumpkin seeds. Can't you just smell that slightly scorched, baked fragrance of the Jack-O-Lantern candle burning up the top of the pumpkin last Halloween? And the aroma of roasting seeds still lingering in the air?

Everyone knows about using cooked sweet pumpkin purée for pie filling—it's an old standard. And you've probably stuffed acorn squash, made brown sugar and butter glazed rings, or experimented with the unusual spaghetti squash. But what about the unknowns such as Sweet Dumplings or Turk's Turbans?

Some of the smaller varieties make ideal containers for a meal or a dessert. Those cute, tangerine-size Jack-Be-Little pumpkins, for example, are the perfect little edible serving dishes for bread puddings and custards. They can also be filled with vegetable purées, such as celery root or beet, or with other cooked vegetables. Cut off their tiny tops, scoop out the shells, rub the outsides with a little oil, then lightly season and roast them in the oven. When cooked till tender, they can be eaten skin and all.

A bigger squash can even become a beautiful tureen for Andre's Eurasian Bistro's Fall Pumpkin and Squash Bisque (page 69). The soup is exotically laced with five-spice, cinnamon, paprika, and nutmeg.

Grocers' produce sections usually cut those huge Hubbards, the most common of the winter squashes, into manageable pieces; but if you've grown one or received a whole one as a gift, they can be monstrous! Be careful when trying to cut them open. Some suggest placing your biggest, sharpest knife lengthwise in the squash and tapping it gently with a wooden mallet until the squash splits in two. Some adamant cooks even admit resorting to throwing a super-daddy one on the pavement to get it open! →

When preparing winter squashes for cooking, scoop out all the seeds and fiber. (Be sure to reserve the seeds of larger squash for toasting.) Most delicious when baked, squash halves or quarters should be placed cut side down on a baking pan and baked in a moderate oven until tender. A faster cooking method is steaming. Peel off the outer skin with a small, sharp knife, then cube the squash and steam until tender.

Squash can also be microwaved on high power. If pierced a couple of times, the tiny types can be done whole in 4 to 6 minutes. Medium-sized ones should be cut open, seeded, covered, and cooked 5 to 8 minutes. Larger squash should be cut in pieces, covered, and microwaved 8 to 10 minutes, or until tender. Sometimes you'll need to add a little water to your cooking vessel for moisture.

To toast the seeds, wash them well, toss with your favorite seasonings, then bake in a 350°F oven, tossing often, until golden and crisp. Seasonings can include soy sauce, Worcestershire, and a dash of Tabasco. Or, for a spicier treatment, use olive oil, cayenne, chile powder, and salt. For a fun twist you could even try a curried version.

All the hard-shelled squash have relatively low moisture content and good potential for long storage. If you want to stock up when the more unusual varieties are available, large winter squash can be kept in a dry 50°F area for a few months. (Delicata and Sweet Dumpling varieties are exceptions; they should be held at room temperature for only a few weeks.) An unheated entryway can store a festive, welcoming display of your squash patch harvest.

—KC

Kale and Tomato Gratin

Boat Street Café

Paired with the sweetness of tomatoes, the mild, crisp flavor of kale makes a great match, here melded in a cheesy custard. This gratin can be served as a side dish alongside grilled or roasted meats, or it can play a more central role as part of a vegetarian entrée.

To slice large leaves such as kale, stack 4 or 5 leaves, roll up the stack lengthwise, and then cut across the bundle to make slices of the size needed. If desired, use halved cherry tomatoes (about 1½ pounds) in place of the larger sliced tomatoes.

1 clove garlic, halved	3 eggs
1 pound kale, rinsed, tough ends trimmed, and cut into ¼-inch-wide slices	2 cups whipping cream
8 small, ripe but firm tomatoes, cut into ½-inch-thick slices	1½ cups grated smoked cheese (such as mozzarella or Gouda) or Gruyère
2 teaspoons chopped thyme	1 cup freshly grated Parmesan cheese
Salt and freshly ground black pepper	1 teaspoon Dijon mustard
	Pinch freshly grated or ground nutmeg

PREHEAT THE OVEN to 400°F. Rub the bottom of a large oval gratin dish (about 14 inches long) with the cut sides of the garlic, then discard the garlic or save it for another use.

SCATTER ABOUT ONE-THIRD of the kale on the bottom of the prepared gratin dish and top with about one-third of the tomato slices, overlapping them slightly. Sprinkle with some of the thyme, salt, and pepper, then repeat the layering twice with the remaining kale, tomatoes, and thyme.

IN A MEDIUM BOWL, lightly beat the eggs, then add the cream, cheeses, mustard, and nutmeg. Whisk to blend evenly, then pour the custard over the vegetables.

BAKE THE GRATIN until it bubbles around the edges and the top is nicely browned, about 25 minutes. Let sit for a few minutes before cutting the gratin into portions to serve.

Makes 6 to 8 servings

Rice Pulao

Raga Cuisine of India

Basmati rice, already wonderfully aromatic, is accented here with
the perfume and flavor of cumin, clove, cardamom, and cinnamon. Traditionally served
alongside the curries and tandooris of Indian cuisine, the rice will be equally at home
with roasted chicken or braised lamb shanks, particularly if some of the same spices
are used in the cooking of the meat.

Cardamom pods come in three forms: green, white (simply bleached green),
and black (also known as brown, not a true cardamom but similar in flavor). Black
cardamom can be hard to find, so look in specialty spice shops or Indian markets.
Use eight pods of green or white if you can't find black.

2 cups basmati rice	2 bay leaves
2 tablespoons vegetable oil	4 cloves
1 teaspoon cumin seeds	¼ teaspoon ground cinnamon
½ large onion, finely chopped	Salt
4 whole green (or white) cardamom pods	3 cups water
4 whole black cardamom pods	

PUT THE RICE in a sieve and rinse it under cold running water until the water runs clear. Set
aside to drain.

HEAT THE OIL in a medium saucepan over medium-high heat. Add the cumin seeds and cook
until aromatic, about 30 seconds. Add the onion and cook, stirring often, until fragrant and
tender, 3 to 4 minutes. Stir in the cardamom, bay leaves, cloves, and cinnamon with salt to
taste, then add the water and bring to a boil over high heat. Stir in the rice, reduce the heat to
low, and cook, covered, until the rice is tender but not mushy, about 10 minutes.

TAKE THE PAN from the heat and let sit for a few minutes before removing the lid. Fluff with
a fork and serve.

Makes 4 to 6 servings

MAIN DISHES

Alder-Barbecued King Salmon with Fennel and Mint

Ivar's Salmon House

For the best results, slice the fennel paper-thin for the salad that accompanies this simply grilled salmon. If you have a mandoline, this is a good time to use it. The recipe was designed with rich and robust king salmon in mind, but other salmon can be used. Look for alder wood chips at hardware stores or other places where grilling equipment is sold.

The smoky aroma and flavor from grilling outdoors over wood chips are integral to this recipe, but if grilling's not an option you could instead broil the salmon indoors.

2 to 3 cups alder wood chips	Juice of 1 lemon
2 fennel bulbs, trimmed, cored, and very thinly sliced	⅓ cup extra virgin olive oil, plus more for cooking salmon
½ cup chopped mint	Salt and freshly ground black pepper
¼ cup thinly sliced green onions, white and pale green parts only	6 king salmon fillet pieces (7 to 8 ounces each), skin and pin bones removed
¼ cup minced flat-leaf (Italian) parsley	

PREHEAT AN OUTDOOR GRILL. Soak the alder wood chips in a bowl of cold water.

IN A LARGE BOWL, combine the fennel, mint, green onions, parsley, lemon juice, and olive oil. Toss the mixture to blend evenly, then season to taste with salt and pepper. Set aside while cooking the salmon.

WHEN THE GRILL IS READY, drain the alder wood chips well and scatter them over the hot coals (or follow the manufacturer's advice for using smoking chips with your grill). Brush the salmon pieces lightly with olive oil and season with salt and pepper. Set the salmon on the pre-heated grill, cover with the lid, and cook, turning once, until done to your taste, 3 to 4 minutes on each side for medium-well, depending on the thickness of the fish.

SET THE GRILLED SALMON FILLETS on individual plates, top with the fennel salad, and serve.

Makes 6 servings

Crab Cakes with Ancho Chile Mayonnaise

Ray's Boathouse

Ray's Boathouse is a classic among Seattle restaurants, and so are Ray's crab cakes among city's seafood lovers. This recipe lets the crab shine, with just a touch of color from parsley and bell pepper and a hint of extra richness from a dash of sherry. Any leftover ancho chile mayonnaise would be great tossed with flaked, cooked salmon to make an awesome salmon salad sandwich, or used as a dip for steamed shrimp.

1 pound Dungeness crabmeat, larger pieces broken up	1 tablespoon dry sherry
	½ teaspoon paprika
¼ cup whipping cream	Pinch celery salt
1 egg, lightly beaten	Dash hot pepper sauce
3 tablespoons finely diced red bell pepper	1½ cups panko crumbs or other dried bread crumbs, more if needed
3 tablespoons chopped shallot	
3 tablespoons chopped flat-leaf (Italian) parsley	Salt and freshly ground black pepper
3 tablespoons freshly squeezed lemon juice	4 tablespoons unsalted butter, more if needed

ANCHO CHILE MAYONNAISE

1 ancho chile	1 tablespoon freshly squeezed lemon juice
1 red bell pepper	1½ teaspoons white wine vinegar
1 cup mayonnaise	½ teaspoon paprika
1 green onion, white and pale green parts only, sliced	¼ to ½ teaspoon ground cayenne pepper
	¼ teaspoon salt
1 clove garlic, chopped	Pinch freshly ground black pepper

FOR THE MAYONNAISE, put the ancho chile in a small bowl and pour hot water over to cover. Set aside to soften for about 30 minutes. While the chile is soaking, roast the bell pepper over a gas flame or under the broiler, turning occasionally to roast evenly, until the skin blisters and blackens, 5 to 10 minutes total. Put the pepper in a plastic bag, securely seal it, and set aside to cool. When cool enough to handle, peel away and discard the skin. Remove the core and seeds and coarsely chop the pepper.

DRAIN THE ANCHO CHILE, remove the stem and seeds, and put it in a food processor or blender with the roasted red pepper. Blend until finely chopped, scraping down the sides a few times. Add the mayonnaise, green onion, garlic, lemon juice, vinegar, paprika, cayenne, salt, and pepper. Pulse until smooth and well blended, then transfer the mayonnaise to a bowl and refrigerate until ready to serve.

SQUEEZE THE CRABMEAT over the sink to remove excess moisture and pick over the meat to remove any bits of shell or cartilage. In a large bowl, combine the cream, egg, bell pepper, shallot, parsley, lemon juice, sherry, paprika, celery salt, and hot pepper sauce. Stir to mix, then add the crab and 1 cup of the panko or bread crumbs. Stir well to mix evenly, then season to taste with salt and pepper.

USING ¼ CUP OF THE CRAB MIXTURE for each one, form the crab mixture into patties, making 16 cakes about 3 inches in diameter. Coat the cakes with the remaining bread crumbs, patting to remove excess, and set the cakes on a tray lightly coated with bread crumbs. (If you have time, refrigerate the cakes, covered with plastic wrap, for an hour or two before frying; they'll hold up better during cooking.)

MELT ABOUT HALF OF THE BUTTER in a large, heavy skillet, preferably nonstick, over medium heat. Working in batches, sauté the crab cakes, turning once, until nicely browned on both sides and heated through, 3 to 4 minutes per side. Add more butter to the skillet as needed and continue frying the remaining cakes.

ARRANGE THE CRAB CAKES on warmed individual plates and drizzle some of the ancho chile mayonnaise over the cakes. Pass the remaining mayonnaise at the table.

Makes 4 servings

Malai Kebab

Raga Cuisine of India

Owner Kamal Mroke offers some background on the recipes served at Raga,
noting that they come "from the Moghul Emperors who ruled India for quite a long time
and were fond of a rich variety of foods." Malai Kebab, a longtime customer favorite, calls
for marinating cubed chicken in an unusual blend of cashews, garlic, ginger, jalapeño, cream
cheese, and cream before grilling. The kebabs can also be baked, if you prefer.
Raga's Rice Pulao (page 98) would be the ideal accompaniment.

6 boneless, skinless chicken breasts (about 6 ounces each)	1 tablespoon vegetable oil
½ cup raw cashews (about 2½ ounces)	2 teaspoons minced or grated ginger or 1 teaspoon powdered ginger
2 ounces cream cheese, cut into pieces	1 cup half-and-half
2 or 3 jalapeño chiles, cored, seeded, and diced	1 teaspoon salt
2 tablespoons freshly squeezed lemon juice	½ teaspoon freshly ground black pepper
4 cloves garlic	

IF USING BAMBOO SKEWERS, soak them in a pan of cold water for about 30 minutes
before using them. Cut the chicken breasts into 1-inch cubes and thread them onto twelve 12-
inch skewers, leaving a little space between the cubes so that they'll cook evenly. Lay the kebabs
in a shallow dish and refrigerate while making the marinade.

PUT THE CASHEWS in a food processor or blender and process until finely chopped. (Do not
overprocess, or the nuts will become a paste.) Add the cream cheese, chiles, lemon juice, garlic,
oil, and ginger and process until smooth. With the blades running, pour in the half-and-half,
then add the salt and pepper and pulse to mix. Pour the marinade over the chicken kebabs,
turning to coat them evenly in the marinade. Cover with plastic wrap and refrigerate for 3
hours.

PREHEAT AN OUTDOOR GRILL. Remove the chicken from the marinade, allowing the
excess to drip off, and grill, turning the skewers every few minutes, until well browned and
cooked through (cut into a large cube to test), 7 to 10 minutes. (Alternatively, you could bake
the kebabs at 425°F for 12 to 15 minutes.) Serve right away.

Makes 4 to 6 servings

City Grilling

It seems that grilling just keeps getting more and more popular. To some it's almost a kind of religion. Light the coals, study the flame, stand guard and protect, feel the heat, poke the coals, discuss them. . . . Seattle's home rotissiers don't get a lot of days to actually practice this outdoor cooking ritual, but when they do they grill like mad, with smoky aromas wafting through the neighborhoods. Restaurants grill year-round and indoors, of course, so they have intricate hood systems to exhaust the smoke.

Grilling is a pretty healthy way to cook and delivers a delicious flavor to almost any food—be it chicken, beef, pork, fish, or veggies. In fact, there isn't much you can't grill.

Chefs love the searing marks that grills give to food. Both Anthony's Home-Port's familiar with a twist Fresh Roasted Corn with Lime and Chile (page 93), which is grilled in the husks, and the eclectic Grilled Ahi in Licorice Root "Tea" with Braised Red Cabbage (page 120), from Salty's on Alki are exemplary.

And certainly great grilled burgers never go out of style, from blue cheese–stuffed, gourmet backyard burgers to The Royal Burger served at Palace Kitchen. This three-tiered, eleven-dollar burger extravaganza is a study in burgermanship: Tier #1 is loaded with the ultimate in burger condiments, ketchup and mustard for sure, horseradish aioli, pickled green tomatoes, grilled onions, and, of course, lettuce. Tier #2 features an organic Oregon beef patty grilled up to perfection and reverently placed on a house made onion bun. And last but not least, housemade frites (French fries) sprinkled with just the right amount of kosher salt comprise Tier #3. That's a burger!

Some grilling connoisseurs like to marinate beforehand. Why? Because it adds taste, zing, and tenderness. The original thought behind marinating was to tenderize tough meat, making it palatable enough to eat. Acids such as vinegar, lemon juice, and wine break down the protein fibers. But these days marinades are used mostly for imparting big flavor to foods.

Marinade ingredients can be very straightforward, as in the simple olive oil and garlic used on the steaks for the Metropolitan Grill's Bruschetta Steak Sandwiches (page 108). Or the components can be more elaborate. Take for instance the bold-flavored Indian dish, Malai Kebab, served at Raga Cuisine of India (page 104). The chicken marinates in an unusual mix of ground cashews, lemon juice, ginger, jalapeño, garlic, half-and-half, and a bit of cream cheese.

The exotic, perfumey flavor of coconut milk infused with cilantro, ginger, lemongrass, and fish sauce makes a divine marinade for chicken breasts or for big juicy shrimp. Alternate them on skewers with shiitake mushrooms, red peppers, and the white ends of green onions—and you'll have a fun, walk-around nosh item for an outdoor grill party. →

And, if made with a minimum of oil and used sparingly, marinades can provide lots of yum factor without a lot of fat. For example, Thai sweet chile sauce mixed with a bit of fresh lime juice and some fresh ginger makes a zippy glaze when brushed lightly on fish. Just remember, when using any sweet ingredients in a marinade, such as sweet chile sauce, honey, sugar, or molasses, to be careful, as they will burn easily. It can get hard to pass that much caramelization off as "well-seared"!

The item you are marinating doesn't have to be swimming in liquid if the marinade is strong enough. Intense flavor sources include chopped garlic, puréed onion, chile powders, citrus zests and juices, chopped fresh herbs, and green onions. To get good coverage while using a small quantity of concentrated ingredients, put boneless, skinless chicken breasts, for example, in a small resealable plastic bag, then add 1 to 2 tablespoons of marinade for each piece of chicken. Squish the air out and seal the bag. Then smoosh the chicken breasts around in the marinade and let it do its thing for at least 4 hours or overnight. For a short cut, freeze extra marinade right in the freezer bags, then just defrost and add in your item to be marinated.

Another technique is to make the marinade thick with herbs and citrus zests for a big flavor punch, then smear on a tablespoon per portion, or push the thick mixture under the skin of poultry and let sit overnight before cooking. Marinades with a lot of acid should be used for a shorter time as the acid tends to start "cooking" the protein.

At Canlis, executive chef Greg Atkinson's favorite grilling tool is a squirt gun that he uses to suppress those tongues of flame that shoot up. He just guns them down with the water pistol. If the kids are joining in, you need to keep them under control—especially if they have "super-soakers," because that could be the end of your fire! It's also fun to toss fruit tree and herb clippings, especially rosemary or thyme sprigs, into your charcoal to give a nice smoky perfume to what you are cooking.

And don't forget about grilling fruit—bananas, pineapple, and even peaches are delicious grilled up on those last lingering embers.

—KC

Plig King Tofu

Bahn Thai

A simple stir-fry of green beans and tofu gets a distinctive boost of flavor from spicy Thai red curry paste. If you'll be serving this alone as a vegetarian main course, it will serve two, but if serving family style with another dish or two, the recipe will serve four or more.

8 ounces green beans, trimmed and cut into 2-inch pieces	Salt
Vegetable oil, for frying	2 tablespoons water
14 to 16 ounces firm tofu	1 cup thinly sliced onion
All-purpose flour, for dredging	1 tablespoon Thai fish sauce (nam pla)
1 tablespoon Thai red curry paste	2 teaspoons sugar
	¼ cup lightly packed Thai sweet basil leaves

BRING A SMALL SAUCEPAN of lightly salted water to a boil and prepare a small bowl of ice water. Add the green beans to the boiling water and blanch for 1 minute. Drain well and put the green beans in the ice water to cool thoroughly. Drain the beans, dry well on paper towels, and set aside.

POUR THE OIL to a depth of 2 to 3 inches into a deep, heavy saucepan and heat over medium-high heat to 350°F. (The oil should come no more than halfway up the sides of the pan.) While the oil is heating, pat the tofu dry with paper towels and cut it into 1-inch cubes. Dredge a few cubes at a time in the flour, coating them evenly and tapping off the excess flour.

WORKING IN BATCHES, gently add the tofu to the hot oil and fry until light brown, 3 to 4 minutes. Use tongs or a slotted spoon to transfer the fried tofu to a plate lined with paper towels. Continue with the remaining tofu, allowing the oil to reheat between batches as needed.

HEAT 1 TABLESPOON vegetable oil in a wok or large skillet over medium heat. Add the curry paste with salt to taste and stir to combine. Add the water and stir to soften the curry paste. Then add the green beans, onion, fish sauce, and sugar and cook until the green beans are crisp-tender, 3 to 5 minutes. Add the tofu and basil and stir gently to coat the tofu evenly with the sauce.

TRANSFER to a warmed serving dish and serve right away.

Makes 2 to 4 servings

Bruschetta Steak Sandwiches

Metropolitan Grill

This is a wonderfully upscale, open-faced steak sandwich, definitely a
knife-and-fork affair. Prime beef is de rigueur at The Met and is available retail at top
butchers and grocery stores (you may need to call ahead to special order). You'll pay top
dollar for the richly marbled prime meat, which represents only about 3 percent of the beef
produced in the United States. You can use choice cuts for a less pricey option, but stick with
the richer ones such as rib-eye (also known as Delmonico and Spencer).

Chefs at The Met cook steaks at room temperature rather than straight
from the refrigerator. Taking off some of the chill in advance of the grill helps
the meat to cook more efficiently and evenly.

3 tablespoons extra virgin olive oil	Salt and freshly ground black pepper
1 tablespoon minced garlic	2 pounds rib-eye steaks, preferably prime

TOMATO AND OLIVE SALSA

1 cup seeded and diced tomato	2 tablespoons minced red onion
3 tablespoons pitted and chopped	2 tablespoons extra virgin olive oil
Kalamata olives	2 teaspoons red wine vinegar
2 tablespoons chopped basil	or balsamic vinegar

BRUSCHETTA

8 French bread slices, 1 inch thick	1 bunch arugula (about 4 ounces),
About ¼ cup extra virgin olive oil	rinsed and trimmed
2 cloves garlic, halved lengthwise	

FOR THE STEAKS, combine the olive oil and garlic with salt and pepper to taste in a shallow
dish or on a plate and stir to mix. Add the steaks, turning to coat them evenly in the seasoning.
Cover and marinate the meat in the refrigerator for at least 1 hour or up to 1 day. Turn the
meat a few times to marinate all sides evenly.

ABOUT AN HOUR before cooking the steaks, take them from the refrigerator and let come to
room temperature.

FOR THE SALSA, combine the tomato, olives, basil, and onion in a medium bowl. Drizzle the olive oil and vinegar over the top and season to taste with salt and pepper. Toss to mix and set aside.

PREHEAT AN OUTDOOR GRILL. The fire should have areas of high heat for searing the meat and lower heat for finishing. Take the steaks from the marinade, allowing excess marinade to drip off, and sear them over the hottest part of the fire, turning once, until well browned, 3 to 4 minutes per side. The steaks should be rare at this point, depending on how thick they are. If you want the steaks cooked more, move them to the low-heat area and continue cooking to the desired doneness, another minute or two per side for medium-rare to medium. (Alternatively, you could broil the steaks about 4 inches below the element, turning once, until cooked to your taste.) Transfer the steaks to a cutting board and let rest, covered loosely with foil, for 10 minutes.

WHILE THE MEAT IS RESTING, prepare the bruschetta. Brush both sides of each bread slice generously with the olive oil and toast on the hot part of the grill or under a preheated broiler, turning once, until the surface is crisp and golden, 1 to 2 minutes per side. Remove the toasts, sprinkle with a little salt, and rub them all over with the cut sides of the garlic cloves.

SET 2 BRUSCHETTA on each plate and top with a layer of arugula. Slice each steak across the grain into $\frac{1}{4}$-inch-thick slices and lay them on top of the arugula. Top the meat with the salsa and serve.

Makes 4 servings

Spaghetti con le Sarde
(Spaghetti with Sardines)

La Medusa

Spaghetti with sardines is one of the signature dishes of Sicily, where the recipe is traditionally made with fresh sardines. Since this version of the recipe includes a lot of pantry ingredients—canned tomatoes, sardines, anchovies, pasta, raisins, nuts—it's the perfect no-fuss meal when you don't have the time or the energy to make a trip to the store.

Be sure to buy the best-quality canned ingredients available. You'd be amazed by the difference in taste and overall quality between a bargain can of sardines and a top-quality brand from Italy. At La Medusa they make it easy for their customers, with their Italian gourmet shop, Salumeria, just a couple blocks away.

1 pound dried spaghetti, preferably imported Italian
2 tablespoons toasted fresh bread crumbs, for garnish

SARDINE SAUCE

1 large fennel bulb
2 tablespoons olive oil
1 large onion, thinly sliced
8 to 10 cloves garlic, crushed or chopped
2 anchovy fillets, minced
2 cans (28 ounces each) whole plum tomatoes, preferably imported Italian, drained

1 can (15 ounces) sardines packed in tomato sauce, preferably imported Italian
Salt and freshly ground black pepper
2 tablespoons pine nuts
2 tablespoons chopped Kalamata olives
2 tablespoons golden raisins

TRIM THE ROOT END and stalks of the fennel bulb, reserving the fronds for use later. Cut the fennel in half lengthwise and cut out the tough core, then thinly slice the halves. Heat the olive oil in a large sauté pan or skillet over medium-high heat. Add the fennel and onion and sauté until golden and tender, 5 to 7 minutes. Add the garlic and anchovies and sauté until the garlic is aromatic and turning golden, 3 to 5 minutes. Add the tomatoes, squishing them with the back of a spoon as you put them in the pan. Stir well and reduce the heat to low. Add the sardines with their sauce, stirring and breaking them up with the side of the spoon. Season to taste with salt and pepper. Simmer, stirring occasionally until the flavors are well blended and the sauce has thickened slightly, 15 to 20 minutes.

WHILE THE SAUCE IS SIMMERING, bring a large pot of salted water to a rolling boil and preheat the oven to 350°F. Scatter the pine nuts in a baking pan and toast, gently shaking the pan once or twice to help the nuts toast evenly, until lightly browned and aromatic, 5 to 7 minutes. Set aside to cool.

WHEN THE WATER IS BOILING, add the spaghetti, stir briefly, and boil until al dente, 8 to 10 minutes. While the pasta is cooking, chop enough of the reserved fennel fronds to make 1 tablespoon. When the sauce is done, take the pan from the heat and stir in the chopped fennel, pine nuts, olives, and raisins.

WHEN THE PASTA IS COOKED, drain it well and put in a warmed large serving bowl. Ladle the sauce over the top and toss gently. Sprinkle with the bread crumbs and serve.

Makes 6 to 8 servings

Grilled Salmon with Lentils
and Brown Butter Balsamic Vinaigrette

Restaurant Zoë

At Restaurant Zoë, chef-owner Scott Staples serves this signature dish accompanied by roasted red and golden beets, warm leek fondue (leeks cooked long and slow, enriched with cream), and a garnish of fried shallots. The vinaigrette will keep one week in the refrigerator; after that it begins to lose its sharpness. It will solidify when cold, but softens again at room temperature.

6 salmon fillet pieces (6 to 7 ounces each), skin and pin bones removed	2 tablespoons olive oil
	1 tablespoon chopped flat-leaf (Italian) parsley

LENTILS

2 tablespoon olive oil	2 bay leaves
½ cup finely diced onion	1½ cups dry lentils, rinsed and drained
½ cup finely diced carrot	1 cup clam juice, fish stock, or water
½ cup finely diced celery	3 cups water, more if needed
2 tablespoons chopped thyme	2 tablespoons unsalted butter

BROWN BUTTER BALSAMIC VINAIGRETTE

½ cup unsalted butter	2 tablespoons chopped shallot
3 tablespoons balsamic vinegar	Salt and freshly ground black pepper
2 tablespoons olive oil	

FOR THE VINAIGRETTE, melt the butter in a small saucepan over medium heat. Continue to cook the butter to evaporate the water, gently swirling the saucepan from time to time to prevent spot burning, until the butter is well browned and has a nutty aroma, 15 to 20 minutes in all. (Keep a close eye on the butter toward the end, to avoid it overcooking, going from nutty brown to bitter black.) As soon as the butter is brown, take it from the heat and carefully strain it through a fine heatproof sieve set over a small bowl. Let the brown butter cool, then whisk in the vinegar, olive oil, and shallot with salt and pepper to taste. Set aside.

FOR THE LENTILS, heat the olive oil in a medium saucepan over medium heat. Add the onion, carrot, and celery and cook, stirring often, until the vegetables are tender and aromatic, 3 to 5 minutes. Add the thyme and bay leaves, then stir in the lentils. Add the clam juice and enough water to cover the lentils by about 1 inch. Bring the mixture to a boil over medium-high heat, then reduce the heat to low and simmer very gently, uncovered, until the lentils are tender, about 30 minutes, adding more water if needed. (The liquid should barely gurgle as it simmers; if it bubbles more rapidly, the lentils risk bursting and becoming mushy.)

WHILE THE LENTILS ARE COOKING, preheat an outdoor grill.

WHEN THE LENTILS ARE TENDER, drain them in a colander set over a bowl to catch the excess liquid, and discard the bay leaves. Heat the butter in a large skillet over medium heat. Add the drained lentils with about ½ cup of the reserved cooking liquid and season to taste with salt and pepper. Reheat, stirring gently from time to time to prevent sticking, 3 to 5 minutes. If they seem dry, moisten with a little more of the reserved liquid (extra cooking liquids can be saved to add to soup or stew). Season to taste with salt and pepper and keep warm over low heat while you grill the salmon.

BRUSH BOTH SIDES of the salmon fillet pieces with olive oil and season to taste with salt and pepper. Grill the salmon over the hot fire until medium-rare, 1 to 3 minutes per side, depending on the thickness of the fish, or longer to suit your taste. (Alternatively, the salmon pieces could be broiled in the oven or pan-seared in a heavy, large skillet over medium-high heat.)

TO SERVE, spoon the lentils in the center of warmed individual plates. Rewhisk the brown butter balsamic vinaigrette (if the dressing is very thick, you can warm it slightly by setting the bowl in a larger bowl of warm water), then drizzle it around the lentils. Lean a piece of salmon up on the lentils and sprinkle the parsley over all.

Makes 6 servings

Eastern Washington

It's amazing what comes over the mountains to Seattle's tables! Washington state is a leading national producer of lentils and other dry peas, sweet cherries, carrots, asparagus, apples, onions, pears, and herbs—and they're all grown in eastern Washington.

Those who have spent weekends past at eastern Washington farms in the heat of summer can probably remember waiting for the brilliant sun to cool off a bit before going out to pick peaches. The branches were loaded with fuzzy, orange globes, their skin kissed with a rosy blush. Can you still smell them just as they were that evening when you were ten? Can you hear the sprinklers tick-tick-tick-ticking and the crickets chirping, and inhale the intoxicating fragrance of peaches perfuming the air?

It can be hard to find tree-ripened fruit in a store these days; in fact, for a while it seemed in danger of completely disappearing. But just in the nick of time the Queen Anne and Admiral Thriftway stores initiated the Peach-O-Rama. These forward-looking grocers sought out farmers who would wait to pick their peaches fully ripe, and then carefully pack them in shallow layers. And it took some seeking! Now, every year these locally owned stores feature super, juice-runs-down-your-arm, genuinely tree ripened peaches—thank goodness!

To peel a peach the quickie way, just boil a big pot of water and immerse the peaches a few at a time for 30 seconds or more, depending on the peach. When the skin starts to get loose, immediately run the peaches under cold water and then slip the skins off.

To make the most of the juiciest, ripe peaches of the season, try the Honey Peach Julep from Sazerac (page 232). The recipe draws its appeal from another eastern Washington product as well—fresh mint.

Of course peaches aren't the only succulent stone fruit Seattleites enjoy from east of the Cascades. Yellow, green, red, and black plums, luscious nectarines, and blushing apricots are among the others. The Savory Nectarine and Shiso Soup (page 59) from Le Gourmand gets an added fillip from hot chiles, an eastern Washington farm product, too.

Nestled at the foot of the Blue Mountains, the Walla Walla valley's rich soil, climate, and water produce an early onion so crisp and mild some claim to eat it like an apple. Walla Walla Sweets—large, round, yellow-skinned onions—are celebrated for their sweetness. The onions were first grown from seeds of Italian origin brought to the valley in about 1900 by a Frenchman. Unlike storage onions, these early summer orbs must be refrigerated. But during their short season, they are the number one choice for eating raw in salads and salsas and on burgers. And they are surely unmatched for crunchy, juicy, deep-fried onion rings.

Another exceptionally fertile agricultural area is the Palouse River basin. Its moist, rich volcanic soil and relatively cool growing season are ideal for producing some of the world's finest lentils. Once commonly referred to as "lowly lentils," these legumes are now highly valued by chefs. Lentils are fiber-rich, high in protein, low in fat, and, unlike many dried beans and peas, there's no need to soak most lentils before cooking them. Their robust, earthy flavor is shown off very well in Restaurant Zoë's Grilled Salmon with Lentils and Brown Butter Balsamic Vinaigrette (page 112).

Less well known, perhaps, is that Washington is the nation's largest producer of hops, a characteristic flavor in beer. If you happen to be driving down a hop-lined road, don't be surprised if you see those Jack-and-the-bean-stalk vines making their way to the sky before your very eyes. Indeed, it has been said that they grow one inch every hour in the heat of an eastern Washington summer!

And then of course there are all those wonderful wine grapes grown there—from luscious Merlot to rich Cabernet to crisp Semillon. So whether you're into beer or wine, eastern Washington raises the crops that produce your favorite libation.

—KC

Pan-Seared Duck Breast with Muscadet Wine Sauce

Brasserie Margaux

You can use either muscovy or Long Island duck breasts; the former tend to be larger and the latter less expensive. Chef Chris Zarkades generally uses muscovy, and prefers to cook the duck to medium, noting that the flesh can have a sort of elastic quality if it's cooked much less than that. In classic French style, the chefs at Brasserie Margaux would cut the carrot and potato into fancy little football shapes, a method called "turning" vegetables, but I've simplified their preparation for this home version (which tastes just as good!). The sauce is finished with a generous amount of butter, which not only adds richness but also a lovely gloss. You can use less, if you prefer, although it should be at least ¼ cup for the best results.

1 small red potato (about 4 ounces), peeled and cut into ½-inch wedges	1 tablespoon olive oil
4 ounces green beans, trimmed and cut into 3-inch lengths	½ cup sliced shallot
	1 tablespoon green peppercorns
1 large carrot, cut into 3-inch matchsticks	¼ cup brandy
2 boneless duck breasts (6 to 8 ounces each)	½ cup whipping cream
Salt and freshly ground black pepper	¼ cup muscadet wine
	½ cup unsalted butter, cut into pieces

BRING A SMALL SAUCEPAN of lightly salted water to a boil and prepare a small bowl of ice water. Add the potato wedges to the boiling water and boil until tender when pierced with a knife, 5 to 7 minutes. Scoop out the potatoes with a slotted spoon and drain in a colander set in the sink. Bring the water back to a boil, add the green beans, and parboil until they are bright green and nearly tender, 2 to 3 minutes. Scoop out the beans with a slotted spoon and transfer them to the ice water to cool thoroughly. Return the water to a boil, add the carrot, and parboil until nearly tender but with some firm bite, about 3 minutes. Drain the carrot and add it to the colander with the potatoes along with the chilled green beans. Let the vegetables drain well while cooking the duck.

PREHEAT THE OVEN to 400°F.

TRIM ANY EXCESS FAT from around the edges of the duck breasts. With the tip of a sharp knife, score the duck skin in a diamond pattern, making slashes not quite to the flesh, and season the breasts all over with salt and pepper. Heat the oil in a heavy ovenproof skillet (cast iron would be great) over medium-high heat. Add the duck, skin side up, to the skillet and sear until nicely browned, 1 to 2 minutes. Turn the breasts over and transfer the skillet to the oven. Bake until the skin side is nicely browned and the breasts are medium, with some pink remaining in the center, 4 to 6 minutes.

TAKE THE SKILLET from the oven and set the breasts aside on a cutting board, skin side up and covered with foil to keep warm. Add the shallot and peppercorns to the skillet and sauté them in the duck fat (use a hot pad, since the skillet handle will be piping hot) over medium-high heat until the shallots are tender, 3 to 4 minutes. Add the brandy and ignite with a long match to flambé, turning your head away slightly from the flames and shaking the pan gently. When the flames have subsided, add the cream and wine and boil to reduce by about half. Stir in the vegetables and reheat for a minute or two, then take the skillet from the heat and whisk in the butter until it has smoothly melted into the sauce. Season the sauce to taste with salt and pepper.

SPOON THE VEGETABLES and sauce onto warmed individual plates. Cut each duck breast on a slight angle into 6 slices, fan the breasts out over the vegetables, and serve.

Makes 2 servings

Orecchiette with Fall Vegetables

Tulio

"Orecchiette is one of my favorite pasta shapes because it holds its texture and is difficult to overcook," explains chef Walter Pisano. He points out that the vegetables can be changed with the season, so feel free to alter the list based on your tastes and what looks best at the market. The same goes for the herbs: use your favorites from among what's freshest from your garden or the store.

Cipollini is a variety of small onion that is available in some Seattle-area stores and farmers' markets. If you can't find cipollini, pearl onions can be used in their place. Chef Pisano prefers chopping the herbs just before adding them to the pasta, which keeps their flavor fresh and their aroma at its peak.

8-ounce piece butternut squash, peeled and seeded	10 tablespoons extra virgin olive oil
2 small zucchini, trimmed	Salt and freshly ground black pepper
6 ounces baby carrots, trimmed	¼ cup blanched almonds
4 or 5 cipollini or pearl onions, peeled	¼ cup dried bread crumbs
1 red bell pepper, cored and seeded	2 tablespoons unsalted butter
1 small or ½ large fennel bulb, trimmed and cored	1 pound orecchiette pasta, preferably imported Italian
½ large eggplant (about ¾ pound), trimmed	8 to 10 basil leaves
1 whole head garlic, plus 4 to 5 whole peeled cloves	¼ cup lightly packed flat-leaf (Italian) parsley leaves
5 or 6 sprigs assorted herbs (such as thyme, rosemary, sage, and/or marjoram)	3 or 4 sage leaves
	1 teaspoon lightly packed marjoram leaves
	6 to 7 ounces fresh goat cheese

PREHEAT THE OVEN to 425°F.

CUT THE BUTTERNUT SQUASH, zucchini, carrots, onions, bell pepper, fennel, and eggplant into roughly equal pieces measuring ½ inch by 1 inch. Combine the vegetable pieces, peeled garlic cloves, and herb sprigs in a large roasting pan. Drizzle 5 tablespoons of the oil over the vegetables, season to taste with salt and pepper, and stir the vegetables to coat them evenly.

ROAST THE VEGETABLES, stirring occasionally, until lightly browned and tender, 30 to 40 minutes. Set the vegetables aside to cool and reduce the oven temperature to 350°F.

PUT THE WHOLE GARLIC HEAD on a piece of foil, drizzle with 1 tablespoon of the olive oil, and wrap securely in the foil. Roast the garlic until soft when pressed, 35 to 40 minutes. Remove the garlic from the foil and let cool. Squeeze the whole tender garlic cloves from their papery sheaths and set aside.

SCATTER THE ALMONDS in a baking pan and toast in the oven, gently shaking the pan once or twice to help the nuts toast evenly, until lightly browned and aromatic, 5 to 7 minutes. Let the almonds cool completely, then put them in a food processor and pulse to chop finely. (Do not overprocess, or the nuts will become a paste.) Add the bread crumbs and pulse until well combined.

MELT THE BUTTER in a medium skillet over medium heat until it foams. Add the almond–bread crumb mixture and sauté, stirring occasionally, until golden brown and toasty smelling, about 5 minutes. Season with a pinch of salt and set aside.

BRING A LARGE POT of generously salted water to a rolling boil. Add the orecchiette and cook until al dente, about 8 minutes.

WHILE THE PASTA IS COOKING, heat 3 tablespoons of the oil in a large saucepan over medium heat. Add the roasted garlic cloves and sauté for a minute or two, then add the roasted vegetables and sauté until they are heated through, 3 to 5 minutes.

WHEN THE PASTA IS DONE, drain it well (but don't rinse) and add the orecchiette to the vegetables. Chop the basil, parsley, sage, and marjoram leaves and add them to the pasta with the goat cheese (roughly crumbled with your fingers) and the remaining 1 tablespoon olive oil. Toss to mix well and season to taste with salt and pepper. Transfer the pasta to a large warmed serving bowl, top with the almond–bread crumb mixture, and serve.

Makes 6 servings

Grilled Ahi in Licorice Root "Tea"
with Braised Red Cabbage

Salty's on Alki

Licorice root is available dried in spice markets and tea shops such as Market Spice or World Spice Merchants at the Pike Place Market. This same preparation would be great with other fish, too, such as swordfish or mahimahi. An additional accompaniment chef Byron Shultz serves with this tuna is butternut squash purée.

4 tuna steaks (6 to 7 ounces each), skin removed
4 tender tarragon sprig tops, for garnish

LICORICE ROOT "TEA"

4 cups chicken stock, preferably homemade	½ teaspoon coarsely crushed black peppercorns
½ cup chopped celery	¼ teaspoon dried thyme
½ cup chopped onion	1 bay leaf
¼ cup chopped carrot	1 star anise
1 piece licorice root (3 to 4 inches), halved	Salt
2 tablespoons sliced shallot	

BRAISED RED CABBAGE

1 tablespoon vegetable oil	¾ cup dry red wine
½ cup thinly sliced onion	1 tablespoon balsamic vinegar
1 shallot, chopped	1 bay leaf
1 clove garlic, chopped	¼ teaspoon fennel seeds, crushed
½ small red cabbage (about ¾ pound), cored and thinly sliced	Freshly ground black pepper

FOR THE LICORICE ROOT "TEA," combine the stock, celery, onion, carrot, licorice root, shallot, peppercorns, thyme, bay leaf, and star anise in a large saucepan and bring just to a boil over high heat. Lower the heat to medium and slowly reduce the liquids by about one-third, 15 to 20 minutes. Strain the "tea" into another saucepan, season to taste with salt, and keep warm over very low heat.

FOR THE BRAISED RED CABBAGE, heat the oil in a large sauté pan or skillet over medium heat. Add the onion and sauté, stirring often, until tender and lightly caramelized, 8 to 10 minutes. Add the shallot and garlic, toss for a minute, then add the cabbage and sauté until the cabbage begins to wilt, about 5 minutes. Reduce the heat to medium-low, stir in the wine, vinegar, bay leaf, and fennel seeds, and braise gently, uncovered, stirring occasionally, until the cabbage is very tender and most of the liquid has evaporated, about 45 minutes. Be careful not to scorch the cabbage; reduce the heat or add a tablespoon or two of water if needed during cooking. Discard the bay leaf and season the cabbage to taste with salt and pepper. Keep warm over very low heat.

PREHEAT AN OUTDOOR GRILL. Season the tuna to taste with salt and pepper, then grill to your taste, about 1 minute per side for rare, 2 to 3 minutes per side for medium-rare to medium. (Alternatively, you could broil or pan-fry the tuna to your taste.)

SPOON THE BRAISED RED CABBAGE into large, shallow soup bowls and top the cabbage with the grilled tuna. Ladle the warm "tea" around the cabbage, garnish with the tarragon, and serve.

Makes 4 servings

Pork Tenderloin with Bing Cherries and Mint

Madison Park Café

Bing cherries are one of the region's most relished summer crops and the plump, sweet fruits are a wonderful complement to this spice-crusted pork tenderloin. But the Bing season comes and goes quickly. I also tried this recipe with chopped plums, which were delicious as well. Another tasty variation would be to grill the tenderloins outdoors, imparting a subtle smoky element to complement the spices.

Beef demi-glace is a highly concentrated reduction of beef stock that adds unparalleled depth of flavor to many sauces. You can make demi-glace at home, although you must not salt your stock, or the reduction will become unpalatably salty. Quality demi-glace (which may need to be diluted before using, read the package) is available in well-stocked grocery stores and gourmet shops Alternatively, use homemade beef stock, which will produce a lighter sauce.

1 teaspoon ground cinnamon	¼ cup crème de cassis (black currant liqueur)
1 teaspoon ground allspice	½ cup pitted Bing cherries
1 teaspoon ground coriander	½ cup beef demi-glace or beef stock,
⅛ teaspoon freshly grated or ground nutmeg	preferably homemade
⅛ teaspoon powdered ginger	1½ teaspoons chopped mint
2 pork tenderloins (about 1 pound each)	¼ cup unsalted butter, cut into pieces
2 tablespoons soy sauce	Salt and freshly ground black pepper
2 tablespoons olive oil	

COMBINE THE CINNAMON, allspice, coriander, nutmeg, and ginger in a small bowl and stir to mix. Sprinkle half of the spice mixture evenly over a piece of plastic wrap or waxed paper slightly longer than the tenderloins. Brush both pieces of pork all over with the soy sauce, then roll 1 of the tenderloins in the spices to coat it evenly. Repeat with the remaining spice mix and the second tenderloin, then wrap each well in plastic wrap and marinate in the refrigerator for at least 6 hours or overnight.

JUST BEFORE COOKING THE PORK, preheat the oven to 375°F.

HEAT THE OLIVE OIL in a large ovenproof skillet over medium-high heat. Discard the plastic from the pork and brown the tenderloins on all sides, 4 to 5 minutes total. Transfer the skillet to the oven and bake until just a touch of pink remains in the center of the pork (about 150°F internal temperature), 12 to 15 minutes.

TAKE THE PORK FROM THE OVEN and set the tenderloins aside on a cutting board to rest, covering them with foil to keep warm. Add the cassis to the skillet (use a hot pad to hold the skillet's piping-hot handle) and cook over medium-high heat for about 1 minute, stirring to lift up cooked bits stuck to the bottom. Add the cherries, demi-glace, and mint. Bring to a boil and boil until reduced by about half, 2 to 3 minutes. Take the skillet from the heat and whisk in the butter until it has smoothly melted into the sauce. Season the sauce to taste with salt and pepper.

CUT THE PORK TENDERLOINS on the diagonal into slices about 1 inch thick. Arrange the slices, slightly overlapping, on warmed individual plates. Pour the cherry and mint sauce over the pork and serve.

Makes 4 servings

Cherries

Flawless, ruby red Bing cherries, icy cold, have to be the perfect snack. Sitting around on a hot day popping them in one by one is the start of a wonderful summer.

Cherries are great mixed in or served over vanilla ice cream, and they can even show up in a fun way in an old American classic—creamy, comforting rice pudding. And you know shortcakes aren't just for strawberries. Fresh pitted cherries make an excellent shortcake. Toss the cherries with a little sugar and kirsch liqueur, and then for the utmost enhancement, put a few dried cherries in your shortcake or scones for the shortcake base. Voila! You have cherry kirsch shortcakes to die for—the perfect ending to a balmy summer night's barbecue.

But there's no reason to restrict these sweet orbs to the dessert course. At Kay Simon and Clay Mackey's Chinook Winery in Prosser, Washington, they often do a summer seasonal feast: salmon grilled over cherry wood, topped off with a lively fresh-cherry salsa flecked with cilantro and ginger. Washing all this down with their luscious merlot is the consummate pairing of food and wine.

Cherries are wonderful in salads made with tender wild greens. Cassis's Yakima Cherry, Walla Walla Sweet Onion, and Basil Salad with Balsamic Vinaigrette (page 85) demonstrates this and is just one excellent example of a restaurant's use of local seasonal produce.

To make a brilliant vinegar for summer vinaigrettes or to perk up winter salads later, boil a quart of distilled or rice wine vinegar and pour it over about a pound of pitted cherries, adding flavorings such as fresh ginger slices, cloves, black peppercorns, thyme sprigs, or whatever suits your fancy. Let the mixture cool to room temperature, then cover and refrigerate for a week. Strain through a fine mesh, then bottle and refrigerate until needed. →

The one drawback to cooking with cherries is getting the seeds out, and this can sometimes be the pits! If you are pitting a lot of cherries, get a large-volume pitter such as the one sold at Sur la Table. It clamps easily onto the side of a picnic table—and outdoors is the ideal place to do this messy chore. You stem the cherries, then load up the hopper and start punching the plunger down like mad. The only hitch is that by the time you are finished you are usually freckled with pink dots! So wear an old shirt; cherry stains are hard to get out.

If you are lucky enough to come upon a load of cherries, consider drying as a great way to preserve the summer's bounty. With their concentrated flavor dried cherries are great to snack on or to add to a winter apple chutney. Or for a real treat forget the raisins and add dried cherries to your favorite oatmeal cookie recipe.

Another way to enjoy your cherries throughout the year is freezing. Simply rinse, pack, and freeze—stems, pits, and all. Delight in them right out of the freezer or let them thaw for about 30 minutes—or pop them in the microwave for 30 to 45 seconds if you just can't wait. They are the best, though, when they still have lots of ice crystals inside. By the way, frozen cherries make fun ice cubes for cold summer drinks.

Of course, you can always just eat a big bowl of cherries for dinner! Once in awhile you want to gorge yourself, and why not when it's something juicy, delicious, and healthy? Cherries are low fat, sodium free, and a great source of fiber and vitamin C. One cup of cherries has only 90 calories—that's about 5 calories each.

1 pound of cherries is equal to:
80 cherries
2 cups sliced, pitted cherries
1½ cups cherry juice

—KC

Pan-Fried Oysters with Jack Daniel's Sauce

Elliott's Oyster House

Pan-frying is a favorite way to enjoy the abundance of local oysters, particularly for folks who aren't keen on slurping the bivalve raw. It's a great use for jarred oysters, which are packed locally and come in a variety of sizes. Extra-smalls are used here, but you could choose another size, depending on how big you like your oysters. The sauce made with Jack Daniel's whiskey adds a nice zip to the crisp fried oysters.

1 cup all-purpose flour	36 extra-small oysters (three to four
1 teaspoon salt	10-ounce jars)
½ teaspoon coarsely ground black pepper	¼ cup vegetable oil

JACK DANIEL'S SAUCE

⅓ cup packed brown sugar	1½ tablespoons soy sauce
¼ cup Jack Daniel's whiskey	2 teaspoons Worcestershire sauce
¼ cup Dijon mustard	

FOR THE JACK DANIEL'S SAUCE, combine the brown sugar, whiskey, mustard, soy sauce, and Worcestershire sauce in a small saucepan. Whisk to mix, then heat the sauce over medium heat, whisking often, until the sugar is dissolved and the sauce is smooth, about 5 minutes. Keep warm over very low heat.

IN A PLATE OR SHALLOW BOWL, combine the flour, salt, and pepper and stir with a fork to mix. Drain the oysters in a colander in the sink. Dredge a few oysters at a time in the seasoned flour, tossing them gently with the fork and patting off the excess flour. As the oysters are coated, set them aside on a lightly floured tray and continue with the remaining oysters.

HEAT THE OIL in a large skillet over medium-high heat. When hot, add some of the oysters, being careful not to crowd them in the pan (you'll need to fry them in batches). Cook the oysters until they are nicely browned on the first side, about 2 minutes. Turn the oysters over and continue to cook until crisp and golden brown, about 2 minutes longer. Transfer the oysters to a plate lined with paper towels, keep warm in a low oven, and continue frying the remaining oysters.

ARRANGE THE FRIED OYSTERS on warmed individual plates. Pour the warm Jack Daniel's sauce into small individual bowls or dishes and set them alongside the oysters. Serve right away.

Makes 4 servings

Enchiladas en Salsa Suiza

El Camino

For these tasty enchiladas, chef Ron Correa uses menonita cheese,
which was first made by Mennonite Germans who settled in and around Mexico City. It is
not commonly available in the Seattle area, although you may find it in specialty Mexican or
Latin American groceries. The white cheese is relatively mild and melts wonderfully.
A decent substitute is mozzarella or a similarly mild, melting cheese.

1 pound boneless, skinless chicken breasts	1 large onion, thinly sliced
¾ cup sesame seeds	Salt and freshly ground black pepper
3 cups prepared salsa verde	12 small white corn tortillas
3 tablespoons vegetable oil	8 ounces menonita cheese or mozzarella cheese,
1½ cups whipping cream	grated

HALF-FILL A SAUTÉ PAN or deep skillet with lightly salted water. Bring the water to a boil,
add the chicken breasts, lower the heat to medium, and simmer until the chicken is just
cooked through at the thickest point, 10 to 15 minutes. Drain the chicken and set aside on a
plate to cool.

PREHEAT THE OVEN to 350°F. Spread the sesame seeds in a baking pan and toast the seeds,
stirring once or twice, until lightly browned and aromatic, 3 to 5 minutes. Let cool completely.
Increase the oven temperature to 450°F. Lightly oil the bottom and sides of a 9- by 13-inch
baking dish.

BRIEFLY GRIND the cooled sesame seeds in a blender. It'll only take a few seconds; if you
overgrind them, you'll have sesame butter. Put the ground seeds in a bowl, then add the salsa
verde to the blender and purée until smooth.

HEAT 1 TABLESPOON of the oil in a medium saucepan over medium heat. Add the puréed
salsa verde, stirring, then stir in the cream and sesame seeds. Bring the sauce to a boil over high
heat, then reduce the heat to medium and cook, stirring occasionally, for 5 minutes to thicken
slightly. Set aside.

WHEN THE CHICKEN IS COOL enough to handle, tear or cut it into thin strips. Heat the
remaining 2 tablespoons oil in a medium skillet over medium heat. Add the onion and sauté
until tender and translucent, 5 to 7 minutes. Take the skillet from the heat and add the
shredded chicken, stirring to mix evenly with the onions. Season to taste with salt and pepper
and set aside in a large bowl.

WIPE OUT THE SKILLET with a paper towel and warm it over medium heat. Add a tortilla to the skillet and heat, turning once, until it softens slightly, about 10 seconds per side. Set the tortilla on the work surface and top with about ⅓ cup of the chicken filling. Fold the tortilla in half to cover the filling and set it in the prepared baking dish. Continue heating and filling the remaining tortillas in the same way, overlapping them slightly in the baking dish.

POUR THE SALSA evenly over the tortillas and sprinkle the cheese over the top. Bake until the cheese is melted and the enchiladas are heated through, about 5 minutes. Let sit for 10 to 15 minutes before serving.

Makes 4 to 6 servings

Coconut Curried Lamb Shanks

Luau Polynesian Lounge

These lamb shanks are richly flavored after the long simmering in the
spice- and coconut-rich braising liquids. The coconut ginger salsa served alongside is the
ideal condiment, a bolt of fresh, bright flavor to complement the rich lamb. Chef Dee Dennis
also suggests serving the shanks with grilled tropical fruit, such as pineapple and mango.
When working with fresh hot chiles—among the hottest of which is the habanero—it's a
good idea to wear plastic gloves, or at least be sure to wash your hands thoroughly
immediately upon finishing, to avoid painful burning.

4 lamb shanks (about 1 pound each)	3 tablespoons honey
3 tablespoons vegetable oil	2 tablespoons red curry paste
1 can (14 ounces) unsweetened coconut milk	2 tablespoons chopped cilantro
¼ cup soy sauce	1 tablespoon coriander seeds
¼ cup Thai fish sauce (nam pla)	5 star anise

COCONUT GINGER SALSA

1 cup freshly grated coconut	½ habanero chile, cored, seeded, and minced,
3 tablespoons chopped pickled ginger	or to taste
2 tablespoons minced lemongrass	Juice of 1 lime
1 tablespoon chopped cilantro	Salt and freshly ground black pepper

PREHEAT THE OVEN to 325°F.

FOR THE SALSA, combine the coconut, ginger, lemongrass, cilantro, chile, and lime juice with
salt and pepper to taste. Stir to mix evenly and set aside.

SEASON THE LAMB SHANKS well with salt and pepper. Heat the oil in a large, heavy pot,
such as a Dutch oven, over medium-high heat. Add 2 of the shanks and brown them well on all
sides, about 5 minutes total. Set them aside on a plate and brown the remaining 2 shanks.
Return the first shanks to the pan (with any juices that have collected on the plate) and add the
coconut milk, soy sauce, fish sauce, honey, red curry paste, cilantro, coriander seeds, and star
anise. Add cold water just to cover the shanks and bring to a boil over high heat. Cover the pot
and braise the lamb shanks in the oven until very tender, about 3 hours.

TRANSFER THE LAMB SHANKS to a platter and cover with foil to keep warm. Skim the fat from the surface of the braising liquid, then strain the liquid through a sieve. Return the liquid to the pot and bring to a boil over medium-high heat. Reduce the liquid until slightly thickened, about 15 minutes. Taste for seasoning and adjust with salt and pepper to taste.

POUR SOME OF THE COOKING LIQUIDS over the lamb shanks and spoon the coconut ginger salsa alongside.

Makes 4 servings

Salmon con Tamarindo

El Camino

Tamarind is a brittle, beanlike pod with tart flesh that is often used in Asian cooking. Here, however, it finds a happy pairing with salmon in a Mexican-inspired dish. Although tamarind has been grown in Mexico since the arrival of the Spanish, it isn't often an ingredient in the cuisine. It is far more commonly used to make a type of *agua fresca,* a popular Mexican drink available in a variety of flavors.

The salmon alone, with its tangy tamarind glaze, would be delicious, so don't feel like you have to prepare the other components if you're looking for a streamlined option. At El Camino, chef Ron Correa serves the fish with *camote,* a blend of yam, sweet potato, and russet potato mashed with cream and a generous dose of chile. The sautéed greens are sometimes treated to a splash of reduced apple cider that has been mixed in equal parts with apple cider vinegar.

4 ounces tamarind pods
¼ cup packed brown sugar
Juice of ½ lemon

4 salmon fillet pieces (6 to 7 ounces each), skin and pin bones removed
Salt and freshly ground black pepper
Cilantro sprigs, for garnish

GREEN ONION OIL

½ cup chopped green onion, white and pale green portions
½ cup vegetable oil
¼ teaspoon salt

CALDILLO SAUCE

4 plum (roma) tomatoes (about 1 pound)
⅓ cup chopped yellow onion
1 teaspoon minced garlic

1 teaspoon cornstarch, dissolved in 2 teaspoons cold water

SAUTÉED GREENS

2 tablespoons vegetable oil
2 teaspoons minced garlic
8 cups rinsed and coarsely chopped cooking greens (chard, mustard, and/or collard)

FOR THE GREEN ONION OIL, combine the green onion, oil, and salt in a blender and purée until fairly smooth. Put the oil in a squeeze bottle, if you have one, or in a small bowl. (You'll have more oil than needed for this recipe; refrigerate the rest and use it in vinaigrette dressings or as a marinade for grilled shrimp.)

PEEL THE HUSKS from the tamarind pods, put the pulpy seeds in a small saucepan, and add just enough water to cover the tamarind. Bring to a boil, then reduce the heat to medium-high and continue cooking until the mixture is thick, about 5 minutes. Stir occasionally to break up the seeds and add water as needed to keep the tamarind moist and not sticking to the bottom of the pan. Pour the pulp into a sieve and set it over a small bowl. Press on the pulp with the back of a spoon until mostly just seeds and fibers remain, scraping the purée from the bottom of the sieve. Return the purée to the saucepan, bring to a boil, and whisk in the brown sugar and lemon juice. Take the pan from the heat and cover to keep warm.

FOR THE CALDILLO SAUCE, put the whole tomatoes in a large pan of cold water and set over high heat until the water is near a boil and the tomato skins just begin to split, about 5 minutes. With a slotted spoon, transfer the tomatoes to a blender, add the onion and garlic, and purée the mixture until fairly smooth. Strain the purée through a sieve set over a medium saucepan. Place the pan over medium-high heat, bring the purée to a boil, and then reduce the heat to medium. Whisk in the dissolved cornstarch and cook until slightly thickened, about 5 minutes. Season to taste with salt, cover, and keep warm over very low heat.

FOR THE SAUTÉED GREENS, heat the oil in a large skillet over medium-high heat. Add the garlic and cook until aromatic, just a few seconds. Add the greens and sauté until tender, 8 to 10 minutes (you may want to add the greens in a couple of batches, allowing some to begin wilting to make room for the rest). Season to taste with salt and keep warm over very low heat.

PREHEAT THE BROILER. Line a broiler pan with foil and oil the foil. Season the salmon pieces with salt and pepper. Set them, skinned side up, on the broiler pan and broil 4 to 5 inches from the heat for 3 minutes. Turn the fish, brush the top with the tamarind glaze, and broil until cooked to taste, 3 to 5 minutes longer for medium-well, depending on the thickness of the fish.

SPOON A POOL OF THE SAUCE onto the center of each warmed individual plate and then spoon the sautéed greens onto the center of the sauce. Lay the salmon on top of the greens, outline the sauce with a border of the green onion oil, and garnish with cilantro sprigs. Serve right away.

Makes 4 servings

Salmon

The Native American tribes of the Northwest coast dined richly, and their most important food was salmon. They identified what they called the five tribes of salmon—Pink, Sockeye, Chinook (or King), Chum, and Coho (or Silver). Settlers told stories of "rivers so thick with salmon you could walk across their backs." According to the Associated Salmon Packers in a booklet dated 1929, the amount of salmon packed after the summer's haul, if the cans were placed end to end, would wrap all the way around the globe—with enough cans left over to stretch from Seattle all the way to New York!

But today all five species of Pacific salmon are at risk in different areas of the Pacific Northwest. Naturally spawning populations of Chinook are about one-third of what their numbers used to be, and still declining, while wild Coho have vanished from more than half of their historic range. The impact of modern human society has critically weakened the fishery, and this once seemingly inexhaustible resource is now endangered.

To save the salmon, and preserve our own quality of life as well, everyone must strive to ensure the health of the Puget Sound ecosystem. The best way to protect the salmon is to protect their habitat—preserving clean, cool water in healthy rivers and streams that offer places to feed on good bugs and larvae and places to rest and hide.

The salmon sold in local grocery stores and served in restaurants is either farm raised or from an area such as Alaska where the species is not yet threatened. So, while we all learn to live in more fish-friendly ways, we can still enjoy eating salmon prepared in its many styles.

A traditional feature at Native American feasts was cedar-staked salmon, slooooow roasted almost vertically, just leaned in slightly beside a driftwood fire. Cooked by radiant heat, the fish was moist and tender with a lightly smoked flavor. This preparation is still enjoyed in a modified way as the ultimate method for cooking salmon.

At Ivar's Salmon House, the restaurant founded by restaurateur and Seattle icon Ivar Haglund, salmon is barbecued in a Native American–style open pit over alder coals, imparting to the salmon's delicate flesh a distinctive, woody perfume. These days you'll find contemporary presentations such as the Alder-Barbecued King Salmon with Fennel and Mint (page 101).

Local menus also showcase salmon presentations with terrific ethnic twists to them. At Fremont's popular El Camino, you'll find the Latin-influenced Salmon con Tamarindo (page 130). Kaspar Donier's menu at Kaspar's touts Steamed King Salmon on Hungarian Paprika Sauerkraut, teeming with caraway seeds (page 153).

In Seattle salmon isn't only barbecued, broiled, or steamed but is also enjoyed in numerous other preparations, from kippered or hard smoked, to pickled and cold smoked. At Fullers, Tequila-Cured Gravlax Salmon (page 40) is accompanied by a coolly contrasting raita made with yogurt, cucumber, red onion, and mint.

When longtime celebrated French chefs Gerard Parrat and Dominique Place left their respective Seattle restaurant posts in 1989 to pursue their dream of smoking perfect, succulent salmon, the result was the incarnation of Gerard & Dominique Seafoods. One of the nation's best salmon smokeries, G&D now ships to well over a hundred restaurants nationwide as well as to Japan. The G&D Nova, a Euro-style cold-smoked salmon, is a delicacy that often appears on Seattle chefs' menus. It's delicious tucked under poached eggs for the ultimate smoked salmon Benedict, or served alongside wasabi-spiked cream cheese and ginger pickled onions. Salmon . . . it's a Seattle way of life, however you enjoy it!

—KC

Steak Teriyaki

Canlis

The secret to good steak teriyaki is to cook it in small batches. You want the meat to sear and the sauce to glaze the meat, which is hard to accomplish if the pan is too crowded. In fact, at Canlis they've perfected the method using two skillets: one hotter pan to sear the meat, then the second pan to continue cooking the meat and to cook the marinade to a glossy glaze. At home, you can streamline to sauté the meat in one skillet over medium-high heat, but be sure to cook in small batches.

Chef Greg Atkinson serves the teriyaki as both an appetizer and a main course. For the former, he uses a smaller portion of beef and includes fresh pineapple and grapes on the plate. He also uses both regular soy sauce and reduced-sodium soy sauce in the recipe, as has been done for decades at Canlis, but admits that when he cooks up the same dish at home, he uses only ½ cup of the regular soy sauce. You can do the same.

2 pounds beef tenderloin, trimmed

TERIYAKI SAUCE

½ cup water	¼ cup Kikkoman soy sauce
⅓ cup sugar	2 tablespoons minced or grated ginger
¼ cup reduced-sodium Kikkoman soy sauce	1 tablespoon chopped garlic

FOR THE SAUCE, combine the water, sugar, soy sauces, ginger, and garlic in a large, shallow dish and stir to blend until the sugar is dissolved. Set aside.

CUT THE BEEF TENDERLOIN into bite-sized pieces. They should measure about 2 inches long and about ½ inch thick. Add the beef to the marinade and stir gently to coat the meat evenly. Cover the dish with plastic wrap and refrigerate for 3 to 4 hours, stirring once or twice.

WHEN READY TO COOK THE MEAT, preheat the oven to 200°F. Heat 1 skillet over medium-high heat and another over medium heat (cast-iron skillets work best). Using tongs, transfer about 1 cup of the meat to the hotter skillet and add about ¼ cup of the marinade. Cook, stirring, for 2 minutes, then transfer the beef to the second skillet (scooping out as much of the marinade as possible with a spatula) and continue cooking until the beef is just cooked to taste and the marinade is reduced to a shiny glaze, about 1 minute longer. Transfer the cooked beef to a heatproof platter and keep warm in the oven while cooking the remaining beef in the same way. (You may need to wipe out the skillets after a couple of batches, since the accumulated marinade might begin to stick.)

TRANSFER THE TERIYAKI BEEF to warmed individual plates and serve at once.

Makes 4 servings

Spicy Polenta with Braised Fennel, Olives, and Goat Cheese

Café Flora

This is an elegantly rustic vegetarian dish, based on a simple recipe of polenta
spiced with red pepper flakes and topped with a flavorful blend of fennel, olives, and
tomatoes, and a sprinkling of goat cheese. A delicious variation substitutes balsamic-roasted
figs for the tomatoes and olives (see page 137). The polenta is broiled here, but it could
also be grilled or sautéed in olive oil.

2 teaspoons fennel seeds	2 tablespoons chopped garlic
4 tablespoons olive oil, plus more	1 teaspoon dried red pepper flakes
for broiling polenta	7 cups water
½ large onion, diced	2 cups coarse yellow cornmeal (polenta)

BRAISED FENNEL

1 fennel bulb	2 cups diced plum (roma) tomatoes
3 tablespoons olive oil	¾ cup Kalamata olives, pitted
Salt and freshly ground black pepper	¼ cup dry white wine
1 cup water	2 tablespoons chopped rosemary
½ large onion, sliced	6 ounces goat cheese, crumbled, for garnish
1 tablespoon chopped garlic	

PUT THE FENNEL SEEDS in a small, dry skillet and toast over medium heat, stirring often,
until the seeds begin to brown and are aromatic, 3 to 5 minutes. Transfer the seeds to a small
plate to cool (they might burn if left to sit in the hot skillet). When cool, coarsely grind them in
a spice grinder or with a mortar and pestle.

PREHEAT THE OVEN to 350°F.

FOR THE BRAISED FENNEL, trim the root end and stalks of the fennel bulb, reserving some
of the fronds for garnish. Cut the bulb in half lengthwise and cut out the tough core. Heat 1
tablespoon of the oil in a Dutch oven or other heavy, deep saucepan over medium heat. When
the oil is hot, add the fennel halves and brown well on both sides, turning often and lightly seasoning with salt and pepper as they cook, 5 to 7 minutes total. Transfer the fennel halves to a
small baking dish, add the water, and cover the dish with foil. Bake until the fennel is tender
when pierced with the tip of a knife, about 30 minutes. Set the fennel aside to cool, reserving
the cooking liquid.

THOROUGHLY COAT a 9- by 13-inch baking dish with olive oil or cooking spray. Heat 1 tablespoon of the oil in the same Dutch oven used for the fennel over medium-high heat. Add the diced onion and ½ teaspoon salt and cook, stirring, for 2 minutes. Add the garlic, red pepper flakes, and ground fennel seeds and cook for 1 minute longer. Add the water and bring to a boil. Whisking constantly, add the cornmeal in a thin, steady stream to the boiling liquid. Continue to whisk until the polenta pulls away from the sides of the pan as you stir, 15 to 20 minutes. Immediately pour the polenta into the oiled baking dish, using an oiled rubber spatula to spread the polenta evenly. Let cool slightly, then refrigerate until fully chilled, at least 1 hour. When the polenta is completely cooled, cut it into 6 squares and then cut the squares on the diagonal into triangles.

PREHEAT THE BROILER. Brush each polenta piece lightly on both sides with olive oil and set on a broiler pan or baking sheet. Broil the polenta about 4 inches from the heat source, turning once, until lightly browned and heated through, about 2 minutes per side. Turn off the oven and keep the polenta warm on a lower rack in the oven.

SLICE THE COOLED FENNEL BULB lengthwise into ¼-inch-wide pieces. Heat the remaining 2 tablespoons of olive oil in a large skillet over medium heat. Add the sliced onion and sauté, stirring often, until tender and translucent, about 5 minutes. Add the garlic and cook for 1 minute longer, then stir in the fennel slices, tomatoes, olives, wine, and rosemary with the braising liquid from the fennel and salt to taste. Cook until well heated through, about 3 minutes.

SET A TRIANGLE OF WARM POLENTA on each warmed individual plate and top with a few spoonfuls of the fennel sauté. Place a second triangle on top of the sauté, at an opposing angle. Top with the remaining fennel sauté, the crumbled goat cheese, and some fennel fronds for garnish. Serve at once.

Makes 6 servings

Balsamic Roasted Figs

If desired, omit the tomatoes and olives from the braised fennel and substitute balsamic-roasted figs. To prepare them, preheat the oven to 350°F. Combine 12 Black Mission figs, halved with stems intact; 2 tablespoons balsamic vinegar; 1 tablespoon olive oil; and salt and pepper to taste and toss to coat well. Place in a small baking dish and bake until tender, 20 to 30 minutes, depending on their ripeness. Set the figs aside to cool, reserving the cooking liquid. You can also add a splash of balsamic vinegar to the final sauté.

Thiebu Djen
(Parsley-Stuffed Halibut with Vegetables and Rice)

Afrikando

Chef Jacques Sarr, born and raised in Senegal, has brought
some new flavors to Seattle, and this recipe is an ideal example. Thiebu Djen
(pronounced cheb-oo-jen), which translates simply as "fish and rice," is a hearty blend of
simmered vegetables and lightly poached halibut. The pockets of stuffing in the halibut are
redolent with parsley, green onions, and fiery habanero chile, and the fish steaks are steeped
in a flavorful stock. The preparation is a bit time-consuming, but the result is a unique feast.
When working with fresh hot chiles—among the hottest of which is the habanero—it's a
good idea to work with plastic gloves, or at least be sure to thoroughly wash your hands
right away to avoid painful burning.

1 cup lightly packed flat-leaf (Italian) parsley leaves	¼ teaspoon salt
1 green onion, white and pale green parts only, coarsely chopped	⅛ teaspoon freshly ground black pepper
	Pinch ground cayenne pepper
1 clove garlic	4 to 6 halibut steaks (about 8 ounces each)
¼ habanero chile, cored and seeded	1 lemon, cut into 4 or 6 wedges, for garnish

VEGETABLES AND RICE

¼ cup vegetable oil	¼ teaspoon ground cayenne pepper
1 cup chopped yellow onion	2 carrots, quartered
¼ cup tomato paste	2 turnips, peeled and quartered
4 cups fish stock, preferably homemade, or water	½ head green cabbage, cut into 4 wedges with core attached
1 bay leaf	½ eggplant, trimmed and cut into 1-inch slices
1 habanero chile	6 ounces cassava (yuca), peeled and quartered (optional)
1 tablespoon minced garlic	
2 teaspoons salt	2 cups basmati rice
½ teaspoon freshly ground black pepper	

FOR THE PARSLEY STUFFING, combine the parsley leaves, green onion, garlic, habanero, salt, black pepper, and cayenne pepper in a food processor and purée to form a finely minced paste.

FOR THE VEGETABLES, heat the oil in a large, heavy pot over medium heat. Add the yellow onion and tomato paste and cook, stirring frequently, until the onion is translucent but not browned, about 5 minutes. Add the stock, bay leaf, whole habanero, garlic, salt, black pepper, and cayenne pepper and bring to a boil. Add the carrots, turnips, cabbage, eggplant, and cassava (if using) and return to a boil. Reduce the heat to medium, cover the pot, and cook the vegetables until they are tender, about 15 minutes, removing quicker-cooking vegetables (eggplant and turnips) earlier as needed. Use a slotted spoon to transfer the vegetables to an ovenproof dish, cover with foil, and set aside in a warm spot while you prepare the halibut steaks. Reserve the cooking liquids in the pot.

SET THE HALIBUT STEAKS on the work surface so that the tapered edge points away from you. Use your thumb to make a cavity in the middle of the fleshy part to either side of the backbone that runs vertically through the fish (much like you would make an indent for the jam in a thumbprint cookie). This is an unusual technique, but the flesh will separate to form a cavity. Be careful not to make a hole all the way through the flesh. Stuff these cavities (2 per steak) with the parsley stuffing.

ADD WATER (1 to 2 cups) to the cooking liquids in the pot to bring the depth to 1 inch. Bring the liquid to a simmer over medium heat, then gently lower the halibut steaks, parsley-stuffed side up, into the bubbling stock and cook until nearly opaque throughout, 6 to 10 minutes, depending on the thickness of the fish. (If the pot isn't wide enough for all the fillets to fit in a single layer, cook them in 2 batches.) With a slotted spatula, transfer the halibut to the dish with the vegetables, cover again with foil, and keep warm in a very low oven. Using a slotted spoon, remove the chile from the pot and set aside in a small dish to serve with the fish, or discard. Reserve the liquids in the pot.

PUT THE RICE in a sieve and rinse under cold running water. When the water runs clear, drain the rice thoroughly. Bring the liquids in the pot to a boil over medium-high heat and add the rice, stirring constantly. Reduce the heat to medium-low, cover, and cook until tender and all the water has been absorbed, 12 to 15 minutes. Take from the heat, let rest for 5 minutes, covered, and then fluff with a fork.

SPOON THE RICE onto a warmed large serving platter, discard the bay leaf, put the halibut steaks in the center, and arrange the vegetables around the edge, alternating them in an attractive pattern. Or, arrange the rice, halibut, and vegetables on warmed individual plates. Garnish with lemon wedges and serve.

Makes 4 to 6 servings

Saucisse de Toulouse

Le Pichet

Do not be put off by the idea of making sausage at home. This recipe is
quite easy: simply grind and season the meat and stuff it in casings. You will need a meat
grinder, either the old-fashioned hand-crank type or an attachment for your stand mixer. A
tapered sausage-stuffing attachment for the grinder is unbeatable in making quick work of
forming the sausages. At Le Pichet, chef Jim Drohman serves these garlicky sausages with a
rich cauliflower gratin (page 90) and crusty bread. The recipe makes a big batch of sausages,
but the extras will keep for a month or so, well wrapped, in the freezer.

Hog casings aren't regularly stocked at most grocery stores but are usually
available at good butcher shops. Call in advance to be sure, in case you need to special order
them. If you prefer, the sausages can be grilled rather than pan-roasted.

4 pounds very lean pork shoulder or leg (boneless)	1 tablespoon salt
1 cup brandy	1 1/2 teaspoons freshly ground white pepper
1 1/2 pounds pork fat	1 teaspoon freshly grated or ground nutmeg
3 tablespoons minced garlic	12 feet hog casing, soaked overnight in ice water
2 tablespoons water	2 tablespoons olive oil

TRIM ALL GRISTLE and silver skin (the tough, white membrane that may cover parts of the
meat) from the lean pork and cut the meat into 1-inch cubes. Put the lean pork in a large bowl,
add 2/3 cup of the brandy, and toss well. Cut the pork fat into 1-inch cubes and put in a
medium bowl. Add the remaining 1/3 cup of the brandy and toss well. Cover both bowls with
plastic wrap and marinate the meat and fat in the freezer for 1 hour, stirring every 15 minutes.
(The pork must be very cold when it is ground.)

COMBINE THE GARLIC, water, salt, pepper, and nutmeg in a small bowl and stir until the
salt is dissolved. Set aside. Drain the hog casing, cut it into 3-foot lengths, and put them in a
colander in the sink (the colander helps avoid having the casings slip down the drain). Run cold
water through each of the casing pieces to rinse them well and place in a bowl of water to
avoid drying out..

USING A 3/8-INCH GRINDER DIE, grind the lean pork meat into a large bowl. Then grind the
fat into the same bowl using a 1/4-inch grinder die. Work quickly so the pork stays cold. Add
the seasonings to the pork, stirring until the mixture is very well combined. Do not overmix or
let the meat become warm, as that will leave the finished sausages dry.

SCOOP OUT ABOUT 1 TABLESPOON of the pork mixture and put the rest in the refrigerator to keep cold. Fry the pork in a small skillet until cooked through and taste for seasoning, adjusting the rest of the sausage mixture if needed.

ATTACH A SAUSAGE STUFFING ATTACHMENT to the grinder, removing the grinding die first, and slide one of the casing portions onto the stuffing tube. Tie a knot at the end of the casing. Refeed the meat through the grinder (without a die attachment) and into the casing. Fill the casing firmly without overstuffing, or the sausages will be too tight to twist into links. If air bubbles are visible through the casing, prick them with a pin. After filling the entire casing, twist it into links each about 6 inches long, making about 20 sausages in all. (If you won't be cooking all of the sausages right away, wrap the extras in a double layer of plastic wrap followed by foil and then freeze.)

PREHEAT THE OVEN to 450°F. Cut the sausages into individual links. Heat the olive oil in a large ovenproof skillet over medium-high heat. Add the sausages and cook until evenly browned on all sides, 5 to 7 minutes. Transfer the skillet to the oven and continue cooking until the sausages are hot through and no longer pink in the center, about 10 minutes longer. Transfer the sausages to warmed individual plates and serve right away.

Makes about 20 sausages

Comfort Foods and Sacred Cows

What are the foods you long for that make you feel oh, so good, warm and fuzzy all over?

For many it's the bubbling, big-flavored Cassoulet served Sunday nights at Cassis. For others it's the perfect, roasted chicken "to order" that Le Pichet touts with seasonal accompaniments such as forest mushrooms. Or what about cooking up some of your own Le Pichet–style, French countryside comfort food like the Gratin de Chou-fleur (page 90) that chef Jim Drohman serves as a bed for his Saucisse de Toulouse (page 140)—very hearty, very delicious!

Everyone has favorites. In restaurants they are sometimes called "sacred cows" or "untouchables"—those items that have become so strongly associated with the establishment that patrons will wreak havoc if the dishes are taken off the menu.

At the resurged and reopened, modern-day El Gaucho they are still serving up those head-turning, magnificent, tableside flaming shish kebabs of the restaurant's first incarnation—along with the complimentary after-dinner, signature platter of fruit and Roquefort cheese for your nibbling pleasure. Opened originally in 1952, closed in 1985, and then opened again with ultimate flair in 1996 by Seattle's preeminent front man, Paul MacKay, El Gaucho's retro touches make today's children of yesteryear's patrons feel oh, so grown up!

At Campagne, chefs and foodies alike clamor for the classic Pâté de Campagne (page 34) served with traditional accompaniments. If you're feeling extra epicurean, you, too, can try whipping it up at home.

What are the Seattle chefs, waiters, and restaurateurs nibbling downtown in after-hour haunts? Well, for sure, the fried chicken at Flying Fish—definitely a comfort food and definitely a delicious bit of home cooking on their sophisticated fish-ified menu.

And of course there are the mashed-potato lovers, meatloaf cravers, and mac-and-cheese junkies. Just look at the comeback of all those classic American retro dishes on restaurant menus. Mashed potatoes show up in variations such as lobster, roasted chile, wild mushroom, blue cheese. . . . It's pretty clear that, deep down, Seattleites have a secret yearning for homey goodness. Take for instance the Ultimate Mac at Icon Grill. The macaroni-and-cheese recipe is a cheese lover's delight, baked up with a humongous amount of cheese and then drizzled "tableside" with more cheese in sauce form. Yum!

Hmmmm, what will the comfort foods be in the 22nd century?

—KC

Roasted Chicken with Caramelized Garlic and Sage

Tulio

This recipe, in which slices of caramelized garlic are slipped under the skin of chicken breasts before baking, is a playful variation on traditional Italian roasted chicken. Chef Walter Pisano typically serves it with lemon risotto.

12 cloves garlic	4 chicken breasts (about 8 ounces each),
¼ cup sugar	bone in and skin on
2 tablespoons unsalted butter	¼ cup olive oil
8 sage leaves	Salt and freshly ground black pepper

CUT THE GARLIC CLOVES lengthwise into slices about ⅛ inch thick. Bring a small saucepan of lightly salted water to a boil and fill a small bowl with ice water. Add the garlic to the boiling water and cook until the garlic is barely tender, 3 to 5 minutes. Using a slotted spoon, transfer the garlic to the ice water. When the garlic has cooled completely, drain it well and pat dry on paper towels, then set the garlic aside in a small dish.

HEAT THE SUGAR in a heavy medium saucepan over medium heat, stirring constantly with a wooden spoon until the sugar melts and turns golden brown, 6 to 8 minutes. Take the pan from the heat and gently stir in the garlic and butter. Avoid overstirring, or the garlic may fall into bits; you want to keep the slices intact. Pour the garlic onto a piece of parchment paper or foil, spreading it out evenly, and set aside to cool.

PREHEAT THE OVEN to 375°F.

FINELY CHOP THE SAGE LEAVES. Working with 1 chicken breast at a time, lift the skin along one edge, being careful not to detach the skin completely, and slip the sage and caramelized garlic slices between the skin and flesh. (There will be some excess garlicky caramel pooled on the paper, but use only the caramel-infused slices for stuffing under the chicken skin.)

HEAT THE OIL in a large ovenproof skillet over medium-high heat. Season the chicken breasts lightly with salt and pepper and add them, skin side down, to the skillet. Cook until the breasts are just browned, 1 to 2 minutes. Turn the pieces over, put the skillet in the oven, and bake until the breasts are just cooked through, 15 to 20 minutes.

TAKE THE BREASTS from the oven, let sit for 5 minutes, then serve on warmed individual plates.

Makes 4 servings

Cumin-Seared Columbia River Sturgeon

Ray's Boathouse

Sturgeon is one of the ugliest and most delicious things to come from Northwest waters. In this recipe, the fish is generously seasoned with cumin, garlic, and curry powder and served with a refreshing tomato vinaigrette. At Ray's Boathouse, chef Charles Ramsayer serves the seared sturgeon with a ragout of white beans, fennel, and chanterelle mushrooms. An ancho chile sauce is drizzled around the fish, delivering some pleasant heat, but you can omit that element of the recipe and still have a wonderful dish.

2 tablespoons ground cumin	½ teaspoon freshly ground black pepper
2 tablespoons granulated garlic (not garlic salt)	6 sturgeon fillet pieces (6 to 7 ounces each),
1 tablespoon Madras curry powder	skin and pin bones removed
1 teaspoon sugar	2 tablespoons olive oil
1 teaspoon celery salt	Sliced green onion, white and pale green parts,
1 teaspoon salt	for garnish

HEIRLOOM TOMATO VINAIGRETTE

½ large heirloom tomato (such as Marvel Stripe), cored, seeded, and chopped	1 teaspoon Dijon mustard
½ shallot, chopped	¾ cup canola oil
¼ cup rice wine vinegar	Salt and freshly ground black pepper

ANCHO CHILE SAUCE

1 large ancho chile
About 1½ cups vegetable stock, preferably homemade

PREHEAT THE OVEN to 400°F.

FOR THE VINAIGRETTE, purée the tomato, shallot, and vinegar in a blender. Add the mustard and pulse to mix. With the blades running, add the canola oil in a slow, steady stream. Season to taste with salt and pepper; set aside.

FOR THE ANCHO CHILE SAUCE, remove the stem and seeds from the chile. Toss the chile in a dry skillet over medium heat to soften it a bit, then put it in a blender with about ¼ cup of the stock. Purée, slowly adding more stock until the chile sauce is smooth and has the consistency of a syrup. Transfer the sauce to a squeeze bottle or small bowl and set aside.

ON A PLATE, combine the cumin, garlic, curry powder, sugar, celery salt, salt, and pepper. Stir with a fork until evenly blended. Dip the top, fleshy side of each sturgeon fillet piece into the cumin rub to coat evenly, patting off any excess.

HEAT THE OIL in a large ovenproof skillet, preferably nonstick, over medium-high heat. When very hot, add the fish pieces, spiced side down, and sear until nicely browned and aromatic, 1 to 2 minutes. (You want the spices to toast and form a nice crust on the fish without burning, which will make them bitter.) Turn the fish pieces over and bake in the oven until just cooked through, about 5 minutes.

WHISK THE TOMATO VINAIGRETTE to reblend, then spoon a pool of vinaigrette in the center of individual plates. Set the sturgeon fillets on the sauce and scatter the green onion over the fish. Drizzle the ancho chile sauce over all and serve, passing any remaining sauce separately.

Makes 4 servings

Lemongrass Rubbed Filet
with Braised Short Ribs and Spicy Red Pepper Sauce

The Painted Table

Asian flavors have become an integral part of Seattle's cooking style.
Here the aroma and flavor of lemongrass, kaffir lime leaves, hot chiles, and ginger impart
wonderful Asian-influenced flavor to both tender filet mignon and rich short ribs. For a
streamlined alternative, you could omit the ribs and serve just the filet steaks (perhaps
slightly larger ones than called for here). When weather permits, the ribs and steak
could be grilled for added flavor.

Chef Tim Kelley serves this aromatic dish with scallion rice cakes,
housemade kimchee, and sautéed pea vines. Simple steamed rice, perhaps with some sliced
green onions tossed in just before serving, would be a perfect and simple accompaniment.
Many styles of kimchee and other pickled vegetables are available in well-stocked
stores and Asian markets. Their piquant, spicy flavor is a wonderful complement
to the richly flavored beef in this recipe.

Be sure to buy the short ribs that have a chunky, squarish shape,
rather than the thinly sliced Korean style of short ribs.

1 stalk lemongrass, trimmed and coarsely chopped	½ cup plus 1 teaspoon brown sugar
3 tablespoons coarsely chopped ginger	½ cup seasoned rice vinegar
6 kaffir lime leaves, coarsely chopped	3 tablespoons dry sherry
6 Thai chiles or other small, hot chiles, stemmed and coarsely chopped	2 tablespoons sesame oil
6 cloves garlic, coarsely chopped	1½ to 2 pounds beef short ribs
½ cup soy sauce	3 cups chicken stock, preferably homemade
	3 tablespoons vegetable oil
	4 filet mignon steaks, about 5 ounces each

SPICY RED PEPPER SAUCE

1 red bell pepper	1 teaspoon Thai fish sauce (nam pla)
2 cloves garlic	1 teaspoon sambal oelek or other hot chile sauce, more to taste
1 teaspoon freshly squeezed lime juice	

FOR THE MARINADE, combine the lemongrass, ginger, kaffir lime leaves, chiles, and garlic in
a small bowl. Stir to mix, then set aside half of the seasoning mixture to use later. Put the rest
of the mixture in a large bowl and add the soy sauce, ½ cup of the brown sugar, the rice

vinegar, sherry, and sesame oil. Stir to mix until the sugar is dissolved, then add the beef short ribs and stir gently to evenly coat them. Cover the bowl with plastic wrap and marinate in the refrigerator for about 5 hours, stirring the ribs once or twice so they marinate evenly.

MEANWHILE, prepare the spicy red pepper sauce. Roast the red pepper over a gas flame or under the broiler until the skin blisters and blackens, turning occasionally to roast evenly, 5 to 10 minutes total. Put the pepper in a plastic bag, securely seal it, and set aside to cool. When cool enough to handle, peel away and discard the skin. Remove the core and seeds and coarsely chop the pepper.

BRING A SMALL SAUCEPAN of water to a boil, add the whole garlic cloves, and boil for 2 minutes. Drain the garlic and repeat with a pan of fresh water. Put the drained garlic in a blender, add the roasted pepper, lime juice, fish sauce, and chile sauce. Purée until smooth and taste for seasoning, adding more chile sauce to taste; set aside until ready to serve. (Refrigerate the sauce if making it more than a few hours in advance, but let the sauce come to room temperature before serving.)

AFTER THE RIBS HAVE MARINATED, preheat the oven to 325°F. Take the ribs from the marinade and pat dry with paper towels. Pour the marinade into a small saucepan, add the chicken stock, and warm the marinade over medium heat. Heat 1 tablespoon of the oil in a heavy medium pot over medium-high heat. Sear the ribs until well browned on all sides, 3 to 5 minutes total, then pour the warm marinade over and cover with the lid. Braise the ribs in the oven until the meat is very tender and begins to fall away from the bones, about 2 hours.

PUT THE REMAINING LEMONGRASS MIXTURE in a food processor (a mini-sized one, if you have it) with the remaining teaspoon of brown sugar and process until very finely minced. Rub the paste over both sides of the filet mignon steaks, set them on a plate, and refrigerate, covered with plastic wrap, while the ribs are braising.

WHEN THE RIBS ARE TENDER, take them from the oven and let cool slightly. Lift the ribs out with a slotted spoon to a plate and use your fingers to separate the meat from the bones and fat. Return the meat to the marinade and keep warm over low heat.

HEAT THE REMAINING 2 TABLESPOONS of vegetable oil in a heavy skillet over medium-high heat. Rub the lemongrass paste from the filet mignon steaks with a paper towel, season the steaks lightly with salt and pepper, and add them to the hot skillet. Pan-fry until cooked to taste, about 2 minutes per side for rare, 3 to 4 minutes per side for medium-rare to medium.

SET THE STEAKS on individual warmed plates and arrange the ribs alongside. Drizzle some of the spicy red pepper sauce alongside and serve.

Makes 4 servings

Morel Mushroom Ravioli
with Chanterelle Mushroom Ragout

The Georgian Room

Executive chef Gavin Stephenson, of the Four Seasons Olympic Hotel,
uses a blend of a special hard-wheat flour (Mondako) and softer pastry flour for this
pasta dough, but everyday all-purpose (made from a blend of high- and low-gluten flours) is
a decent substitute. White truffle oil is one of those gourmet products that packs a great deal
of flavor into a small—albeit expensive—package. The oil is redolent with the flavor and
aroma of Italian white truffles and a little goes a long way, whether in the form of
a quick drizzle over linguine or a thin-crust pizza or stirred into mashed potatoes.
Once you buy the bottle for this recipe, you'll be glad to have it on the shelf.

Ravioli pans make the forming of ravioli quick and tidy. They come in a variety of
sizes and styles, but try to find one that will make two-inch-square ravioli. You can also form
the ravioli freestyle, as described in the recipe.

1 ounce dried morel mushrooms	1 teaspoon white truffle oil
½ russet potato (about 8 ounces)	1 pound chanterelle mushrooms, wiped clean,
Salt and freshly ground black pepper	trimmed, and halved or quartered if large
5 tablespoons unsalted butter	2 cups veal or beef stock, preferably homemade
2 shallots, minced	2 tablespoons chopped flat-leaf (Italian) parsley
2 tablespoons brandy	

PASTA DOUGH

2 cups all-purpose flour	2 tablespoons olive oil
¼ cup fine semolina flour, plus more	½ teaspoon salt
for rolling out dough	1 whole egg, lightly beaten with 1 tablespoon
2 whole eggs	water, for sealing pasta
2 egg yolks	

FOR THE PASTA DOUGH, combine the all-purpose flour and semolina flour in a food
processor and pulse once or twice to mix. Lightly beat together the whole eggs, egg yolks, oil,
and salt in a small bowl. Add this mixture to the flour and pulse just until evenly blended. Turn
the pasta dough out onto a work surface and knead for a few minutes to make a smooth, soft
dough. Wrap the pasta dough in plastic and set aside at room temperature for 1 hour.

PUT THE MORELS in a small bowl and add warm water to cover. Let soak until the mushrooms are rehydrated, about 15 minutes. Lift the mushrooms out of the water and put them into another small bowl, discarding the water and grit from the first bowl. Cover the mushrooms again with warm water and soak again for about 15 minutes. Drain the mushrooms and pat dry on paper towels, then finely chop the morels and set aside.

PEEL THE POTATO, cut it into chunks, and put it in a medium saucepan. Add cold water to cover and a pinch of salt. Bring to a boil, lower the heat to medium, and simmer, uncovered, until the potato is tender when pierced with a knife, about 15 minutes. Drain the potato well and purée it by passing it through a ricer or by pressing it through a sieve with the back of a wooden spoon. Set aside in a medium bowl in a warm spot.

MELT 1 TABLESPOON of the butter in a medium skillet over medium-high heat. Add about half of the shallots and sauté until tender and aromatic, 30 to 60 seconds. Add the morels and sauté until they are slightly crisp, about 3 minutes. Add the brandy and cook until the liquid has evaporated, about 1 minute longer. Season to taste with salt and pepper. Add the morels and truffle oil to the potato purée, stirring to blend evenly. Taste the filling for seasoning, then set aside to cool while rolling the pasta dough.

CUT THE PASTA DOUGH into quarters. Roll out 1 portion with a pasta machine, beginning at the thickest setting (setting 1) and progressing to thinner settings until you reach a thickness of about $\frac{1}{16}$ inch (setting 6 or 7), using a bit of semolina as needed to prevent sticking. The pasta sheet should be about 5 inches wide and more than 2 feet long. Cut the sheet in half crosswise and set 1 sheet over a ravioli pan, pressing it gently into the depressions to make room for the filling. Add about 1 teaspoon of filling to each depression, then lightly brush the edges with the egg-water mixture. Top with the other half of the pasta sheet, pressing gently to seal. Roll a rolling pin over the ravioli pan to cut and form the ravioli. Turn them out onto a surface lightly dusted with semolina flour and repeat with the remaining pasta and filling. If you don't have a ravioli pan, lay one half of each pasta sheet on the work surface and top with 2 rows of 1-teaspoon mounds of filling, leaving a $\frac{1}{2}$-inch border around each mound. Brush around the mounds with the egg-water mixture, top with the other half of the sheet, and press gently to seal and securely enclose the filling. Use a pasta cutter or sharp knife to form individual ravioli.

BRING A LARGE POT of salted water to a rolling boil.

WHILE THE WATER'S HEATING, prepare the chanterelle ragout. Heat 2 tablespoons of the butter in a large skillet over medium-high heat. Add the chanterelle mushrooms and sauté until they are tender and begin to turn golden brown, about 5 minutes. Add the remaining shallots and sauté for 1 minute longer, stirring. Add the stock and cook to reduce the liquid by about three-quarters, 5 to 7 minutes. Season to taste with salt and pepper. Keep the ragout warm over very low heat.

ADD THE RAVIOLI to the boiling water and when they float to the surface, count about 3 minutes longer for them to be fully cooked. When done, remove them from the water with a slotted spoon and drain well in a colander set in the sink. Discard the pasta water, add the remaining 2 tablespoons butter to the pan, and let it melt before returning the ravioli; toss gently to coat the ravioli in butter. Season to taste with salt and pepper.

STIR THE PARSLEY into the chanterelle ragout and spoon it into warmed shallow bowls or rimmed plates. Place the ravioli over the ragout and serve immediately.

Makes 6 to 8 servings

Wild Mushrooms

When it's fall in the Northwest and the air gets damp and the rains start to come, mushroom enthusiasts, foodies, and chefs start heading for the woods to scope out their favorite spots. At this time of year you may find in the forests— or the markets—the gigantic cauliflower mushroom which grows on stumps, white or golden chanterelles, brilliant red lobster mushrooms, or the perfumey, coveted matsutake.

Mushrooming is the perfect Northwest outdoor sport. These aren't just little wooded paths that fungi foragers take to find the elusive wild mushrooms; these are hikes into the deep of the woods. It can be quite a workout plowing around over fallen trees and uneven, rough terrain, but it's all worth it to see a chanterelle's orange head poking out of a blanket of fuzzy moss or peeking from a bed of Douglas fir needles. Just remember, do respect our Northwest bounty and there'll always be plenty for all.

Chanterelles are typically found in second-growth forests (about 60 to 80 years old) as early as August and sometimes as late as Thanksgiving, depending on the date of the first big frost. The two most common types of chanterelle are the yellow *Cantharellus cibarius* and the white *C. subalbidus*. They like to grow under fir trees and vine maples and rarely are found when cedar trees are present.

The spring delights are *Boletus edulis*, also known as porcini in Italian or cèpe in French, and the morel, one of the richest tasting mushrooms. Just a little will do in a recipe for these flavors are intense.

Morels fruit in two types of habitat and they are saprophytic (meaning they eat dead plant material). In areas where they are naturalized, they fruit every year. It is usually a grassy area where natural composting occurs or along a stream where leaves drop to give them food. The other type of habitat is in disturbed areas, such as logged areas or forest burns, where the morels will come up only once because there is no continuous source of food. Sometimes they are even found growing out of soil that has been temporarily disturbed, such as for a new lawn or new garden beds.

Predicting where and when these jewels will appear is a true art. The three key elements are timing, temperature, and elevation. There are also many biological indicators, such as the appearance of other plants and flowers blooming.

There are actually three types of morels: False morels, Early morels, and True morels. The False morel, a *Gyromitra,* should not be eaten. It has a gnarly, brainlike appearance and can be quite large, even as big as your fist. The Early morel, or *Verpa,* is characterized by the way its stem is attached up under the cap, only at the top of the mushroom. *Verpas* can be eaten but do upset many people's stomachs. All lust after the True morel, the *Morchella* species. The name most often given to the variety in this part of the country is *Morchella elata.* Its cap is attached all along the stem.

When seeking True morels, the best bet is to look in the eastern Cascades on south-facing slopes in April and May and then on north-facing slopes as the season progresses into June or sometimes even into August. May is usually the peak of the season.

At the Dahlia Lounge, chef Matt Costello serves a delicious Orcas Island Rack of Lamb with Spring Pea Flan and Morels (page 172), a dish that screams of spring in Seattle! Morels also dry beautifully and can easily be substituted in recipes for fresh ones. Just cover with tepid water and soak for 40 minutes or until soft.

Chanterelles are excellent when sautéed in a little butter or olive oil with some garlic, then deglazed with white wine and a few fresh herbs tossed in. The flavor of chanterelles is definitely brought out by a squeeze of fresh lemon. They are wonderful over a big, fat, juicy steak or as a main ingredient in a dish such as the Wild Mushroom Terrine with Goat Cheese Caillé and Berry Vinaigrette (page 42) that Thierry Rautureau serves at Rover's. Oh, so Northwest!

At The Four Seasons, Morel Mushroom Ravioli with Chanterelle Mushroom Ragout (page 148) is an excellent way to get a little of the best of both wild mushroom seasons.

Patrice Benson, a past president of the Puget Sound Mycological Society and longtime mycophagist (someone with an interest in eating mushrooms), has taken many a chef to her secret foraging grounds—after swearing them to silence of course. She's taught them her fungi-finding gift, and then coerced them (easily!) into whipping up some mushroom delicacies for the Mycological Society's famous fall mushroom show.

Why all the secrecy? With much wild mushroom habitat being destroyed by logging and development, many species are more difficult to find every year. So that's why 'shroomers keep their prime spots a secret. →

As mushroom-savvy chefs know, when preparing any type of edible wild fungus it is very important to cook it thoroughly, as some undesirable compounds are broken down by heat. For example, fresh morels contain a substance, destroyed by heat, that causes upset stomachs when eaten raw. Cooking also enhances the mushrooms' flavor and releases their nutritional elements.

Many traditional dishes can be kicked up a few notches by the addition of wild mushrooms; add them to mashed potatoes, scrumptious eggs Benedict with crab, or oyster stew. Sautéed and marinated, wild mushrooms are often seen on local menus in luscious warm mushroom salads with local greens.

Just remember when you're out foraging that there are many poisonous mushrooms. Be sure of what you're picking. Hunt with an experienced mushroomer or join a mycological society and link up with one of their field trips. To find one near you, call the Puget Sound Mycological Society, 206/522-6031.

—KC

Steamed King Salmon on Hungarian Paprika Sauerkraut

Kaspar's

Of course, other varieties of salmon can be used for this recipe, but the richness of king salmon is perfect with the tangy character of the paprika-scented sauerkraut. The quality of the sauerkraut plays a big role in this recipe, so choose a good-quality brand that isn't overly strong in flavor.

2 tablespoons vegetable oil	1 bay leaf
1 medium onion, chopped	1 teaspoon caraway seeds
1 green bell pepper, cored, seeded, and finely diced	½ teaspoon salt
	1 small russet potato
1 clove garlic, chopped	½ cup whipping cream
2 cups sauerkraut, rinsed and well drained	4 king salmon fillet pieces (6 to 7 ounces each), skin and pin bones removed
1 cup dry white wine	
½ cup water	1 teaspoon minced thyme
8 juniper berries	Salt and freshly ground black pepper
2 tablespoons sweet Hungarian paprika	

HEAT THE OIL in a large skillet over medium heat. Add the onion, bell pepper, and garlic and sauté until the vegetables are tender and aromatic, 5 to 7 minutes. Add the sauerkraut, wine, water, juniper berries, paprika, bay leaf, caraway, and salt and stir until well combined. Reduce the heat to low, cover, and simmer 20 minutes.

PEEL AND GRATE THE POTATO and stir it into the sauerkraut. Cover and simmer until the potato is tender and the flavors are well melded, about 30 minutes longer, then stir in the cream. The sauerkraut mixture should be moist but not soupy. If it's very wet, uncover the pan and cook for a little while longer; if it becomes dry while cooking, add a bit more water.

SEASON THE SALMON with the thyme and salt and pepper to taste. Set the salmon fillets over the sauerkraut, cover the skillet, and cook over medium heat until the salmon is done to your taste, about 10 minutes for medium-well, depending on the thickness of the fillets.

SPOON THE SAUERKRAUT on warmed individual plates and set the salmon fillets on top. Serve right away, telling your guests to keep an eye out for the juniper berries, as they're quite strongly flavored and not meant to be eaten.

Makes 4 servings

Pan-Seared Alaskan Cod
with Green Beans, Niçoise Olives, and Smoked
Paprika Vinaigrette

Cassis

For this cod dish, chef Charlie Durham uses fresh Pacific lingcod from Alaska,
the fillets of which tend to be thicker and fleshier than other cod fillets. Try to avoid buying
thin cod fillets, which don't have the texture and flavor of Alaskan cod and have wetter flesh
that won't sear well. You could use halibut instead, if it looks better than
the cod that's available at the store.

Pimentón de La Vera, a wonderful smoked paprika from Spain, adds a distinctive
earthy perfume and flavor. It is available in specialty spice shops and gourmet stores.

4 Alaskan cod fillet pieces (6 to 7 ounces each), skin and pin bones removed	2 teaspoons smoked paprika (pimentón de La Vera)
⅓ cup plus 4 tablespoons olive oil	½ cup Niçoise olives, including 1 tablespoon brine
½ cup kosher salt	
1 pound green beans, trimmed	3 tablespoons sherry vinegar
1 teaspoon minced garlic	Salt and freshly ground black pepper

BRUSH THE COD PIECES with about 1 tablespoon of the oil and season to taste with salt and pepper. Set the cod on a plate and refrigerate until ready to cook.

BRING 2 QUARTS of water to a boil with the kosher salt and prepare a large bowl of ice water. Add the green beans to the boiling water and boil until slightly tender but still bright green, 2 to 3 minutes. Drain the beans and put them in the ice water to cool thoroughly. When fully cooled, drain the beans well and set aside on paper towels.

HEAT 1 TABLESPOON of the olive oil in a small saucepan over medium heat. Add the garlic and sauté until fragrant and just lightly browned, about 1 minute. Take the pan from the heat and stir in the paprika, then let cool to room temperature. When cool, whisk in the 1 table-spoon of brine from the olives, ⅓ cup of the oil, and the sherry vinegar. Season the vinaigrette to taste with salt and pepper and set aside.

PREHEAT THE OVEN to 400°F. Heat the remaining 2 tablespoons oil in a large, heavy skillet over medium-high heat. When the oil is very hot and just begins to smoke, carefully add the cod pieces, shaking the pan gently to keep the fish from sticking. (The fish pieces shouldn't be crowded in the pan; cook in 2 batches if needed.) Sauté until the fish is nicely browned on the first side, about 2 minutes, then turn the fish and transfer the skillet the oven. Continue cooking until the fish is just opaque through, about 4 minutes longer. (Cooking time will vary with the thickness of the fish.)

TRANSFER THE FISH to a plate and cover with foil to keep warm. Add the green beans to the skillet and sauté over medium-high heat until just heated through, 1 to 2 minutes. (If the skillet is gunky from the fish, you can either wipe it out first or use another skillet instead, adding another tablespoon of oil.)

ARRANGE THE BEANS in the center of warmed individual plates and top with the cod. Spoon the olives around the fish. Rewhisk the vinaigrette to blend, drizzle it over the cod and beans, and serve.

Makes 4 servings

Paella

Andaluca

Paella is one of the world's greatest one-dish meals. This version from chef Wayne Johnson uses a combination of sausage, chicken, and seafood, all baked together on a bed of saffron-infused Arborio rice. It's an elaborate dish, with a number of steps before it goes in the oven, but the results are worth the work. Look for top-quality chorizo sausages, preferably freshly made. Some chorizo can be quite fatty and strongly flavored and can easily overpower the other ingredients in the dish.

1 large red bell pepper	8 ounces boneless, skinless chicken thighs, cut into 1-inch pieces
1 medium tomato	
¼ cup olive oil	1 pound asparagus, trimmed and cut into 4-inch lengths
½ small red onion, cut into ½-inch julienne	
1 cup diced carrot	1 cup fresh or thawed frozen peas
8 ounces chorizo sausage links, cut into 1-inch pieces	8 ounces Manila clams, scrubbed
	8 ounces small mussels, scrubbed and debearded
	8 ounces medium shrimp, peeled and deveined

PAELLA BROTH

4 cups chicken stock, preferably homemade	½ to 1 teaspoon dried red pepper flakes
1 tablespoon minced garlic	½ teaspoon turmeric
1 teaspoon saffron threads	

TOMATO BUTTER

¼ cup unsalted butter, at room temperature	1 teaspoon minced flat-leaf (Italian) parsley
1 teaspoon tomato paste	1 teaspoon minced thyme

RICE

1 tablespoon unsalted butter	2½ cups Arborio rice
½ cup diced yellow onion	2 cups chicken stock, preferably homemade

ROAST THE BELL PEPPER over a gas flame or under the broiler, turning occasionally to roast evenly, until the skin blisters and blackens, 5 to 10 minutes total. Put the pepper in a plastic bag, securely seal it, and set aside to cool. When cool enough to handle, peel away and discard the skin. Remove the core and seeds and cut the pepper into julienne strips.

BRING A MEDIUM PAN of water to a boil and fill a medium bowl with ice water. With the tip of a sharp knife, score an X on the bottom of the tomato. Add the tomato to the boiling water and blanch until the skin begins to split, 20 to 30 seconds. Scoop the tomato out with a slotted spoon and put it in the ice water for quick cooling. When cool, drain the tomato, then peel away and discard the skin. Quarter the tomato lengthwise and scoop out and discard the seeds. Dice the tomato and drain on paper towels. Set aside.

FOR THE PAELLA BROTH, combine the chicken stock, garlic, saffron, red pepper flakes, and turmeric in a small saucepan and bring just to a boil, stirring once or twice. Take the pan from the heat and set aside.

FOR THE TOMATO BUTTER, combine the butter, tomato paste, parsley, and thyme in a small bowl and mix with a fork until well blended. Set aside.

TO PARCOOK THE RICE, melt the butter in a heavy saucepan over medium heat. Add the yellow onion and sauté until just tender and translucent, 5 to 7 minutes. Add the rice and cook, stirring constantly, until the rice is evenly coated in butter, 1 to 2 minutes longer; do not let the rice brown. Stir in about ½ cup of the chicken stock (*not* the paella broth) and cook, stirring, until the rice has absorbed most of the liquid, 2 to 3 minutes. Add another ½ cup of the stock and continue cooking and stirring, until the liquid has been absorbed. Repeat this process twice, using the rest of the stock; the rice will finish cooking in the oven. Set aside in a warm spot.

PREHEAT THE OVEN to 400°F.

HEAT THE OLIVE OIL in a 14-inch paella pan or other large ovenproof skillet over medium-high heat. Add the red onion and carrot and sauté until the onion is tender and translucent, 3 to 5 minutes. Add the chorizo and chicken pieces and cook until just beginning to brown, 3 to 5 minutes. Take the pan from the heat, stir in the rice and tomato butter, then slowly pour in the paella broth, stirring gently so that the rice is evenly moistened by the broth. Scatter the roasted pepper, asparagus, and peas over the rice.

BAKE THE PAELLA until nearly all of the liquid has been absorbed, 15 to 20 minutes. Take the pan from the oven, scatter the clams, mussels, and shrimp evenly over the surface, and continue baking until the rice is tender, the shrimp are just cooked through, and the clams and mussels have opened, 5 to 8 minutes longer.

WHEN THE PAELLA IS DONE, discard any clams or mussels that failed to open. Scatter the diced tomato over the top and set the paella dish in the center of the table on a heatproof platter or a large trivet. Scoop out the rice, vegetables, meat, and seafood for each serving.

Makes 6 to 8 servings

Lamb Chops with Arugula Pesto

The Hunt Club

This award-winning recipe pairs the flavorful lamb chops with a pesto sauce
made from peppery arugula rather than basil. Scattered on the plate are sweet, oven-dried
cherry tomatoes, a wonderful complement. Chef Brian Scheehser serves the lamb with
butternut squash ravioli and a luxurious (and labor-intensive) lamb essence.

1 pint cherry tomatoes
18 lamb rib chops (about 2½ pounds total)

ARUGULA PESTO

1 tablespoon pine nuts
1 bunch arugula (about 4 ounces),
rinsed and trimmed
2 tablespoons freshly grated Parmesan cheese

1 teaspoon chopped garlic
½ cup extra virgin olive oil
Salt and freshly ground black pepper

PREHEAT THE OVEN to 250°F. Line a baking sheet with foil and lightly oil the foil. Stem the
cherry tomatoes and cut them in half through the stem end. Lay the tomatoes, skin side down,
on the baking sheet and bake until dried and slightly leathery looking, about 1½ hours.

WHILE THE TOMATOES ARE OVEN-DRYING, prepare the arugula pesto. Heat the pine
nuts in a small, dry skillet over medium heat until lightly browned and aromatic, about 5 minutes, shaking the pan often to toast them evenly. Transfer the nuts to a plate to cool completely.
Combine 1 cup of the arugula (moderately packed, about half of the bunch), the Parmesan
cheese, garlic, and pine nuts in a food processor or blender and blend until smooth. With the
blades running, add the oil in a slow, steady stream. When all of the oil has been added, season
the pesto to taste with salt and pepper; set aside.

JUST BEFORE SERVING, preheat the boiler. Arrange the lamb chops on a lightly oiled broiler
pan and broil 3 to 4 inches from the heat source, turning once, until cooked to taste, about 2
minutes per side for rare, 3 to 4 minutes per side for medium-rare.

ARRANGE 3 LAMB CHOPS on each warmed individual plate. Scatter the oven-dried tomatoes between the chops and add a small pile of the remaining arugula leaves alongside. Drizzle
the arugula pesto over and around the chops and serve.

Makes 6 servings

"Blue Plate Special" Lingcod
with Sour Cream, Red Onion, and Fresh Dill

Chinook's at Salmon Bay

When Chinook's opened in 1988, the intention was to have a rotating
blue plate special at this Fishermen's Terminal restaurant. But this lingcod with sour cream
has been that "special" since day one. Nowadays, regulars would put up a fight if
the kitchen ever tried to take it off the menu.

1 cup dry white wine	1 cup mayonnaise
1 teaspoon salt	½ cup sour cream
6 lingcod fillet pieces (6 to 7 ounces each), skin	¼ cup minced red onion
and pin bones removed	1 tablespoon minced dill, plus sprigs for garnish
1 cup dried bread crumbs	

COMBINE THE WINE and salt in a shallow dish and stir until the salt is dissolved. Add the
fish pieces, turn to coat evenly, then cover and marinate in the refrigerator for 1 hour, turning
the pieces once or twice. Take the fish from the marinade, allow the excess to drip off, and
dredge the pieces in bread crumbs. Arrange the breaded fillets in a baking dish in a single layer.

PREHEAT THE OVEN to 375°F.

COMBINE THE MAYONNAISE, sour cream, red onion, and minced dill in a small bowl and
stir to mix evenly. Spread the mayonnaise topping on each piece of fish, covering the surface
completely. Bake the fish until opaque through and the topping is golden, 15 to 20 minutes.

SET THE LINGCOD on warmed individual plates, garnish with sprigs of dill, and serve.

Makes 6 servings

Thai Basil–Seared Mahimahi
with Red Curry Lobster Essence

Roy's

This rich and luxurious dish includes one of those elaborate restaurant-style sauces that takes time and effort but pays off with outstanding flavor. It begins with roasting lobster heads, which may sound barbaric, but it echoes a similar step in the making of beef or veal stock: roasting develops and intensifies the flavor. Start by steaming 2 whole lobsters; enjoy the tails for dinner one night, and save the heads for this recipe. (The well-cleaned heads could be frozen for up to two weeks before using.) If you're not up for tackling lobster heads, you could roast the shells from about two pounds of shrimp and proceed as directed, although the resulting flavor won't be as pronounced.

At Roy's, the fish is served atop a mash of sweet potatoes embellished with roasted garlic, and the plate is garnished with taro chips. You can easily make taro chips at home, deep-frying the peeled and thinly sliced root until crisp and lightly browned.

6 sprigs Thai basil, rinsed and dried	Salt and coarsely ground black pepper
4 mahimahi fillet pieces (6 to 7 ounces each), skin removed	2 tablespoons olive oil

RED CURRY LOBSTER ESSENCE

2 Maine lobster heads, well cleaned	1 stalk lemongrass, trimmed and sliced
1 tablespoon olive oil	1 tablespoon chopped cilantro
1 teaspoon chopped ginger	2 tablespoons Thai red curry paste
1 teaspoon chopped garlic	1 tablespoon tomato paste
½ cup chopped onion	½ cup water
¼ cup chopped carrot	1 can (14 ounces) unsweetened coconut milk
¼ cup chopped celery	1 cup whipping cream

PREHEAT THE OVEN to 350°F.

FOR THE LOBSTER ESSENCE, using a cleaver or a large, heavy knife, cut each lobster head into 2 or 3 pieces, lifting off and discarding the feathery gills that are found inside. Put the shell pieces in a roasting pan and roast them until aromatic and lightly browned, about 20 minutes. While the lobster shells are roasting, pull the leaves from 2 sprigs of the basil, reserving the leaves with the remaining sprigs for the mahimahi; the stems will be used in the lobster essence.

HEAT THE 1 TABLESPOON OIL in a large saucepan over medium heat. Add the ginger and garlic and sauté until aromatic and beginning to soften, 1 to 2 minutes. Add the onion, carrot, and celery and sauté until fragrant and tender, about 5 minutes. Stir in the leafless Thai basil stems, lemongrass, and cilantro, followed by the curry and tomato pastes. Add the water and stir to soften the pastes. Stir in the coconut milk and cream, then add the roasted lobster heads. Bring just to a boil, reduce the heat to medium-low, and simmer for 1 hour, stirring occasionally. Strain the lobster essence through a fine sieve into a small saucepan and keep warm over very low heat.

PUT THE RESERVED BASIL LEAVES in a pile on the cutting board and, using a sharp knife, cut across the leaves to make fine shreds (you should have about ¼ cup lightly packed shredded basil). Season the fish with salt and pepper, then scatter the basil on the surface of the mahimahi pieces, pressing to help it adhere. Heat the 2 tablespoons oil in a large, heavy skillet over medium-high heat. When hot, add the fish pieces, basil side down, and sear for 1 minute. Turn the fish pieces over, reduce the heat to medium, and continue cooking until the fish is just opaque through (peek into a thicker portion with the tip of a knife), 5 to 7 minutes longer.

SET THE MAHIMAHI FILLETS on warmed individual plates, spoon the warm lobster essence around, and garnish with the remaining sprigs of basil.

Makes 4 servings

Chefs' Secrets

Have you ever wondered how chefs make what they do look so easy?

Well, sometimes it is easy and sometimes not. Good cooking has many facets—lots of practice and hard work, a true feel for cooking, and a few tried-and-true tricks of the trade. Every cook and chef has these special secrets up their sleeve, from a piece of equipment that makes their life easier to a little procedure that is a smack-in-the-head, "Why didn't I think of that?" experience.

How do chefs make putting out 200 dinners seem so effortless? What makes that beautiful golden crust on their chicken so crisp and the inside so tender and juicy? What makes that sauce so rich tasting and their plates always look so special? It's really four simple secrets:

Number 1—and foremost—Mise en place: Putting out meal after delicious meal, constantly pulling together multiple fabulous dinners at once or whipping out a cocktail party at the drop of a hat . . . it all comes down to mise en place, a French phrase that translates to "everything in its place." What it really means is that you have everything that can possibly be done in advance done, and everything that must be done at the last minute "staged," that is, organized and ready to go. This can be done in a home kitchen, too.

First, make a plan of action. Figure out your menu. Have a good mix of easy, simple dishes and more challenging ones. Remember to consider what item will be cooked where. For instance, don't plan on baking rolls at the same time you've got a roast in the oven because they will probably need to be cooked at different temperatures. When having appetizers, choose one item that's hot and a couple of cold ones.

On a copy of your menu, write next to each item what the serving vessel is or what plate it's going on. Do you need a serving utensil? And what pieces of cutlery will be needed for the place setting? Then list out for each course each component that's going on the plate, and star what needs to be prepped. Next to each item draw a diagram of the dish's presentation, if it's complicated. On this list include a loose timeline of what you're doing when.

Prepare "kits" for each item on the menu. The day of serving, create mise en place trays, and then on your list highlight each item as you tray it up. Use small dishes to hold cut herbs or tiny prepped items.

It may be a bit more work ahead of time than you're used to, but it will give you a lot more time to spend with your guests. Since you have everything prepped, there will be no need to get stressed out! Go ahead. Try this out with one of the more complicated recipes here, such as Roy's Thai Basil–Seared Mahimahi with Red Curry Lobster Essence (page 160).

Number 2—Finishing in the oven: Many restaurant dishes are started on a stovetop burner—either sauteed or seared in a very hot pan, then transferred to a preheated oven to finish cooking. This gives the chef a few minutes to finish the sauce or other accompaniment for the dish and also gives the salmon steak, pork loin, or duck breast a nice "crust" with a juicy interior. Take for instance the recipe for Pork Tenderloin with Bing Cherries and Mint from Madison Park Café (page 122). The tenderloin is browned in a skillet before finishing in the oven, making cooking more consistent.

Number 3—Reducing: This refers to evaporating sauces, stocks, and other liquids to concentrate their flavors, as in the Coconut Curried Lamb Shanks (page 128) from Luau Polynesian Lounge. The important things to remember are to use medium-high heat, so the liquid doesn't boil too vigorously which can cloud it, and to wait to salt the item until after you reduce—otherwise it's likely to be oversalted. Reducing is also used to turn balsamic vinegar into a syrup or a nice local merlot into a thick glaze.

Number 4—the last but in no way the least—Plating: Chefs have a knack for breathtaking presentations, which often utilize special cuts for vegetables. But you don't have to have professional knife skills to achieve spectacular looks for your dishes.

The one implement to never be without is a Japanese mandoline. Basically, it's a heavy plastic rectangular frame that holds any one of several blades, as well as a guiding plate that can be adjusted according to the desired thickness of the cut. Many chefs prefer the Japanese mandoline over the French (metal) type because it's simpler to use, cheaper, and, most importantly, doesn't collapse on you at critical moments! In the Seattle area Uwajimaya carries one favorite brand, Benriner, which can be used for making those paper-thin cuts and hair-like, ultra-skinny vegetables.

Another favorite gadget is a spiral cutter, also available in shops that stock Asian cooking utensils. This device can turn vegetables into beautiful, long, curly strands. Spiral-cut golden yellow and red beets make fabulous, crunchy poufs to garnish a salad!

Probably most chefs who do brilliant platings have dabbled in the visual arts at some point in their lives. This fact is obvious when looking at Chef Kerry Sears' platings at Cascadia. Indeed, his beautiful drawings of vegetables, from leeks to beets to scallions, grace the walls of many of his friends' homes.

These days, you'll also see in the back kitchen dozens of squirt bottles filled with brilliant sauces, oils, and reductions. What a wonderful palette to paint the plate with! Alongside the array of flavorful pigments, there will likely be containers of fluffy herb salads for making high poufs of greens, crackly transparent shards of tuiles and brittles to stand tall on the plate, and tiny, brunoise-cut vegetables for sprinkling over just about everything for a striking finish.

—KC

Smothered Game Hens

Kingfish Café

At the popular Kingfish Café on Seattle's Capitol Hill, the Coaston sisters, Leslie and Laurie, serve this wonderfully fragrant game hen dish with herbed biscuits. Alter your favorite biscuit recipe by adding some fresh herbs and black pepper to the dough, and serve the hens in the same Southern style featured at Kingfish.

If you don't have room to roast the hens and vegetables at the same time, roast the vegetables first. They can be reheated in the sauce prior to serving, but the hens will be best if served right after roasting.

It's easy to split Cornish game hens with a good pair of poultry or other kitchen shears. Cut down the center of the breast on each bird, then turn the bird over and snip down both sides of the backbone, which can be discarded (or frozen to add to your next batch of chicken stock).

2 Cornish game hens (about 1 ¼ pounds each), split and patted dry with paper towels	8 ounces small button mushrooms, wiped clean, trimmed, and halved
Salt and freshly ground black pepper	8 ounces new potatoes, quartered
½ cup all-purpose flour	1 head garlic, separated into cloves and peeled
¼ cup vegetable oil	2 cups whipping cream
2 cups dry sherry	¼ cup Dijon mustard
¼ cup olive oil	1 cup fresh or thawed frozen peas
2 tablespoons thyme leaves	1 tablespoon minced green onion, for garnish
2 tablespoons minced basil	1 tablespoon minced flat-leaf (Italian) parsley, for garnish
8 ounces baby carrots, trimmed	
1 red onion, cut into large dice	1 tablespoon minced red bell pepper, for garnish

PREHEAT THE OVEN to 375°F.

SEASON THE HALVED HENS with salt and pepper, then dredge them with the flour, patting to remove the excess flour. Heat the vegetable oil in a large skillet over medium heat. Brown 2 hen halves at a time until nicely browned, about 5 minutes per side. Transfer the hens to a baking dish (the pieces can overlap slightly if necessary), reserving the skillet for cooking the sauce. Pour 1 cup of the sherry into the baking dish, cover with foil, and roast the hens until the juices run clear when the thigh is pierced with a knife, 45 to 50 minutes.

IN A MEDIUM ROASTING PAN, combine the olive oil, 1 tablespoon of the thyme, 1 tablespoon of the basil, and a generous dose of pepper. Stir to mix, then add the carrots, onion, mushrooms, potatoes, and garlic. Toss to mix and roast until the vegetables are all tender, about 40 minutes, stirring once or twice during cooking so that they will roast evenly.

WHILE THE HENS and vegetables are roasting, prepare the sauce. Pour out all but about 2 tablespoons of the oil from the skillet used to brown the hens. Heat the remaining oil over medium-high heat, then whisk in the remaining 1 cup sherry. Bring to a boil, scraping to lift up the flavorful bits stuck to the pan, and boil until reduced by about half. Whisk in the cream, mustard, the remaining 1 tablespoon thyme, and the remaining 1 tablespoon basil with pepper to taste. Reduce the heat to medium-low and simmer, whisking occasionally, until the sauce thickens and is reduced by about one-third, about 10 minutes.

WHEN THE ROASTED VEGETABLES ARE TENDER, add them to the sauce with the peas and warm until heated through. Taste the sauce for seasoning, adding salt and pepper to taste. (You can also add some of the flavorful cooking juices from the hen roasting pan.)

TO SERVE, set a roasted hen half in the center of a warmed large shallow bowl or rimmed plate, and ladle the sauce and vegetables over. Scatter the plates with the green onion, parsley, and bell pepper, and serve.

Makes 4 servings

Alaskan Halibut with Tagliatelle of Vegetables, Beurre Blanc, and American Caviar

The Hunt Club

Chef Brian Scheehser transforms a variety of vegetables into long, thin strips to replicate tagliatelle pasta and serves them as a colorful bed for the grilled halibut. When it's not grilling season, you could pan-roast the halibut instead, browning the fish on the stove top and then roasting in a 400°F oven until just cooked through.

1 large carrot, trimmed	2 tablespoons olive oil
1 medium zucchini, trimmed	6 halibut fillet pieces (6 to 7 ounces each),
1 medium yellow squash, trimmed	skin and pin bones removed
1 large leek, white and pale green	1 ounce American caviar (such as white
parts only, split	sturgeon, whitefish, or salmon)

BEURRE BLANC

¼ cup dry white wine	1 cup unsalted butter, cut into 1-inch cubes
1 shallot, finely chopped	and chilled
2 tablespoons freshly squeezed lemon juice	Salt and freshly ground white pepper
2 tablespoons whipping cream	

IF YOU HAVE A MANDOLINE, use it to cut the carrot, zucchini, squash, and leek lengthwise into thin slices, then use a chef's knife to cut the slices lengthwise into strips about ½ inch wide. If you don't have a mandoline, cut a small slice from one side of the zucchini, squash, and carrot so that they will sit securely on the cutting board, then use a good, sharp knife to cut the lengthwise slices carefully. Slightly fan out the layers of each leek half and lay it flat on the cutting board, then cut lengthwise into ½-inch-wide strips.

FOR THE BEURRE BLANC, combine the wine, shallot, and lemon juice in a small saucepan. Bring to a boil over medium-high heat and boil, stirring occasionally, until nearly all the liquid has evaporated, about 5 minutes. Add the cream and reduce slightly, 2 to 3 minutes longer. Whisk in the butter, bit by bit, careful that the butter melts creamily without becoming oily. Move the pan off the heat as needed to avoid overheating. Season to taste with salt and pepper, and set aside in a warm spot or over a pan of barely simmering water until ready to use. Do not overheat the sauce or it will separate.

HEAT THE OLIVE OIL in a large skillet over medium-high heat. Add the carrot and sauté until it begins to soften, 1 to 2 minutes. Add the zucchini, yellow squash, and leek and continue cooking until all the vegetables are al dente—tender but with a bit of crunch left—3 to 5 minutes longer. Set aside in the skillet.

PREHEAT AN OUTDOOR GRILL. Season the halibut to taste with salt and pepper, and grill the fish, turning once, until nicely browned and just cooked through, 3 to 5 minutes per side, depending on the thickness of the fillets. (Alternatively, you could broil or pan-fry the halibut.) Gently reheat the vegetables while the halibut is cooking.

SPOON THE VEGETABLES into the center of warmed individual plates and top with a piece of halibut. Spoon the beurre blanc over the halibut, garnish with dollops of the caviar, and serve.

Makes 6 servings

Grilled Pork with Pumpkin Poblano Tamales
and Green Chile Sauce

Yakima Grill

There's no way around the fact that making tamales at home is time-consuming, but the delicious results are worth the effort. This style of tamale isn't stuffed. Instead, the masa harina is blended with pumpkin purée and roasted poblano chiles and steamed in corn husks. The tamales are topped with a tomatillo and poblano sauce and served alongside grilled pork chops. Cotija is a hard, crumbly Mexican cheese with a moderately strong flavor. Masa harina is flour made from dried corn, used to make tamales and tortillas, and is available in Mexican grocery stores.

About 20 dried corn husks	1 teaspoon ground cumin
6 pork loin chops (about 8 ounces each)	¼ teaspoon ground cayenne pepper
Olive oil, for brushing	Pinch freshly grated or ground nutmeg

GREEN CHILE SAUCE

1 tablespoon cumin seeds	2 poblano chiles, cored, seeded, and julienned
¼ cup extra virgin olive oil	1 cup chicken stock, preferably homemade
1 clove garlic, minced	1 bunch cilantro, chopped (about 1 cup)
2 large onions, chopped	Salt and freshly ground black pepper
1 pound tomatillos, husks removed, chopped	

PUMPKIN POBLANO TAMALES

4 poblano chiles	2 cups fresh or canned pumpkin purée
1 cup unsalted butter, at room temperature	1½ cups masa harina
1½ teaspoons baking powder	¼ cup grated cotija cheese
¾ teaspoon salt	¼ cup milk

FILL A POT or large baking dish with cold water, add the corn husks, and soak overnight. (For a shortcut, you could pour hot water over the husks and let them sit for a few hours.)

FOR THE GREEN CHILE SAUCE, put the cumin seeds in a small, dry skillet over medium heat and toast, stirring often, until they begin to brown lightly and smell aromatic, 3 to 5 minutes. Transfer the seeds to a small dish to cool (they might burn and become bitter if left in the hot skillet), then grind the cumin seeds in a spice grinder or with a mortar and pestle.

HEAT THE ¼ CUP OIL in a large saucepan over medium-high heat. Add the garlic, and sauté until fragrant, 30 to 60 seconds. Add the onions, tomatillos, and chiles and sauté, stirring frequently, until the vegetables are tender, 10 to 15 minutes. Add the stock, cilantro, and cumin with salt and pepper to taste, then simmer over medium-low heat, uncovered, until the sauce is slightly thickened, about 20 minutes; set aside.

FOR THE TAMALES, roast the poblano chiles over a gas flame or under the broiler, turning occasionally to roast evenly, until the skin blisters and blackens, 10 to 15 minutes total. Put the chiles in a plastic bag, securely seal it, and set aside to cool. When cool enough to handle, peel away and discard the skin. Remove the core and seeds and chop the chiles; set aside.

RINSE THE CORN HUSKS well and cut about 1 inch off the tapered tip of each husk to square it slightly. Pat dry on paper towels and set aside.

COMBINE THE BUTTER, baking powder, and salt in the bowl of a stand mixer fitted with the paddle attachment. Whip the mixture until fluffy. Add the pumpkin, masa harina, cheese, milk, and roasted chiles and mix until well combined. Alternatively, blend the ingredients in a large bowl using electric beaters to cream the butter, then stir in the remaining ingredients.

CUT LONG, THIN STRIPS from a few of the corn husks to use as ties for the tamales. Spoon about ⅓ cup of the prepared filling down the center of 1 of the corn husks, leaving at least 1 inch of each end uncovered. Fold one side of the husk over the filling and roll up to enclose the filling fully. (You can overlap 2 smaller husks, as needed.) Tie both ends securely with husk strips. Repeat with the remaining filling to make 12 tamales in all.

SET A STEAMER RACK inside a large pot and add a few inches of water to the pot. Arrange the tamales on the rack, alternating their positions so the steam can circulate well. Put the lid on the steamer, bring the water to a boil, and steam over medium-high heat until the filling is nearly firm and no longer gooey (you'll have to remove a tamale and open it up to check), about 1 hour. Keep an eye on the water level in the pot, adding more boiling water as needed to keep it from going dry.

WHILE THE TAMALES ARE STEAMING, preheat an outdoor grill. Brush the pork chops with olive oil and season with the cumin, cayenne, nutmeg, and salt and pepper to taste. When the grill is very hot, grill the chops until just cooked through, 4 to 6 minutes per side. (Alternatively, pan-fry the pork chops over medium-high heat.) Arrange the pork chops on individual plates and reheat the sauce. Set 2 tamales, husks partially opened, next to each chop and spoon some of the green chile sauce over the tamales. Pass the remaining sauce at the table.

Makes 6 servings

Peppers

On Labor Day at Taste of Washington Farms in the Pike Place Market, there are bins and bins of colorful peppers—and Gayle Krueger's beauties are sure to be among them.

Krueger Pepper Gardens has 40 acres in peppers in their fields south of Yakima. With more than 75 varieties, there's a hot-pepper side of the road and a sweet-pepper side. The Kruegers also grow squash and melons, several types of tomatoes, and other produce.

Gayle's parents, Ermen and Chloetta Krueger, started growing peppers more than 50 years ago. The family became interested in peppers after a neighbor, Mr. Christoff, who was growing some Bulgarian peppers, gave the Kruegers their first seeds. Later, Italian families would come from western Washington to hunt pheasants on the Kruegers' land. They brought seeds of different types of peppers and asked the Kruegers to grow them. The next year they brought their friends, and that's how the whole "you-pick" thing started. The Kruegers stuck an apple-box U-Pick sign in front of their carport in Wapato and more people came. Chloetta used to make chiles rellenos and give out samples. Then everybody wanted the recipe, and the peppers.

Word of mouth took it from there. Next they added tomatoes. And eggplant for the Europeans. And tomatillos for the Mexicans. It wasn't long before everyone—friends, neighbors, customers—started sending them seeds. People wrote home and had seeds sent. Immigrants brought seeds from Hungary, Romania, Mexico, Greece, Japan, Thailand, and Bulgaria.

Gayle Krueger encourages pepper experimentation. "Often people have a recipe for a certain variety," he says, "but you can interchange for temperature, taste, and color." For instance, the curly goat horn pepper, a sweet hot, is good for adorning vinegar. To spice up dill pickles, though, you might try the Bulgarian carrot pepper. (Watch out if you go picking at Krueger's; one of the youngsters might try to make you eat one of these. It looks like a sweet little orange carrot, but it'll blow your head off!)

A delightful introduction to poblano peppers is provided by the Grilled Pork with Pumpkin Poblano Tamales and Green Chile Sauce from Yakima Grill (page 168). The recipe uses these mild-to-medium piquancy, glossy dark green chiles in both the tamales and the sauce.

The Krueger gardens sport a rainbow of sweet bells in red, orange, yellow, gold, lime, purple, green, and even blue. All these colors make it easy to prepare tiny diced pepper confetti, a great way to dress up any dish

Seattle area markets now carry a wide range of peppers. If you want your grocery store to carry more varieties, just ask.

—KC

Yassa au Poulet
(Chicken in Onion-Mustard Sauce)

Afrikando

In this traditional dish from the West African nation of Senegal, *yassa* is
the name of the spicy onion-mustard sauce and *au poulet,* meaning "with chicken," is a
reminder that French is spoken throughout the country. The simple stew has a surprising
blend of flavors that range from the sweet onions to the tangy mustard to the hot habanero.
Steamed jasmine rice would be the ideal starch alongside, ready to soak up flavor from the
delicious sauce. Chef Jacques Sarr uses bouillon cubes here, but if you prefer to leave them
out, you can use chicken stock in place of the water added to the sautéed onions,
and season the sauce to taste with salt before serving. The habanero chile
is among the hottest of the chile family, so wear plastic gloves or be sure
to wash your hands thoroughly right away to avoid painful burns.

¼ cup vegetable oil	1 habanero chile, cored, seeded, and chopped
4 large onions, chopped	2 tablespoons freshly squeezed lemon juice
1 cup water	1 teaspoon freshly ground black pepper
½ cup Dijon mustard	4 chicken breasts (about 8 ounces each), bone in
4 cloves garlic, minced	2 carrots, chopped
3 or 4 chicken bouillon cubes	1 cup green olives

HEAT THE OIL in a large, heavy pot, such as a Dutch oven, over medium-high heat until it
begins to smoke. Add the onions and sauté, stirring frequently, until tender and just lightly
browned, 10 to 12 minutes. Add the water, mustard, garlic, bouillon cubes, chile, lemon juice,
and pepper and stir to mix. Add the chicken and carrots, nestling the chicken down into the
onions, and reduce the heat to medium. Simmer, covered, until the chicken is cooked through
but still tender, about 25 minutes.

JUST BEFORE SERVING, drain the olives, add them to the sauce, and heat through. Set the
chicken breasts on warmed individual plates, spoon the onion-mustard sauce over the chicken,
and serve.

Makes 4 servings

Orcas Rack of Lamb
with Spring Pea Flan and Morels

Dahlia Lounge

Matt Costello, chef of the Dahlia Lounge, relishes the spring deliveries of local lamb from Wild Currant Farm on Orcas Island. Here, the lamb is paired with fresh peas and morels, which are also highly anticipated spring treats. For the perfect springtime meal, chef Costello likes to serve steamed or roasted asparagus with the lamb.

For a full restaurant-style presentation, the lamb racks would be "frenched," which means that all excess meat is scraped from the exposed bone ends for a tidy look. You can ask the butcher to do this for you, or you can carefully scrape away the tissue with the back of a small knife. You'll need to start with about 1½ pounds of peas in the shell to get the 1½ cups of shelled peas needed. Fresh peas are important in this recipe. The results using packaged peas would not be nearly as good.

2 whole racks of lamb (about 1 pound each), trimmed
2 tablespoons olive oil

SPRING PEA FLAN

1½ cups freshly shelled peas	3 eggs, lightly beaten
1¼ cups whipping cream	¾ teaspoon salt

ROASTED MORELS

½ pound morels or other fresh wild mushroom, wiped clean and trimmed	2 teaspoons minced thyme
	Salt and freshly ground black pepper
2 tablespoons olive oil	

BEURRE BLANC

½ cup plus 1 tablespoon unsalted butter	½ cup dry white wine
1 tablespoon minced shallot	1 tablespoon whipping cream

FOR THE FLAN, preheat the oven to 300°F. Brush four ½-cup ramekins with melted butter, put them in a baking pan, and set aside.

BRING A MEDIUM SAUCEPAN of lightly salted water to a boil, add the peas, and cook for 2 minutes. Drain the peas, run cold water over them in the colander, and drain thoroughly. Purée the peas in a food processor, then run the peas through a food mill or press them through a fine sieve with a rubber spatula to remove the skins.

COMBINE THE PEA PURÉE, cream, eggs, and salt in a mixing bowl and whisk together well. Ladle the pea custard into the prepared ramekins, and add hot water to the baking dish to come about halfway up the sides of the ramekins. Cover the pan loosely with foil and bake the flans until just set, about 35 minutes. A knife inserted in the center of one of the flans should come out clean; the custard will be soft, but it will firm up slightly as it cools. Take the ramekins from the water bath and cover them with the foil to keep warm. Increase the oven temperature to 425°F.

FOR THE MORELS, put the mushrooms in a bowl and toss them with the olive oil and thyme. Season to taste with salt and pepper and toss again. Scatter the mushrooms on a baking sheet and roast until lightly crisp and golden brown around the edges, about 15 minutes. Set aside.

TO ROAST THE LAMB, reduce the oven temperature to 400°F. Season the lamb with salt and pepper. Select an ovenproof sauté pan or skillet large enough to hold both racks. Heat the oil in the pan over medium-high heat until hot but not smoking. Add the lamb, meat side down, and sear until browned, 3 to 4 minutes. Transfer the pan to the oven and roast the lamb, turning once, until a meat thermometer registers 120°F for rare, about 15 minutes, or cook the lamb longer to your taste. Remove the lamb from the oven and let sit for 5 to 10 minutes before serving.

WHILE THE LAMB IS ROASTING, make the beurre blanc. Cut ½ cup of the butter into small chunks and refrigerate until needed. In a small saucepan, melt the remaining tablespoon of the butter over medium heat. Add the shallot and sauté until tender, 1 to 2 minutes. Add the wine, bring to a boil, and boil until reduced by two-thirds, about 3 minutes. Add the cream, bring to a boil, and reduce the mixture by half, 1 to 2 minutes longer. Whisk in the butter, bit by bit, careful that the butter melts creamily without becoming oily. Move the pan off the heat as needed to avoid overheating. Take the sauce from the heat, season to taste with salt, and stir in the roasted mushrooms. Set the pan aside in a warm spot, or over a pan of barely simmering water, until ready to use; do not overheat the sauce or it will separate.

RUN A KNIFE around the edge of each pea flan and invert each one onto a warmed plate. Spoon the beurre blanc and roasted morels around the flans. Carve the lamb racks into chops, set the chops around the flan on each plate, and serve.

Makes 4 servings

Kasu Black Cod

Waterfront

The pairing of the yeasty kasu (the lees produced during sake brewing) with
rich black cod (also known as sablefish, and not a true cod) gives an inimitable, rich flavor
and silky texture. Chef Vicky McCaffree suggests serving the fish with Asian greens in a
ponzu dressing or with a seaweed salad. The richness of black cod means
the portion sizes can generally be smaller than with other fish.

Note that the recipe needs to be started at least three days in advance of when it is to be
cooked and served, so be sure to plan ahead. The long marinating allows natural sugars in
the kasu paste to be absorbed into the fish. When grilled or pan-seared, the sugars create a
beautiful caramelized crust that is typical of the popular dish. Kasu paste is available in
Asian markets, such as Seattle's Uwajimaya, and at some well-stocked grocery stores.

6 black cod fillet pieces (4 to 5 ounces each), skin on
1 to 2 tablespoons kosher salt
2 tablespoons vegetable oil

KASU MARINADE

1 pound kasu paste (sake lees) | ¼ cup freshly squeezed orange juice
¼ cup mirin (sweet Japanese cooking wine) | 2 tablespoons sugar

LAY THE COD PIECES on a plate and sprinkle both sides of each piece with the salt. Cover
the plate with plastic wrap and marinate overnight in the refrigerator.

THE NEXT DAY, make the kasu marinade. Combine the kasu paste, mirin, orange juice, and
sugar in a food processor and pulse until well mixed. Blend in a few tablespoons of water to
give the marinade a thick but pourable consistency.

RINSE THE SALT from the cod and pat dry with paper towels. Lay them again on a plate and
pour the kasu marinade over them, turning the fish pieces so they are evenly coated. Cover
with plastic wrap and refrigerate for 2 to 3 days.

TO COOK, take the fish pieces from the marinade, allow the excess to drip off, and pat the fish dry with paper towels. Heat the oil in a large, heavy skillet over medium-high heat. Add the fish pieces and pan-sear until the black cod is just cooked through and the surface has a nice caramelized glaze, 2 to 3 minutes per side. (You could also grill the fish, although you need to take care in handling the fish because black cod is quite delicate.)

IF YOU WANT to do your guests a favor (as they do at Waterfront), pull out the pin bones before serving; they're much easier to remove after the fish is cooked than before. Serve on warmed individual plates.

Makes 6 servings

DESSERTS

Spoon Cheesecake

Tulio

"I have never been a big fan of cheesecake," says chef Walter Pisano. "But I know how many people like cheesecake, so I developed this 'cake' in a glass." He sometimes serves the Spoon Cheesecake with biscotti, which add the flavor and crunch you'd otherwise get from a crust.

Using "average" part-skim ricotta cheese from the grocery store will give less than average results. Seek out a good-quality whole-milk ricotta, such as Polly-O brand, for the smoothest and tastiest results.

¾ cup sugar	Juice and grated zest of 1 lemon
¼ cup mascarpone cheese	1 teaspoon vanilla extract
2 tablespoons cream cheese	1 teaspoon almond extract
1 container (about 15 ounces) whole-milk ricotta cheese	½ teaspoon freshly grated or ground nutmeg
	Fresh berries, for garnish (optional)

IN A STAND MIXER fitted with the whip attachment or with electric beaters, cream together the sugar, mascarpone, and cream cheese. Purée the ricotta cheese, lemon juice and zest, vanilla extract, almond extract, and nutmeg in a food processor until very smooth and well blended, 2 to 3 minutes. Add the ricotta mixture to the mascarpone mixture and blend well.

SPOON THE CHEESE MIXTURE into wine or martini glasses or small bowls. Top with a few seasonal berries, if using, and refrigerate until well chilled, at least 2 hours, before serving.

Makes 4 servings

Fresh Blackberry Tart

Chez Shea

This simple but elegant tart from Chez Shea in the Pike Place Market is ideal
for the Seattle area's summer boon of blackberries. It's also a great showcase for other
seasonal berries—wild strawberries, marionberries, salmonberries, lingonberries—whether
playing solo or as an ensemble. The thin layer of white chocolate on the base of the tart
offers a surprising touch of sweetness, an ideal complement to the tart's other elements.

2 ounces white chocolate, preferably Belgian, coarsely chopped
1½ pints fresh blackberries

PASTRY

6 tablespoons unsalted butter, at room temperature	1 egg yolk
	¾ cup all-purpose flour
2 tablespoons powdered sugar	1½ teaspoons whipping cream

PASTRY CREAM

¾ cup half-and-half	2 tablespoons cornstarch
¼ cup water	2 egg yolks
¼ cup granulated sugar	1 teaspoon vanilla extract

FOR THE PASTRY, combine the butter and powdered sugar in the bowl of a stand mixer. Beat
with the paddle attachment until well blended and smooth. Scrape down the sides of the bowl,
then add the egg yolk and mix until well blended. Scrape down the sides of the bowl again.
Add half of the flour and mix the dough until it is crumbly. Add the remaining flour and the
cream and mix until a soft ball forms. Wrap the dough in plastic and chill until firm, about
30 minutes.

PREHEAT THE OVEN to 425°F.

ROLL OUT THE CHILLED DOUGH on a lightly floured work surface into a round large
enough to line an 8- or 9-inch removable-base tart pan. Gently transfer the dough to the tart
pan, pressing it well into the corners and trimming and fluting the edges. Line the pastry with
foil and partially fill it with pie weights or dried beans. Bake for 8 minutes. Take the pan from
the oven, remove the weights and foil, and continue baking until the pastry is lightly browned
and cooked through, about 3 minutes longer. Set aside to cool.

PUT THE WHITE CHOCOLATE in a small heatproof bowl. Set the bowl over a pan of simmering (not boiling) water and melt the chocolate slowly, stirring occasionally. Take the bowl off the pan when a little more than half of the chocolate has melted and stir until completely smooth. Spread the chocolate in a thin, even layer over the bottom of the pastry.

FOR THE PASTRY CREAM, put the half-and-half and water in a small saucepan and bring just to a boil over medium-high heat. Meanwhile, whisk the sugar and cornstarch together in a small bowl. Add the egg yolks and beat until light yellow and well combined. Slowly add half of the half-and-half to the yolk mixture, whisking constantly. Whisk this back into the saucepan and cook over medium heat, whisking vigorously, until the pastry cream thickens, about 5 minutes. Take the pan from the heat and whisk in the vanilla. Pour the pastry cream into a heatproof bowl and let cool before refrigerating to chill thoroughly. (To prevent a skin from forming, lay a piece of plastic wrap directly on the surface of the pastry cream.)

WHEN THE PASTRY CREAM is fully chilled, add it to the prepared tart shell, spreading it into an even layer. Arrange the blackberries on top, crowns up, and refrigerate for at least 1 hour before serving. Remove the outer rim of the tart pan and cut the tart into wedges to serve.

Makes 8 servings

Pear and Rose Hip Sorbet

Le Gourmand

"Yum," declared chef-owner Bruce Naftaly on the recipe he sent in for this simple but delicious sorbet. I have to agree. It screams fall, when the pears are ripe and sweet and rose hips are plump and aromatic. The pear comes through as a predominant flavor, with the rose lingering on your palate after each bite. Serve the sorbet as an ideal palate-cleansing course for a fancy dinner party.

In the past, chef Naftaly has used the French pear brandy called Poire Williams, but today he uses the outstanding pear brandy from Clear Creek Distillery in Portland, Oregon. Fresh rose hips are not available retail, so you'll have to collect your own if you are using fresh ones (make sure that they're untreated, unsprayed, and clean). They are fat and red when "ripe." The kitchen at Le Gourmand usually relies on hips from the rugosa roses in the restaurant garden.

2 cups fresh pear cider	1 tablespoon pear brandy
2 ripe pears, peeled, cored, and diced	1 teaspoon rose water
¼ cup fresh rose hips or 2 tablespoons dried	

COMBINE THE CIDER, pears, and rose hips in a medium saucepan and simmer over medium heat until the pears are soft, 5 to 10 minutes, depending on their ripeness. Purée the pears in a blender or food processor, then strain the purée through a fine sieve, using a rubber spatula or the back of a large spoon to press on the solids. Let the purée cool, then stir in the pear brandy and rose water. Refrigerate the sorbet base until well chilled.

POUR THE CHILLED BASE into an ice cream maker and freeze according to the manufacturer's instructions. Transfer to an airtight freezer container and freeze until set, at least 2 hours. Before serving, let the sorbet sit at room temperature for a few minutes to make scooping easier.

Makes about 1 quart

Northwest Fall Fruits: Pears and Apples

In the fall, when apple and pear trees have had their sagging, fruit-laden branches relieved, Seattle chefs stir up desserts such as Bartlett pears poached in a good Oregon Pinot Noir or warm apple cranberry pie topped with a slice of melting, sharp Tillamook cheddar cheese. Such recipes warm the soul as the dry, autumn-colored leaves fall to the ground.

Is there anything better on a brisk, sunny fall day than biting into a clean-tasting, crisp perfumey apple? Can't you just hear that snapping, crunchy sound of a really good one?

Only a few years ago the Red Delicious variety dominated apple production, but that's changed quite a lot. People's tastes evolve and have brought on a more sophisticated lineup of new apples with a sweet/sour tang. With chefs demanding variety, some of the old favorites have come back, along with plenty of new cultivars. Old-time varieties may seem new to the younger set, but older Washingtonians remember growing up with Winesap or Jonathan apples in their backyards.

The ever-popular Rome, known for its baking aptitude, has now lost out to the sweet, firm Cameo, and to the Fuji that holds its shape amazingly well when cooked. Cameo apples are the star of the Palace Kitchen's Cameo Apple Salad with Treviso, Arugula, Oregon Blue Cheese, and Cider Vinaigrette (page 74), a perfect first course for a fall harvest dinner.

Other popular varieties include the versatile Gala—a light apple with a perfumey sweet flavor, and juicy, creamy flesh under a light red-pinky striped exterior—which is great for just munching, and that bright green standby, Granny Smith, so delish whether baked up in pies or eaten as a crunchy tart snack. Grannies are also delectable simmered in a homemade, spiced-apple relish to dollop on crostini with soft goat cheese or to cozy up to a pork roast.

There are so many types of pears that sometimes it's hard to come up with enough ideas to fully utilize their bounty. One traditional favorite is in a seasonal green salad with a red wine and blue cheese vinaigrette. Finely julienned with apple, celery, and celery root, pears are also a source of sweet crispness in a fruit slaw. Or try whipping up Le Gourmand's Pear and Rose Hip Sorbet (page 182), a light, sweet ending to a hearty fall meal.

The world's best pears are grown in rich fertile soils, cool air, and warm sun. These ideal conditions are found in eastern Washington as well as in California and Oregon, which produces pears that are world-famous. Together these West Coast states produce 95 percent of the nation's commercially grown fresh pears.

Perhaps the most familiar pear is the greenish-yellow skinned Bartlett, but more and more varieties are being seen in the markets. From brilliant Red →

Crimson and Red Bartletts to brownish-gold Bosc, from large Anjou to tiny Seckel, there's a range in both color and size.

Petite Seckel pears are fun to cut in half, core, and fill with a little dollop of Gorgonzola mixed with cream cheese and a few toasted walnuts. The ultra-sweetness of these pears is a fine foil for savory flavors. The fruits, ranging from 2 inches to even smaller, their olive-green skins often blushed with red, are really spectacular pickled whole with a bit of cinnamon and cloves, or star anise and peppercorns, then served alongside lamb or roast duck, turkey, or ham.

Pastry chefs' fall menus are full of delicious pear delights from open-face pear tarts baked in an almond crust to Gorgonzola stuffed poached pears, so perfect enjoyed with a glass of luscious port.

Pears are one of the few fruits that do not mature well if ripened on the tree. Therefore, they are picked before they are ripe, then packed carefully, stored, and then shipped, usually still unripened. That's why you'll often find firm, unripened pears in the store. It's easy to ripen a pear. Just place in a paper bag and leave it out at room temperature. When the pear yields to gentle pressure near the base of the stem, it is ready to eat. Refrigerate till needed, and for the best flavor bring it back to room temperature before eating. In general, summer pears such as Bartletts change color as they ripen, whereas winter pears do not. Therefore, depend on the gentle thumb test, not color, as your guide to ripeness.

To preserve these fall beauties—both apples and pears—try drying them. Cut the fruit in thin slices, core, seeds and all, and dry them in a hydrator. Then string them on thread—they not only look great hanging but also make for a fun, walk-by, impromptu nibble.

—KC

Bing Cherry Cake

Nell's

This dessert is similar to the French *clafouti,* a rustic dessert of fruit—traditionally cherries—baked in a simple batter. In this variation from chef Philip Mihalski, the "cake" is mostly fruit, with just enough batter to hold the cherries together. Choose a baking dish that's broad and shallow enough to hold the fruits in a snug, even layer. When the batter seeps in around the cherries, they should still be visible in dimples on the surface. The cake is best eaten the day it's made.

1½ pounds Bing cherries, pitted	½ cup sugar
½ cup milk	½ teaspoon baking powder
2 eggs	¼ teaspoon salt
1 teaspoon vanilla extract	½ cup unsalted butter, cut into small pieces,
1 cup all-purpose flour	at room temperature

PREHEAT THE OVEN to 350°F. Butter and flour a 10-inch round tart pan (not with a removable base) or an oval gratin dish about 12 inches long.

ARRANGE THE CHERRIES in a single layer in the prepared pan. They should be snug, but not too tightly packed, to allow room for the batter to flow around them.

COMBINE THE MILK, eggs, and vanilla in a small bowl and whisk gently to blend. Combine the flour, sugar, baking powder, and salt in the bowl of a stand mixer and mix well. Add the butter and half of the egg mixture to the dry ingredients. Mix at medium speed with the paddle attachment for about 1 minute. Add the remaining egg mixture in 2 batches, mixing well after each addition. (Alternatively, mix the batter by hand with a large wooden spoon, being careful to blend the butter fully into the batter.) The batter should be thick but loose enough to pour.

USING A SPOON OR SPATULA, spread the batter over the cherries, just covering them. Shake or tap the dish gently to help the batter settle around the fruit. Bake until the top is lightly browned and a toothpick inserted into the center comes out clean, about 30 minutes. Cool the cake slightly. Serve the cake warm, cutting it into wedges or scooping it out with a large spoon.

Makes 8 servings

Chocolate Hazelnut Kisses

The Painted Table

Pastry chef Patric Gabre-Kidan typically lets these cookies sit out a full day
after piping and before baking. "The object is for the cookie to form a crust that will bake
up crispy while leaving the inside moist," he explains. At home, you can let the cookies sit
for about an hour before baking to achieve something of the same effect. The cookies do
strike a wonderful balance between a slight crispness around the edges
and a soft chewy center. Perfectly addicting.

For best results, form the cookies with a pastry bag fitted either with a
large plain or star tip. If you use a star tip, be sure that its points are open enough
to avoid being blocked by the ground nuts.

1 ¼ cups hazelnuts	1 tablespoon honey
1 cup sugar	1 teaspoon vanilla extract
¼ cup cocoa powder	2 egg whites
1 tablespoon unsalted butter, melted	

PREHEAT THE OVEN to 350°F. Scatter the hazelnuts in a baking pan and toast, gently
shaking the pan once or twice to help the nuts toast evenly, until lightly browned and aromatic,
10 to 12 minutes. Transfer the nuts to the center of a lightly dampened kitchen towel, wrap the
towel around the nuts, and rub the nuts around vigorously (but carefully, since they're hot) to
remove as much of their skins as possible. Let the nuts cool completely.

IN A FOOD PROCESSOR, grind the cooled hazelnuts with the sugar until very fine. Add the
cocoa powder, butter, honey, and vanilla. Pulse until well blended. In a small bowl, beat the egg
whites with a fork to break them up a bit but not make them too frothy. Add about half of the
egg whites to the processor and pulse a couple of times, then add the remaining egg white and
pulse again. You're looking for a paste that's smooth but firm enough to hold its shape.

FIT A PASTRY BAG with a large plain or star tip and fill the bag with the dough. Line 2 heavy baking sheets with parchment paper. Squeeze a small dot of the dough under each corner of each paper lining to adhere it to the baking sheet (this will make piping easier). Squeeze the dough onto the paper in big rosettes or teardrop shapes, making each cookie about 1½ inches across and with at least 1 inch between the cookies. Give the cookies a bit of height as you pipe. If you make them too flat, they'll be more crisp than chewy when baked. Let the cookies sit for 1 hour before baking.

REHEAT THE OVEN to 350°F.

BAKE THE KISSES until they are just set on the outside, about 8 minutes. The cookies will firm up as they cool and you want the insides to remain tender and chewy. Transfer the kisses to a wire rack to cool and serve soon, or store in an airtight container for a few days.

Makes about 2½ dozen cookies

Bananas Foster

Luau Polynesian Lounge

Red bananas are a smaller, starchier variety than the more common yellow eating bananas, although the latter can be used if red ones cannot be found. Be sure to use a high-proof rum, such as Lemon Hart or Bacardi 151, for this recipe, to ensure that you'll be able to flambé with a flourish when sautéing the bananas. At Luau, the dessert is brought to your table still flaming, the result of a final splash of the rum ignited just before serving. You can do the same at home if you dare, but "make sure to avoid curtains during delivery," note owners Thomas and Jessica Price.

½ cup pecan pieces

4 tablespoons unsalted butter

12 ripe red bananas or 8 medium-ripe small
yellow bananas, peeled

¼ cup dark rum

4 good scoops Tahitian or other top-quality
vanilla bean ice cream

SAUCE

1½ cups packed brown sugar

⅓ cup dark rum

Juice of 1 orange, plus 1 teaspoon grated zest

Juice of 1 lemon, plus 1 teaspoon grated zest

Juice of 1 lime, plus 1 teaspoon grated zest

1 cinnamon stick

2 tablespoons unsalted butter

PREHEAT THE OVEN to 350°F.

FOR THE SAUCE, combine the brown sugar, rum, citrus juices and zests, cinnamon stick, and butter in a small saucepan. Bring to a boil over medium-high heat, stirring to dissolve the sugar. Reduce the heat to medium-low and simmer uncovered until slightly thickened, stirring occasionally, about 15 minutes. Set aside in a warm spot.

WHILE THE SAUCE IS SIMMERING, scatter the pecans in a baking pan and toast, gently shaking the pan once or twice to help the nuts toast evenly, until lightly browned and aromatic, 5 to 7 minutes. Set aside to cool.

MELT THE BUTTER in a large skillet over medium-high heat and cook until the butter is a light brown with a nutty aroma, 3 to 5 minutes. Add the bananas and brown them on all sides, about 5 minutes total. Add the rum and ignite it with a long match to flambé, turning your head away slightly from the flames and shaking the pan gently. When the flames have subsided, spoon the sauce over the bananas and cook, basting the bananas a few times until the sauce thickens slightly, 5 to 7 minutes.

PUT THE BANANAS on individual dessert plates and spoon the sauce over them. Place a scoop of ice cream alongside and scatter the toasted pecans over each serving.

Makes 4 servings

Old Chatham Camembert
with Pear and Dried Cherry Chutney

Earth & Ocean

Seattle area diners have been relishing a rekindled love of quality cheese of late, with both regional and well-chosen international cheeses showing up in a number of guises on menus, beginning with appetizers and on through dessert (as in the Honey-Chevre Cheesecake with Blueberry-Port Sauce, page 198) or this savory alternative to a sweet finish for the meal.

At the sleek and stylish Earth & Ocean restaurant in Seattle's W Hotel, chef Johnathan Sundstrom consistently offers appetizer options that highlight outstanding cheeses from near and far. Among his favorites is this Camembert from the Old Chatham Sheepherding Company in New York, made with sheep's milk rather than the cow's milk used for the traditional cheese produced in the Normandy region of France. You can use other mild, creamy cheese, such as Brie, if you prefer. You'll surely have chutney left over, but the extra will be tasty alongside a pork roast or with pan-roasted duck breasts.

1 cup whole blanched almonds (about 5 ounces)	Juice of 1 lemon
4 tablespoons extra virgin olive oil	8 ounces Camembert, cut into 8 wedges
Sea salt and freshly ground black pepper	2 tablespoons minced chives
1 fennel bulb	1 baguette, warmed and sliced
1 bunch watercress (about 4 ounces), washed, trimmed, and separated into small bundles	

PEAR AND DRIED CHERRY CHUTNEY

3 ripe, firm Bartlett pears, peeled, cored, and cut into ½-inch dice	½ cup red wine vinegar
	½ cup finely chopped onion
½ cup tart dried cherries	1 cinnamon stick
½ cup sugar	1 bay leaf

PREHEAT THE OVEN to 350°F.

SCATTER THE NUTS in a baking pan and toast in the oven until lightly browned and aromatic, gently shaking the pan once or twice to help the nuts toast evenly, about 5 to 7 minutes. Put them in a small bowl and set aside to cool. When cool, drizzle 2 tablespoons of the olive oil over with a generous pinch of salt and toss to evenly coat the nuts; set aside.

FOR THE CHUTNEY, combine the pears, cherries, sugar, vinegar, onion, cinnamon stick, and bay leaf in a medium nonreactive pan and stir gently to mix. Cook the chutney over medium-low heat until the pears are just starting to break down, 30 to 40 minutes depending on the ripeness of the pears. Take the chutney from the heat and drain off about ½ cup of the juice into a small dish; set aside. Remove the cinnamon stick and bay leaf from the chutney and let cool.

TRIM THE ROOT END and stalks from the fennel bulb. Cut the bulb in half lengthwise and remove the tough core. Cut the fennel lengthwise into thin julienne strips. In a medium bowl, combine the fennel and watercress. Sprinkle the fennel and watercress with the lemon juice, the remaining 2 tablespoons of oil, and salt and pepper to taste. Toss gently to coat.

TO SERVE, put a piece of Camembert just off center on each salad plate. Spoon a tablespoon or so of chutney to one side of the cheese and add a small mound of the salad along the other side. Sprinkle the edges of the plate with the almonds, chives, and some pepper. Drizzle the reserved chutney juice over all and serve with the warmed baguette.

Makes 8 servings

Local Cheesemakers

Washington state has long been known for its dairy farms, which are among the most productive in the nation. Then in the 1980s, as in other parts of the country, the small-scale production of artisanal cheeses became an extension of our dairy culture and part of the local food scene here. These specialty cheeses are often sold through local farmers' markets, and several cheesemakers bring their wares to the annual Taste of Washington Farms at Pike Place Market during Labor Day weekend as well as to Seattle Tilth's Organic Harvest Fair.

Artisanal—that is, handcrafted—cheeses have much more individual character than commercially produced cheeses. The cheesemaker has more control over the product, attending to the cheeses individually and aging them according to his or her judgment, rather than following a factory schedule. If pasteurized milk is used for a farmstead cheese, the milk has usually been pasteurized at a lower temperature than that used for commercial cheese, so the cheese doesn't taste "cooked" . . . and so it tastes better.

Another source of variation in the cheese begins with the diets the animals are fed. Subtle differences in the milk also occur as the animals are usually rotated through a property's different pastures where a range of forage is available to them.

Sally Jackson makes a variety of cheeses from milk produced by her own herd at her farm in Oroville near the Canadian border. Jackson's products ➤

include both soft and hard goat cheeses, sheep's milk cheeses (both fresh and aged), and semihard cow's milk cheeses. They are often flavored with such ingredients as jalapeño pepper and garlic or dried tomatoes and oregano. Sally Jackson's cheeses caught the attention of Northwest chefs early on in the American cheese renaissance, and today her cheeses are delivered to restaurants and retail cheese shops throughout the Seattle area.

At Quillisascut Cheese Company, in Rice, just east of Franklin D. Roosevelt Lake, Lora Lee and Rick Misterly make specialty cow- and goat-milk cheeses, produced from their herd of 38 goats and 2 Jersey cows. Quillisascut's luscious, raw-milk, aged Manchego cheese is well known among Seattle chefs and foodies, as is the company's creamy smooth and slightly tangy chèvre, so perfect in chef Walter Pisano of Tulio's recipe for Orecchiette with Fall Vegetables (page 118).

Roger Wechsler, owner of Samish Bay Cheese since 1999, is a relative newcomer in the arena. He produces all organic cheeses from a small herd of Jersey cows, even raising their feed on his certified organic dairy farm in Bow.

The old European tradition of after-dinner cheese is finally finding acceptance with local diners. After years of trailblazing persistence by "cheese plate pusher" chefs in the late '80s and early '90s, the custom has hit its stride in the Seattle dining scene and foodies are going down that delicious, postprandial fromage path. Consistent with its French bistro concept, Cassis serves French, Spanish and Basque cheeses. And Tom Douglas offers Samish Bay's excellent organic gouda on his cheese menu at the Palace Kitchen along with other stunners from the James Cook Cheese Company—Seattle's Retail Cheese Guru.

James Cook imports fine European farmstead cheeses, including the world-renowned British selections of Neal's Yard dairy of London. Seattleites line up to get on the baby Stilton list early enough to receive one of these coveted blue-veined delights in time for the winter holidays. The cheeses carried by James Cook can also be purchased through his website, www.jamescookcheese.com.

"The saddest way to eat cheese is cold," laments Cook. Except for young cheeses, such as fresh chèvre-style goat cheese or creamy ricotta, the only way to eat cheese is tempered at room temperature for an hour or so before serving. This will not only improve its texture but also enhance its taste and aroma.

—KC

Lavender-Honey Ice Cream

Cassis

All of the ice creams served at Cassis are made in-house by pastry chef Shannon Baker. If you're a big fan of the flavor and aroma of lavender, use the upper end of what's called for; the lesser amount produces a more subtly flavored ice cream. Either way, this is a rich, dense, delicious ice cream—a treat for any serious ice cream lover.

3 cups whipping cream	Pinch salt
2 cups milk	12 egg yolks
2 to 4 tablespoons dried lavender flowers	1 cup honey
Grated zest of 1 orange	1 tablespoon Grand Marnier (optional)

COMBINE THE CREAM, milk, lavender, orange zest, and salt in a medium saucepan and bring just to a boil over medium-high heat. Take the pan from the heat and let sit, covered, for 1 hour.

REHEAT THE CREAM MIXTURE just to a boil, then strain through a fine sieve into a medium bowl, reserving the saucepan for cooking the custard (wipe it out with paper towel, if needed). Whisk the egg yolks, honey, and Grand Marnier (if using) in a large bowl until well blended. Slowly whisk the hot cream into the yolk mixture until well combined, then return it to the saucepan. Cook the custard over medium heat, stirring constantly with a wooden spoon, until it is thick enough to coat the back of the spoon, about 10 minutes. Strain the custard through a fine sieve placed over a bowl and let cool to room temperature, then refrigerate to cool completely.

WHEN CHILLED, pour the custard into an ice cream maker and freeze according to the man- ufacturer's instructions. Transfer to an airtight container and freeze until set, at least 2 hours.

Makes 1 1/2 quarts

Hawaiian-Style Coconut Cake

Canlis

For almost fifty years, Canlis imported Hawaiian cakes from Deelite Bakery in Honolulu. When chef Greg Atkinson started at Canlis in 1997, he was determined to duplicate the famous cakes in his own kitchen. Deelite Bakery wouldn't part with the recipe, but after a couple of years of experimenting, Atkinson came up with a cake light enough and flavorful enough to replace the original. "I can still tell the difference," chef Atkinson says, "but I've come to like my 'imitation' even more than the original."

This recipe leaves plenty of room for variations. For macadamia cake, replace the syrup and the coconut with macadamia nut syrup and chopped toasted macadamias. Or for a Northwest-style cake, try hazelnuts on the surface and use hazelnut syrup or Frangelico liqueur for saturating the cake. The syrups used are the kind that would be used in coffee drinks, such as those from Seattle-based Da Vinci Gourmet.

2 tablespoons coconut-flavored syrup
2 cups sweetened shredded coconut

SPONGE CAKE

3 whole eggs | ¼ teaspoon salt
3 egg yolks | ½ cup plus 1 tablespoon cake flour
½ cup granulated sugar |

WHIPPED CREAM FILLING

2 cups whipping cream
¼ cup powdered sugar
1 tablespoon vanilla extract

PREHEAT THE OVEN to 350°F. Butter an 8-inch square cake pan and line the bottom with parchment paper, then butter the paper as well.

FOR THE CAKE, in the bowl of a stand mixer or in another large bowl, whisk together the whole eggs, egg yolks, sugar, and salt. Set the bowl over a pan of hot water and whisk until lukewarm. Whip on high speed until the eggs have more than doubled in bulk, about 5 minutes. Sift the flour over the surface of the egg mixture and fold together just until well combined. Spread the batter evenly in the prepared pan.

BAKE THE CAKE until it is golden brown and the center springs back when pressed lightly with your finger, 10 to 12 minutes. Invert the cake into a wire rack covered with another piece of parchment paper, then peel away the parchment from the bottom of the cake. Let cool completely.

FOR THE FILLING, whip the cream until soft peaks form, then add the powdered sugar and vanilla and continue whipping until the cream holds stiff peaks. Refrigerate until ready to use.

USING A LARGE SERRATED KNIFE, trim the crusts off the outside edges of the cooled cake and carefully cut the cake into 2 even layers. Drizzle the layers with the coconut syrup. Put the bottom layer on a serving plate and spread the top with about one-quarter of the cream filling. Set the second layer on top and use the remaining whipped cream to cover the sides and the top of the cake completely. Press the coconut onto the sides and top of the cake. Refrigerate until ready to serve.

Makes 8 to 10 servings

Apricot, Rose, and Saffron Tart

The Herbfarm

Chef Jerry Traunfeld borrows exotic and fragrant flavors from India and
the Middle East for this distinctive tart. Fresh apricots are first baked separately, so that
they won't give off moisture in the custard filling, while the saffron, rose geranium, and
vanilla are steeped in the cream that will be used for the custard. If you don't have fresh rose
geranium leaves, rose water, available in ethnic markets and well-stocked grocery stores,
will give a similar result. Turbinado is an unbleached sugar product with a blonde color
and slight molasses flavor that works well for caramelizing the top of the tart.
Regular granulated sugar can be used in its place, however.

1 ½ pounds ripe but firm apricots
¼ cup granulated sugar
2 tablespoons turbinado or granulated sugar

ALMOND SHORTBREAD CRUST

⅓ cup raw almonds, whole or sliced	5 tablespoons unsalted butter, cut into ½-inch
¼ cup granulated sugar	cubes and chilled
¾ cup all-purpose flour	1 egg yolk
¼ teaspoon salt	

CUSTARD

½ cup whipping cream, more if needed	8 saffron threads
¼ vanilla bean or ¼ teaspoon vanilla extract	1 whole egg
8 medium rose geranium leaves or	1 egg yolk
1 ½ teaspoons rose water	6 tablespoons granulated sugar

FOR THE ALMOND SHORTBREAD CRUST, process the almonds and sugar in a food
processor until very finely ground. Add the flour and salt and pulse just to mix. Add the butter
and pulse until the mixture has the consistency of coarse cornmeal. Add the egg yolk and pulse
just until it is incorporated (the dough will not come together in a ball).

PUT A 9-INCH REMOVABLE-BASE TART PAN on a baking sheet and pour the crust mixture into the pan. Spread it out evenly, then use your fingers to form the crust, pressing firmly
against the bottom and up the sides of the pan to create an even layer. If the crust mixture
begins to stick to your fingers, refrigerate it for 5 to 10 minutes before continuing. When the
crust is evenly formed, refrigerate for at least 1 hour.

PREHEAT THE OVEN to 400°F.

LINE THE CRUST with a piece of buttered parchment paper or foil, buttered side down, and partially fill it with pie weights or dried beans. Bake the crust until the top edge is lightly browned, 16 to 18 minutes. Reduce the oven temperature to 350°F. Take the crust from the oven and remove the weights and paper. (If there are any holes at this point, the crust will still be soft enough to press them gently closed.) Return the crust to the oven and continue baking until the bottom is lightly browned, 8 to 10 minutes longer. Set aside on a wire rack to cool completely. Reheat the oven to 400°F.

HALVE THE APRICOTS, remove the pits, and toss the halves with the ¼ cup granulated sugar in a large bowl. Spread the apricots out on a baking sheet, cut side down and in a single layer. Bake them until they soften, about 20 minutes, then set aside to cool. Reduce the oven temperature to 350°F.

FOR THE CUSTARD, put the cream in a small saucepan and bring it to a boil over medium-high heat. While the cream heats, split the vanilla bean portion in half and scrape out the seeds. Add the vanilla bean and seeds to the hot cream with the rose geranium leaves and saffron (if using vanilla extract or rose water, they will be added later), pushing them under the surface of the liquid with a spoon, and immediately take the pan from the heat. Cover the pan and set aside to steep for 30 minutes. Strain the cream though a fine sieve into a large liquid measuring cup, pressing down firmly on the flavorings to extract all of the liquid from the leaves. Check the measurement on the infused cream; if there is less than ½ cup, top it off with additional cream. Combine the whole egg, egg yolk, and sugar in a small mixing bowl and whisk to blend, then add the infused cream with the rose water and/or vanilla extract (if using).

ARRANGE THE APRICOT HALVES, cut side up and very close together or slightly overlapping, in a ring at the outer edge of the tart crust. Reserve 3 or 4 halves and use them to fill in the center of the ring. Put the baking sheet with the tart on the center oven rack, and pour the custard over the apricots, letting it settle into any open spaces. Do not fill the crust too high or the custard will leak over the edge. Bake the tart until the filling is set in the center, about 40 minutes. Set aside to cool to room temperature.

JUST BEFORE SERVING, preheat the broiler and position the oven rack about 4 inches from the heat source. Carefully remove the outside ring from the tart pan and replace it upside down over the top to cover the exposed crust. Evenly sprinkle the tart with the turbinado sugar. Place the tart under the broiler until the sugar melts and the edges of the apricots brown.

REMOVE THE UPSIDE DOWN RING and transfer the tart to a serving plate. Cut into wedges to serve.

Makes 8 servings

Honey-Chèvre Cheesecake with Blueberry-Port Sauce

Cassis

The touch of tangy flavor from the goat cheese balanced by the aromatic sweetness of the honey makes this crustless cheesecake a pleasant change from the traditional. Pastry chef Shannon Baker prefers baking with fireweed honey because of its heady flavor, though you can use your favorite honey instead.

Since the pod of the vanilla bean isn't used in this recipe (only the seeds that are scraped from the inside), you can plunge it into a dish of granulated sugar to "steep," thereby creating vanilla-scented sugar to use in baking or as the sugar for caramelizing a crème brûlée.

1 pound cream cheese, at room temperature	½ cup mascarpone cheese
8 ounces fresh goat cheese	½ cup sour cream
¾ cup sugar	3 eggs
1 vanilla bean or 1 teaspoon vanilla extract	2 tablespoons freshly squeezed lemon juice
½ cup honey	1 tablespoon brandy

BLUEBERRY-PORT SAUCE

1 pint blueberries	3 tablespoons sugar
¼ cup port	Juice of ½ lemon

PREHEAT THE OVEN to 350°F. Butter a 10-inch springform pan, line the bottom with parchment paper, and then butter the paper.

USING A STAND MIXER fitted with the paddle attachment, cream the cream cheese, goat cheese, and sugar until light and fluffy. With a small, sharp knife, split the vanilla bean in half lengthwise, and use the tip of the knife to scrape out the seeds into the cheese mixture (or add the vanilla extract, if using). Add the honey, mascarpone, and sour cream and mix thoroughly, scraping the sides of the bowl, until there are no lumps. Add the eggs one at a time, mixing for 30 seconds between each addition and scraping the sides of the bowl before adding the next egg. Add the lemon juice and brandy and mix again.

POUR THE CHEESECAKE BATTER into the prepared pan. Bake until it begins to set around the edges but is still a little soft in the center, about 1 hour. Take the cheesecake from the oven and set on a wire rack to cool, then refrigerate for at least 2 hours.

WHILE THE CHEESECAKE IS CHILLING, make the sauce. Combine the blueberries, port, and sugar in a small saucepan. Bring just to a boil over medium-high heat, stirring occasionally, then take the pan from the heat. Stir the lemon juice into the sauce and set aside to cool.

WHEN THE CHEESECAKE IS WELL CHILLED, remove the sides from the springform pan and cut the cake into wedges. Drizzle some of the blueberry sauce over and around each piece, and serve.

Makes 10 to 12 servings

Putting Foods Up

Whether by drying, pickling, canning, or freezing, preserving has always been a way of life in the Northwest. When produce is at its peak in the summer, who doesn't want to stock up and stretch out the time a little on all the season's goodness? But what do you do with those abundant fruits and vegetables?

For many local foodies, the harvest's bounty conjures up childhood memories of picking bushels of fruits and vegetables in the hot summer sun, then lugging them home where the real work began—sterilizing dozens of jars then blanching, peeling, pitting, and packing the day's pickings. Rows and rows of colorful, artfully packed jars in brilliant hues of purple, red, orange, and green, filled with pepper pickled peaches (juicy Freestones or Elbertas), green minted pears, rosy Tilton apricots, vegetable chow-chow, bread-and-butter pickles, Marionberry preserves, and brandied Bing cherries lined the pantry and cellars of Seattle homes.

A lot of people love homemade canned goods but are too intimidated by the procedure to process them by the traditional method, or are too crunched for time to labor away in the kitchen all day waiting for each batch to be ready from the water bath. More common nowadays are quick put-up jobs that sustain the season's gifts and that can be stored for a few months without having to haul out the canner. Most of the time, preserves, jams, purées, and fruit syrups are frozen, and pickled foods are refrigerated.

Pickling has always been popular—using everything from asparagus to cherries to dilled pearl onions and beets. Big crocks of sauerkraut and dill pickles curing on kitchen counters used to be a summertime standard. With today's schedules, refrigerator pickles are a fast and easy option. Clean quart jars are packed with a mixture of vegetables, and then vinegary brine is boiled and quickly poured into the veggie-packed jars. The lids are screwed on and the jars cooled to room temperature, then refrigerated. In just two days you have delicious pickles to bring to a picnic or enjoy at a backyard barbecue. The only tears shed are the ones that may form if you get too big a whiff of the boiling pickling liquid. But be forewarned—the pungent, wafting aroma may bring the neighbors begging for some of your pickles.

Making fruit vinegars is also super easy, and these are a favorite ingredient on chefs' menus, plus they last for a year refrigerated. To make them, sweet ripe berries are infused in white wine vinegar. It makes the most beautiful vinaigrette: Whisk together one part of the vinegar to three parts good olive oil, add a little finely chopped shallot and some salt and pepper, and you have the perfect foil for tender gourmet greens.

For those city folk who like to get out for culinary field trips, there are many U-pick berry fields near Seattle. It's easy to pack up a picnic and spend the day picking, sampling, and enjoying the outdoors. Returning home with several flats of fruit, dedicated city preservers make homemade jams—the perfect way to make the summer fruits bring joy all year long. For a quickie dessert, you can toss some freezer jam with a few fresh, sliced peaches, nectarines, or cherries, add a dash of dark rum, and serve over vanilla ice cream. And when it's blustery cold or drizzling rain outside, you'll have sunny memories of picking the brilliant berries, or the fragrance of bubbling jam will waft back under your nose, filling your head with summery reflections as you take a bite of your jam-spread, crisp sourdough toast in the morning!

So take a little time to prolong the flavors of summer. It's not that hard, and you'll be glad you did when the skies turn gray.

—KC

Chocolate Chai Tea Soufflé Cake

Waterfront

This isn't a traditional featherlight soufflé. Created by pastry chef Jessica Campbell, it is more like a soufflé crossed with a very moist chocolate cake. The hint of spice from the chai (spice tea)—as well as the touch of cardamom in the whipped cream—is a wonderful contrast to the chocolaty cake.

Here is a helpful hint for recipes that call for adding eggs one at a time to a batter. There's nothing worse than slipping while cracking an egg and dropping the whole thing, shell and all, into the batter. To avoid disaster, crack each egg first into a small dish, then tip the egg from the dish into the batter.

½ cup unsalted butter, at room temperature	⅛ teaspoon salt
1¼ cups packed brown sugar	2 tablespoons extra-strong brewed chai tea
3 eggs	¼ cup hot water
1 teaspoon vanilla extract	¾ cup whipping cream
1 cup all-purpose flour	2 tablespoons powdered sugar
¼ cup plus 1 teaspoon cocoa powder	¼ teaspoon ground cardamom
½ teaspoon baking soda	

PREHEAT THE OVEN to 350°F. Butter six ¾-cup ramekins and dust the insides with granulated sugar, shaking out the excess.

IN A STAND MIXER fitted with the paddle attachment, combine the butter and ¾ cup of the brown sugar and beat until light and fluffy. Add the eggs, one at a time, and beat until well blended, scraping down the sides as needed. Beat in the vanilla.

SIFT THE FLOUR, ¼ cup of the cocoa powder, baking soda, and salt into a medium bowl. Add the dry ingredients to the wet ingredients all at once and mix on low speed just until blended. Add the tea and continue blending; the batter should be smooth.

POUR THE BATTER into the prepared ramekins, filling them about two-thirds full. Combine the remaining ½ cup brown sugar, the remaining 1 teaspoon cocoa powder, and the hot water. Stir to mix, then spoon the mixture into the center of each cake, making an indentation with the spoon.

SET THE RAMEKINS in a baking dish and add hot water to the dish to come about halfway up the sides of the ramekins. Bake the cakes until a wooden toothpick inserted into the center of the cake comes out clean, 30 to 40 minutes. Transfer the ramekins to a wire rack to cool slightly.

WHILE THE CAKES ARE COOLING, beat the cream until soft peaks form, then add the powdered sugar and cardamom and continue beating for a few seconds to mix evenly and form medium peaks.

TO SERVE, gently tap the sides of the ramekins to help loosen the cakes before turning them out onto individual plates. Add a good dollop of the cardamom whipped cream alongside, then serve.

Makes 6 servings

Nectarine Blackberry Crisp

Anthony's HomePort

Use any of the season's best berries, such as blueberries, marionberries, huckleberries, or a combination, for this great summer treat. You can also use peaches in place of the nectarines. The amount of sugar you'll need for the fruits depends on their sweetness and your own personal taste. Serve the warm crisp with top-quality vanilla ice cream, crème fraîche, or whipped cream.

½ cup sugar
¼ cup all-purpose flour
2½ pounds nectarines, pitted and cut into ½-inch wedges

1½ pints fresh blackberries
Pinch salt

TOPPING

1 cup all-purpose flour
¾ cup sugar
1 teaspoon baking powder

1 egg, lightly beaten
½ cup unsalted butter, melted

PREHEAT THE OVEN to 350°F. Butter a 9- by 13-inch baking dish.

COMBINE THE SUGAR and flour in a large bowl and stir to mix. Add the nectarines and blackberries and toss gently until the fruit is well coated. Scatter the fruit in an even layer in the prepared baking dish and set aside.

FOR THE TOPPING, mix the flour, sugar, and baking powder in a medium bowl. Add the egg and stir until the mixture is crumbly. (Using your fingers to pinch and mix the topping will help to create an even texture.) Sprinkle the crumbs over the fruit filling, then drizzle the melted butter over the top.

BAKE THE CRISP until the crust is golden brown and the nectarines are tender, about 1 hour. Set aside to cool at least slightly before serving. Serve warm or at room temperature.

Makes 8 to 12 servings

Cinnamon Ice Cream

La Medusa

Cinnamon lovers, take note: this is an addictive, rich ice cream that'll have you hooked at first bite. At La Medusa, the ice cream is often served with mini biscotti, but any simple cookie would be great alongside. Or imagine serving it with apples that have been lightly sautéed in butter, cinnamon, and a touch of brandy. Delicious.

For a shortcut, so you can freeze the ice cream sooner, do a quick chill on the thickened base mixture: set the bowl inside a larger bowl of ice water, stirring occasionally, until fully chilled.

2 cups whipping cream	3 eggs
1 ¼ cups milk	1 cup sugar
2 cinnamon sticks	2 teaspoons ground cinnamon

SLOWLY HEAT THE CREAM, milk, and cinnamon sticks in a medium saucepan over medium heat just until the liquid comes to a boil. Take the pan from the heat and let sit until the mixture has a good cinnamon aroma, about 30 minutes.

WHILE THE MIXTURE IS STEEPING, whisk together the eggs, sugar, and ground cinnamon in a medium bowl. Slowly pour about half of the heated cream mixture into the eggs, whisking constantly. Whisk this back into the saucepan and cook over medium heat, stirring constantly with a wooden spoon, until the mixture is thick enough to coat the back of the spoon, about 10 minutes. Strain through a fine sieve into a medium bowl and let cool to room temperature, then refrigerate until well chilled.

WHEN COLD, pour the mixture into an ice cream maker and freeze according to the manufacturer's instructions. Transfer the ice cream to an airtight container and freeze until set, at least 2 hours.

Makes 1 quart

Flan with Caramelo Drizzle

El Camino

This coconut-spiked dessert is a blend of simple components that together
make a luxurious finale to a meal: rich custard, an even richer caramel sauce, and the
refreshing finish of toasted coconut and fresh raspberries. Don't be tempted to make the flan
with reduced-fat coconut milk, as the results will be disappointing. The oven temperature
chef Ron Correa calls for is quite low, so that the custard cooks slowly,
which results in a silky texture.

2 cups milk	6 tablespoons sugar
1¼ cups unsweetened coconut milk	1 cup sweetened shredded coconut
2 whole eggs	½ to 1 cup fresh raspberries
3 egg yolks	8 sprigs mint, for garnish

CARAMELO

1 cup sugar	1 cup whipping cream
½ cup water	1½ teaspoons vanilla extract

PREHEAT THE OVEN to 230°F. Lightly oil eight ½-cup ramekins or custard cups with nonstick cooking spray or flavorless oil.

COMBINE THE MILK and coconut milk in a medium saucepan and bring just to a boil over
medium-high heat, stirring constantly. Take the pan from the heat. In a large bowl, whisk
together the whole eggs, egg yolks, and sugar until well blended, then slowly whisk in the
heated milk, blending well. Let the mixture stand for 5 minutes.

LADLE THE FLAN MIXTURE into the prepared ramekins. Put the ramekins in a baking pan
and add boiling water to the pan to come about halfway up the sides of the ramekins. Bake
until the tops are golden brown and the centers are set (insert the tip of a knife into the center
of a ramekin; it should come out clean), about 3 hours. Halfway through cooking, carefully
take the pan from the oven and rotate it 180 degrees so that all the flans will cook evenly.
When done, take the ramekins out of the baking pan and let cool on a wire rack, then refrigerate for at least 2 hours.

SHORTLY BEFORE SERVING, make the caramelo. Combine the sugar and water in a
medium saucepan and cook over medium heat, stirring occasionally, until the sugar is dissolved, 5 to 7 minutes. Continue cooking, without stirring, until the mixture reaches a deep
caramel color, about 15 minutes longer. Slowly and carefully stir in the cream and vanilla,

stirring constantly for 5 minutes. (If the caramel solidifies when the cream is added, don't worry; it'll soften up again as it continues to heat.) Set aside to cool until tepid and slightly thickened, stirring occasionally.

WHILE THE CARAMELO is cooling, preheat the oven to 375°F. Spread the coconut in a baking pan and toast, stirring a few times to help the coconut toast evenly, until golden, 4 to 5 minutes. Set aside to cool.

RUN A SMALL, sharp knife around the edges of the ramekins. To unmold each ramekin, set a dessert plate upside down on top, hold the two firmly together, and invert them, patting the ramekin gently to free the flan. Lift off the ramekin. Drizzle the caramelo over each flan, sprinkle with the coconut and raspberries, and then garnish with a sprig of mint.

Makes 8 servings

Gateau de Riz Façon Grand-Mère
(Old-Fashioned Rice Pudding)

Le Pichet

Despite the name, the inspiration for this recipe isn't chef Jim Drohman's grandmother. Instead, it is a grandmotherly woman who was his concierge when he lived in Paris. A glass loaf pan will produce the most even heat distribution, but a regular metal loaf pan can be used instead, though the pudding should bake at 400°F if you are using metal.

The plum compote is just one of many fruit compotes that chef Drohman likes to serve with this dessert, noting that the sweetness of the fruit is a particularly good complement. A stream of cream poured around the rice pudding is the final flourish in this outstanding, rustic dessert.

1 cup sugar	½ cup long-grain white rice
6 tablespoons water	2 eggs
5 cups milk	Whipping cream, for serving
2 vanilla beans or 2 teaspoons vanilla extract	

PLUM COMPOTE

1 pound plums, pitted and coarsely chopped	2 star anise
½ cup sugar	2 tablespoons brandy
2 tablespoons freshly squeezed lemon juice	

COMBINE ½ CUP of the sugar and 3 tablespoons of the water in a small saucepan and cook over medium heat, stirring occasionally, until the sugar dissolves, 1 to 2 minutes. Increase the heat to medium-high and continue cooking, without stirring, until the mixture reaches a deep caramel color, 7 to 10 minutes longer. Take the pan from the heat, then slowly and carefully stir in the remaining 3 tablespoons water to stop the cooking process. Pour the caramel into a 5- by 9-inch glass loaf pan and set aside to cool.

PUT THE MILK in a medium saucepan. Split the vanilla beans in half lengthwise, scrape pit the seeds, and add the bean pods and seeds to the milk. (If using vanilla extract, it will be added later.) Heat the milk over medium-high heat, stirring occasionally, until it just begins to boil. Stir in the rice, reduce the heat to medium-low, and simmer, uncovered, stirring occasionally, until the rice is tender and the mixture has the consistency of a thick porridge, about 40 minutes. Toward the end, you may need to stir constantly to keep the rice from sticking to the bottom of the pan.

PREHEAT THE OVEN to 450°F and position the oven rack in the lower third of the oven.

WHEN THE RICE IS DONE, take the pan from the heat and remove the vanilla bean pods. Whisk together the eggs and remaining ½ cup of sugar in a small bowl until the mixture is a pale yellow, about 1 minute. Whisk in the vanilla extract, if using. Quickly stir the egg mixture into the rice and stir until well combined.

CAREFULLY POUR THE RICE CUSTARD into the prepared loaf pan. Bake until the caramel starts to bubble up around the sides of the custard, 12 to 15 minutes. Let the rice pudding cool for a few minutes, then refrigerate until well chilled, 2 to 3 hours.

FOR THE PLUM COMPOTE, combine the plums, sugar, lemon juice, and star anise in a medium saucepan and add cold water to just barely cover. Cook over medium heat, stirring occasionally, until the plums are very tender and the sauce has thickened, 20 to 30 minutes. Take the pan from the heat and let cool slightly, then stir in the brandy. Let cool to room temperature.

TO SERVE, run a knife around the edges of the loaf pan and invert the rice pudding onto a cutting board. Cut the pudding into thick slices and set them on individual plates. Pour some cream around the slices and spoon the plum compote alongside. This dessert also works well as a plattered dessert with the compote and cream passed separately.

Makes 8 servings

Raspberry and Peach Shortcakes
with *Honey Whipped Cream*

Six Degrees

Two of the region's favorite summer crops make a perfect partnership in one of the season's simplest desserts: shortcake. You could also use fresh boysenberries and other seasonal berries for this variation on the classic strawberry shortcake. The flaky, biscuit-style shortcakes are embellished with the grated zest of lemon and orange for added aroma and flavor.

4 cups peeled and sliced ripe peaches (about 2½ pounds whole peaches)	2 tablespoons honey
½ cup sugar	2 cups fresh raspberries
2 cups whipping cream	2 tablespoons crème de cassis

SHORTCAKES

3 cups all-purpose flour	Grated zest of 1 small orange
3 tablespoons plus 1 teaspoon sugar	Grated zest of 1 small lemon
2 tablespoons baking powder	1½ cups plus 1 tablespoon whipping cream, more if needed
½ teaspoon salt	
½ cup unsalted butter, cut in small pieces and chilled	

COMBINE THE SLICED PEACHES and sugar in a medium saucepan and cook over medium heat, stirring gently, until the sugar is melted and the peach juices just come to a boil, 5 to 7 minutes. Take the pan from the heat and let the fruit cool completely.

PREHEAT THE OVEN to 375°F.

FOR THE SHORTCAKES, sift the flour, 3 tablespoons of the sugar, the baking powder, and salt into a large bowl, then add the butter and orange and lemon zests. Use a pastry blender to cut the butter into the flour until it has the texture of cornmeal, with only occasional pea-sized bits of butter. (Alternatively, you can sift the dry ingredients into a food processor, add the zests and butter, and pulse until blended and crumbly; transfer the mixture to a large bowl before continuing.) Add 1½ cups of the cream and stir gently just until the dough holds together, adding 1 to 2 tablespoons more cream if the dough seems a bit dry.

TRANSFER THE DOUGH to a lightly floured work surface and pat it out to a thickness of about 1 inch, lightly dusting your fingers with flour as needed to avoid sticking. Cut the dough into eight 3-inch rounds. You may need to gather up dough trimmings to cut the last couple of shortcakes, but don't form the trimmings into a ball and re-roll the dough, which will make shortcakes that don't rise well. Instead, simply draw larger pieces of the trimmings together and pinch the edges gently to join them.

BRUSH THE TOPS of the shortcakes lightly with the remaining 1 tablespoon of cream and sprinkle the remaining teaspoon of sugar lightly over them. Put the shortcakes on a baking sheet, leaving at least 1 inch between them, and bake until nicely puffed and golden brown, 15 to 18 minutes. Transfer the shortcakes to a wire rack to cool.

JUST BEFORE SERVING, whip the 2 cups cream with the honey until soft peaks form. Cut each shortcake in half horizontally with a serrated knife and set the bottom halves on individual plates. Top the lower halves with a generous dollop of the whipped cream, then spoon the cooled peaches and some of their juices over and sprinkle with the berries. Drizzle the crème de cassis over the fruit, top with the remaining halves of shortcake, and serve.

Makes 8 servings

Beautiful Berries

Huckleberries, pink and purple. Strawberries, domestic and wild. Himalayas, alias railroad blackberries, and tiny tart wild ones. Marionberries, boysenberries, tayberries. Raspberries, red, black, and gold. Salmonberries. Green-gold gooseberries, blueberries, cranberries. . . . Chefs are extremely fortunate to live in this land of berries.

It's hard to tell when summer begins in Seattle. Some years it's grey and rainy until July. But local strawberries are one sure signal that summer's here. Everyone yearns for the first local berries. Although the season is short and the picked berries don't last long, they are sweeter and more intensely flavored than any imports. Only when you've tasted their intense, perfect sweetness can you be sure summer is really here.

Piled over shortcake is probably the most popular way strawberries are enjoyed. But on the non-dessert side, too, strawberries have multiple possibilities. Often appearing on Seattle menus in a spinach salad with thin slivers of sweet Walla Walla onion and glazed almonds, dressed with a poppy seed vinaigrette, they make a light and refreshing summer salad.

After they first burst into summer with strawberries, the farmers' markets later abound with "caneberries": raspberries, followed by their kissin' cousins, marionberries, tayberries, boysenberries, and loganberries. The last three are blackberry-raspberry crosses but are technically considered blackberries. (Raspberries' "cores" pull out when the berries are picked, blackberries' don't.) ➤

Many Seattle backyards also have heirloom raspberries growing in them. Big, juicy, and dark red, these berries may not look as perfect as some of the new hybrids but they exude flavor like you've never had before. A handful of these rouge babies will make you sit up straight and say "Raspberry!" or fall over swooning with berry delicious goodness.

Around the same time, plump blueberries start showing up on Seattle's tables—usually by the Fourth of July. August brings on the big, fat blackberry varieties—"railroad" blackberries that line the city's side streets. Then there are the delicious, wild mountain blackberries. Every summer teams of pickers scour the Cascades and Olympics to hand-pick these teeny tiny local delicacies for Anthony's Nectarine Blackberry Crisp (page 204).

All those berry options send Seattle area pastry chefs into a frenzy to slump, grunt, cobbler, and crisp their way through the summer whipping up delicious baked berry treats.

And then in the fall comes the crimson cranberry.

Along with blueberries and Concord grapes, cranberries are one of the few fruits native to North America. Recipes using them date back as far as the 18th century, and well before that Native Americans made pemmican, a survival cake of crushed cranberries, melted fat, and dried deer meat. Early American sailing vessels carried cranberries, which are high in vitamin C, to prevent scurvy. The cranberry gets its name from Dutch and German settlers who called it the "crane berry" because of the way its light pink flower petals twist back, resembling the head and bill of the sand hill crane. Over the years the name was shortened to cranberry.

The Pacific Northwest is one of the nation's major cranberry-growing areas. A compatible use of wetlands, cranberry farming provides habitat for many varieties of birds as well as other animals and plants. The berries grow on vines in sandy, acidic peat soil, commonly know as bogs.

Look for these tart, jewel-like berries in their dried, raisinlike form in a fluffy oversized muffin alongside your morning latte. Cranberries are also a perfect foil for their seasonal contemporaries in salads of winter greens with slices of crisp apples and spicy toasted walnuts, tossed with a blushing pink cranberry vinaigrette. And they're delicious cozied up to a roasted chicken in a savory chutney or relish or in a fragrant apple cranberry pie with a Tillamook Cheddar crust. What more could you ask for from the season's last berry?

—KC

Earl Grey Sorbet

Kaspar's

Chef-owner Kaspar Donier says that it was a batch of leftover iced tea that inspired this refreshing sorbet. Sometimes he serves it as a sort of "iced tea float," adding a generous scoop of the sorbet to a glass of unsweetened iced tea, noting that the sorbet slowly sweetens the tea. Chef Donier suggests fresh fruits alongside, particularly tropical fruits such as litchi, mango, and papaya.

3¾ cups water	6 Earl Grey tea bags
1½ cups sugar	Juice of 1 lemon

COMBINE THE WATER and sugar in a medium saucepan and bring just to a boil over medium-high heat, stirring occasionally to dissolve the sugar. Take the saucepan from the heat and add the tea bags. Set aside to steep, covered, for 30 minutes.

REMOVE THE TEA BAGS, squeezing them to remove as much flavorful liquid as possible, and refrigerate the sorbet base until well chilled, at least 1 hour. Stir in the lemon juice, then pour the mixture into an ice cream maker and freeze according to the manufacturer's instructions. Transfer the sorbet to an airtight container and freeze until set, at least 2 hours. Before serving, let the sorbet sit at room temperature for a few minutes to make scooping easier.

Makes about 1 quart

Baked Hawaii

Roy's

At Roy's, this tropical island–inspired update on the Baked Alaska
is served with thin, crisp gingersnaps. Believe it or not, a blowtorch is the best tool for
browning the meringue topping, although it doesn't have to be the big, unwieldy one from
your garage or shop. Smaller, more genteel culinary versions of the blowtorch are available,
much handier for browning a meringue or caramelizing sugar on top of a crème brûlée. If
you don't have one, the Baked Hawaii can be slipped under your broiler, although the
browning will not be nearly as even.

MACADAMIA NUT CAKE

¼ cup chopped macadamia nuts (about 1 ounce)　¼ cup sugar
4 tablespoons all-purpose flour, sifted　½ teaspoon vanilla extract
1 egg

COCONUT ICE CREAM

¾ cup sweetened shredded coconut
1½ cups top-quality vanilla ice cream

CHAMBORD BERRY SAUCE

½ cup mixed fresh berries (such as blackberries, boysenberries, and/or raspberries)
¼ cup Chambord (black raspberry liqueur) or other berry liqueur

MERINGUE

3 egg whites
⅓ cup sugar

FOR THE CAKE, preheat the oven to 375°F. Butter an 8-inch square or round cake pan, line
the bottom with parchment paper, and butter the paper.

PUT THE MACADAMIA NUTS in a food processor with 1 tablespoon of the flour and pulse
to chop very finely. Set aside. In a stand mixer or using electric beaters, beat the egg with the
sugar until light and fluffy, 2 to 3 minutes. Add the vanilla, then fold in the macadamia nuts
and the remaining 3 tablespoons of flour until thoroughly blended. Spread the cake batter
evenly in the prepared pan.

BAKE THE CAKE until lightly browned on top and the center springs back when gently pressed with your finger, 8 to 10 minutes. Invert the cake onto a wire rack, peel away and discard the paper, and then let cool completely. Leave the oven set at 375°F.

SPREAD THE COCONUT in a baking pan and toast, stirring a few times to help the coconut toast evenly, until golden, 4 to 5 minutes. Set aside to cool. Meanwhile, put the ice cream in a medium bowl and set aside to soften slightly, about 5 minutes. Add the cooled toasted coconut to the ice cream and stir vigorously to mix well. Return the ice cream to the freezer to refreeze fully.

FOR THE SAUCE, combine the berries and liqueur in a small bowl and stir to mix, gently mashing the berries against the side of the bowl. Set aside.

FOR THE MERINGUE, using a stand mixer or electric beaters, whip the egg whites until medium-firm peaks form. Slowly add the sugar and continue beating until firm peaks form (check by lifting the whip out of the meringue to see how well it holds its shape).

CUT THE MACADAMIA NUT CAKE into four 3-inch rounds, saving the trimmings for a snack. Top the cake with rounded scoops or mounds of the coconut ice cream. Spread the meringue over the cake and ice cream, covering them fully and forming small peaks by lifting the knife directly up from the surface of the meringue. Using a small blowtorch or a very hot broiler, brown the meringue evenly. Transfer to individual plates, spoon the berry sauce around the edges, and serve.

Makes 4 servings

Pinchineta
(Almond Tart)

Harvest Vine

Carolin Messier de Jiménez, co-owner with husband Joseph of Madison Valley's cherished Harvest Vine, is the dessert doyenne of this outstanding Basque restaurant. Her desserts perfectly balance comfort with finesse, as is true with this free-form almond tart that offers simple flavors in a delicious package.

For the lemon zest used to infuse flavor into the egg custard, simply peel away the vibrant yellow layer from the lemon in broad strips with a vegetable peeler. The size and shape don't matter much, since the zest will be strained out later. Trimmings from the puff pastry can be cut into slender strips, sprinkled with grated cheese, sesame seeds, and/or poppy seeds, and baked for delish cocktail snacks.

½ cup chopped almonds	1 egg, lightly beaten
1 package (1 pound; 2 sheets) puff pastry, thawed	½ cup sliced almonds
	Powdered sugar, for garnish

EGG CUSTARD

1 cup milk	⅓ cup granulated sugar
1 vanilla bean, split lengthwise	2 tablespoons all-purpose flour
Zest from ½ lemon	3 egg yolks

FOR THE EGG CUSTARD, combine the milk, vanilla bean, and lemon zest in a small saucepan and bring just to a boil over medium-high heat. While the milk is heating, combine the granulated sugar and flour in a small bowl and whisk to mix. Add the egg yolks and whisk until well blended. Strain the hot milk into the sugar-yolk mixture, whisking constantly. Return the custard to the saucepan and cook over medium heat, whisking often, until the custard is thickened and just begins to boil, 5 to 7 minutes. Transfer the custard to a heatproof bowl and let cool slightly, then lay a piece of plastic wrap directly on the surface of the custard (to prevent a skin from forming) and let cool completely. (If making the custard in advance, refrigerate until ready to use.)

PREHEAT THE OVEN to 375°F.

SCATTER THE CHOPPED ALMONDS in a small baking pan and toast, gently shaking the pan once or twice to help the nuts toast evenly, until lightly browned and aromatic, about 5 minutes. Set aside to cool. (Leave the sliced almonds untoasted.)

CUT A 9-INCH CIRCLE from 1 sheet of the puff pastry dough and set it on a baking sheet. Leaving a ½-inch border untouched, prick the rest of the dough with the tines of a fork. Brush the full surface of the pastry round with some of the beaten egg. Spread the custard over the center of the pastry, just up to the border, and sprinkle the toasted chopped almonds over the custard. Cut another 9-inch circle from the second sheet of pastry and lay it evenly over the first, pressing lightly around the edges to seal. Using the back of a knife, press down on the seam every ½ inch or so around the pastry, to reinforce the seal and make a fluted edge. Brush the top of the dough with more beaten egg and sprinkle the sliced almonds evenly over the top.

BAKE THE ALMOND TART until the dough is nicely browned and puffed, 30 to 35 minutes. Take the tart from the oven and dust the top with powdered sugar. Cut into wedges to serve on individual plates while still warm.

Makes 8 servings

Lemon Rosemary Biscotti

Still Life in Fremont Coffeehouse

Biscotti have become a nearly cliché cookie, showing up in a vast array of guises. It's a trend that makes this recipe that much more refreshing, thanks to the clean flavors of lemon zest and rosemary. This is absolutely just the thing to accompany an afternoon cup of tea or after-dinner cup of coffee.

3 eggs, separated	1 teaspoon baking powder
1¾ cups sugar	1 cup chopped walnuts (optional)
½ teaspoon vanilla extract	2 tablespoons grated lemon zest
½ cup unsalted butter, melted and cooled	1 tablespoon minced rosemary
3¼ cups all-purpose flour	

PREHEAT THE OVEN to 350°F. Line a heavy baking sheet with parchment paper, or lightly butter the baking sheet. (If your baking sheet is less than 15 inches long, you'll need to prepare 2 baking sheets, or cook the biscotti in 2 batches.)

BEAT THE EGG WHITES and ¾ cup of the sugar in a stand mixer or with electric beaters until the mixture is thick, about 4 minutes, scraping down the sides once or twice. When you lift the beaters, a ribbon of the mixture should fall gently onto the surface and hold its shape for a few seconds. Set aside.

IN A LARGE BOWL, whisk together the egg yolks, the remaining 1 cup sugar, and the vanilla until well blended and the mixture is a pale yellow. Add the melted butter and whisk until well combined. Fold in about one-quarter of the egg whites to lighten the batter, then gently fold in the remaining egg whites until evenly blended.

SIFT THE FLOUR and baking powder into a separate bowl. Add the walnuts (if using), lemon zest, and rosemary; stir to blend evenly. Stir the dry ingredients into the wet ingredients just until well mixed.

SCRAPE THE DOUGH out of the bowl onto a lightly floured work surface and divide the dough into 2 equal portions. Form each portion into a log 2½ inches wide and 15 inches long. Set the logs on the prepared baking sheet with a few inches between them. (Or position the logs on the diagonal if using shorter baking sheets.) Bake until the logs are firm to the touch, 30 to 35 minutes. Transfer the logs to a wire rack and let cool for about 15 minutes. Leave the oven set at 350°F.

WHEN THE LOGS ARE COOL, use a serrated knife to cut them on the diagonal into ¾-inch-thick slices beginning in the center of each log. Arrange the slices, cut side up, on 2 baking sheets (you don't need parchment paper or buttered sheets for this second baking) and bake until they begin to brown, about 15 minutes, turning the biscotti over halfway through. Let cool completely on wire racks and serve, or store in an airtight container for up to a week.

Makes about 3 dozen

DRINKS

Absolut Mandarin Martini

Salty's on Alki

The bar at Salty's is a long-cherished spot to sit and sip while taking in the downtown cityscape from the perspective of West Seattle's Alki neighborhood. Here's one house concoction that you might consider as you enjoy the view. Bar manager Tim O'Brien uses a premium California vermouth for this martini, King Eider from Duckhorn Vineyards in Napa Valley. You can also use other good-quality dry vermouth in its place.

2 fluid ounces Absolut Mandarin vodka
½ fluid ounce King Eider dry vermouth
Lemon twist, for garnish

FILL A ROCKS GLASS WITH ICE. Pour the vodka and vermouth over the ice, garnish with the lemon twist, and serve. Alternatively, shake the vodka and vermouth on ice in a cocktail shaker, then strain into a chilled martini glass to serve "up."

Makes 1 serving

Cadillac Margarita

Santa Fe Café

I had the pleasure of being asked by the late (and sorely missed) Tom Stockley to join him and a few others in judging the city's best margaritas for a *Seattle Times* article. Of course, Santa Fe Café, where the margaritas are a house signature, was on our agenda. This Cadillac Margarita is a premium option from their list. Their House Margarita uses the same proportions, with Cuervo Gold tequila in place of the top-shelf Sauza, and Triple Sec in place of the Cointreau.

To salt the rim of a cocktail glass, pour some coarse (such as kosher) salt onto a plate. Rub a lemon wedge around the rim of the glass to moisten it, then dip the rim in the salt.

1½ fluid ounces Tres Generaciones Sauza tequila
¾ fluid ounce Cointreau
Lime slice, for garnish

LEMON MIX

¾ cup freshly squeezed lemon juice
¼ cup simple syrup (page 225)

FOR THE LEMON MIX, combine the lemon juice and simple syrup in a small pitcher or bowl and stir to blend. Cover the mix with plastic wrap and refrigerate until ready to use. (You'll have enough for about 3 margaritas.)

FOR AN "UP" MARGARITA, fill a cocktail shaker with ice and add 2½ fluid ounces of the lemon mix with the tequila and Cointreau. Cover the shaker and shake until very cold, then strain into a chilled margarita or martini glass. Garnish with the lime slice and serve.

FOR A BLENDED MARGARITA, combine the ingredients in a blender with a handful of ice cubes and pulse to blend. Pour into a margarita glass or tumbler, garnish with the lime slice, and serve.

Makes 1 serving

Strawberry Spice and Everything Nice

Sazerac

A great summer refresher, this blended drink balances the sweetness of ripe strawberries with hints of warm spiciness from the spiced rum, aromatic Tuaca liqueur, and a touch of vanilla.

1 handful (about 1 cup) ice cubes
4 large strawberries, stemmed, plus another stem-on for garnish
1½ fluid ounces spiced rum
1 fluid ounce Tuaca

1 fluid ounce crème de cassis
1 fluid ounce freshly squeezed lime juice
1 fluid ounce simple syrup (page 225)
Few drops vanilla extract

PUT THE ICE, stemmed strawberries, rum, Tuaca, cassis, lime juice, simple syrup, and vanilla in a blender and blend at high speed until smooth. Pour the cocktail into a large glass, garnish with the remaining strawberry, and serve.

Makes 1 serving

Simple Syrup

Simple syrup, which is a basic ingredient in many different drinks, will keep indefinitely at room temperature.

1 cup sugar
1 cup water

Combine the sugar and water in a small saucepan over medium-high heat. Bring to a low boil and cook for approximately 3 to 4 minutes, stirring occasionally, until the mixture becomes a very light syrup. Let cool, then keep covered at room temperature. Makes 1¾ cups.

Elsie's Bloody Mary

Hattie's Hat

A favorite Ballard gathering spot for decades, Hattie's Hat is the essence of no-frills, inviting dining and drinking. A beloved constant here was Elsie Barros, who retired in 1999 after 27 years of bartending. This recipe, one of her most popular standbys, is still served at Hattie's today.

Of course, bartenders rarely make drinks by following a precise recipe. (Elsie herself was known to add a generous extra splash of vodka when mixing this classic.) The horseradish and Worcestershire should make themselves known by changing the texture and color of the tomato juice a bit, and the celery salt and hot pepper sauce are more a question of taste. Optional additions include the juice of a lemon and/or a tablespoon of olive brine. Drinks at Hattie's are lavishly garnished. Choose your favorites from among the choices listed here.

4 cups tomato juice	10 shakes hot pepper sauce
2 tablespoons prepared horseradish	8 grinds freshly ground black pepper
15 to 20 shakes Worcestershire sauce	Vodka
14 shakes celery salt, plus more for garnish	

GARNISHES

Pickled green beans	Large pimento-stuffed green olives
Pickled cherry peppers	Lime and lemon slices

COMBINE THE TOMATO JUICE, horseradish, Worcestershire sauce, celery salt, hot pepper sauce, and black pepper in a juice pitcher and shake or stir until well blended. Taste the mix for seasoning and refrigerate until ready to serve.

FILL A TALL GLASS WITH ICE and pour 1 to 2 fluid ounces of vodka over the ice. Shake or stir the chilled Bloody Mary mix and fill the glass with it. Garnish with the pickled beans, peppers, olives, lemon slices, and/or lime slices. Add a final quick shake of celery salt on top and serve.

Makes 1 quart (for 4 to 6 servings)

The Priestess

Restaurant Zoë

It's fun to watch a master mixologist at work, which is just what you get to do
sitting at the bar at Belltown's Restaurant Zoë. This spiced, aromatic hot drink, created by
barman Ryan Magarian, is an ideal way to ward off the chill of a winter's night,
or a night any time of the year.

1 bag orange spice tea	½ fluid ounce Tuaca
1 teaspoon sugar	½ fluid ounce Hennessy brandy
¾ cup boiling water	Orange twist, for garnish
1 fluid ounce spiced rum	

PUT THE TEA BAG in a heatproof brandy snifter or glass mug with the sugar. Add the boiling
water and let steep for about 5 minutes, stirring once or twice to help the sugar dissolve.
Remove the tea bag and stir in the rum, Tuaca, and brandy. Garnish with the orange twist
and serve.

Makes 1 serving

Hawaiian Punch

Luau Polynesian Lounge

Think of this punch as a sort of Island sangria. Owner–bar master Thomas Price
says the spicier the red wine, the better. He suggests Carchelo (a mourvèdre blend from
Spain), a Rioja wine, or maybe a zinfandel. This is a great recipe for parties—the perfect
drink for those colorful little paper umbrellas. Just make a few batches in pitchers
and chill, adding ice right before serving.

Fruit purées are becoming more widely available. Look for them in specialty food
sections or with frozen juices. If you can only find concentrated fruit juice, be sure to
dilute it as directed before measuring the amount needed in this recipe.

1 bottle (750 ml) red wine	½ cup guava purée or nectar
1½ cups freshly squeezed orange juice	⅓ cup passion fruit purée or juice
½ cup Cointreau	3 or 4 orange slices, halved, for garnish

IN A PITCHER, combine the red wine, orange juice, Cointreau, guava purée, and passion fruit
purée. Stir to mix and refrigerate until ready to serve. Fill tall glasses with ice and pour the
punch over the ice. Or, add ice cubes to the pitcher and let your guests serve themselves. Either
way, garnish each serving with a half slice of orange.

Makes 6 to 8 servings

Silver Rocket

Four Seasons Olympic Hotel

When barmaster Michael Vezzoni realized his menu didn't list many martini-style
drinks that included tequila, he set about to find a combination to suit the Mexican spirit.
There's just a touch of tequila here, combined with a touch of fruitiness from Cointreau and
pear brandy. The vodka smoothes and balances the flavors in this unique and subtle cocktail.
Clear Creek is a European-style distillery based in Portland, Oregon, that produces outstanding eaux-de-vie from a variety of local fruits.

2½ fluid ounces Chopin vodka
¼ fluid ounce Patron silver tequila
⅛ fluid ounce Clear Creek pear brandy

⅛ fluid ounce Cointreau
Lime twist, for garnish

FILL A COCKTAIL SHAKER with ice. Add the vodka, tequila, pear brandy, and Cointreau.
Shake the cocktail lightly, then strain into a chilled martini glass. Garnish with the lime twist
and serve.

Makes 1 serving

Cocktails

The cocktail is back—and its return is obviously not just a quick craze. From the resurgence of the martini to the exploding popularity of sidecars and manhattans, everyone from Gen Xers to thirty- and forty-somethings has rediscovered the pleasure and art form of the mixed drink.

Martinis were the cat's meow in the '50s. In advertisements of the period you see men pondering: to shake or to stir? What's the point here? Some old cocktail books proclaim that when a martini's shaken, it bruises the gin and dilutes it with melting ice. But other mixologists prefer shaking because of the tiny ice flakes that are strained out into the martini.

Whatever the mixing method, the true secret to a perfect martini is that it must be very cold and made with a high-quality brand liquor. (Fanatics keep their martini glasses chilled in the fridge.) Be it vodka or gin, martinis are the overall favorite in the cocktail scene.

With people generally drinking less, the trend is to have one or two perfect cocktails, made with premium liquor. In Seattle this pursuit of perfection shows up in the Martini Classic Challenge, a "shake, stir, and swizzle off" among select Seattle restaurants. Since the Challenge was started in 1992, Oliver's in the Mayflower Park Hotel has won the most awards for its Classic Martini (page 235).

But, as with other fashions, today's trendy tastes demand something new. To stay ahead of the curve, restaurants must not only excel at the standards but invent signature drinks as well. On the specialty cocktail front, Seattle bartenders have set the bar at a new level.

Many Seattle establishments offer creative martinis. The Four Seasons' repertory ranges from the award-winning Copper Illusion, a perfectly stirred potion of gin spiked with Cointreau and Campari—very reminiscent of an Italian Negroni but in martini form—to their newest Ultraviolet Martini (page 239), which begins with a wash of grappa, and then blends gin and vodka with Chambord and cassis. It's served up with a blueberry garnish.

Restaurant Zoë's namesake drink is intoxicatingly delightful in every respect—to the eye, the nose, and the palate. From the mixture of lemon rum, with just a whisper of blue curaçao, fresh lime sour, and fresh mint, shaken then served up in an oversized martini glass, to the simple garnish of a single floating mint leaf, the Zoë Cocktail is a study in the new cocktail creation. At Waterfront restaurant the cocktail of choice is their Rain City Punch (page 236). A retro twist on rum punch—pineapple juice, dark rum, amaretto, sweet and sour, and Chambord, swizzled up with a splash of soda—it makes for a refreshing tropical escape.

And, as in the rest of the country, the Nuevo Latino groundswell is lapping at the Seattle cocktail scene. Fandango serves a thirst-quenching Mojito (page 237), the classic Cuban cocktail with lime, rum, and mint leaves, while the Santa Fe Café rides the premium tequila wave with a signature Cadillac Margarita (page 224) based on Tres Generaciones Sauza.

In the summer, cocktail sippers line up at Belltown's Axis to get a refreshing Watermelon Kazi (page 240)—vodka, lime, and fresh, sweet watermelon chunks hand-shaken and served up ice cold. Can't you just taste it? When the local melons are ripe, you can shake up some for your own supper sippin'.

And Seattle favorites aren't just found in trendy, cosmopolitan downtown. Imbibers make for the Wallingford neighborhood for the Hawaiian Punch at Luau Polynesian Lounge (page 228), and Bloody Mary enthusiasts head to up-and-coming, arty Ballard for Elsie's Bloody Mary (page 226), served up at weekend breakfast at Hattie's Hat.

Local bartenders are also brewing up exciting after-dinner beverages, and of course you find a lot of exciting, spiked coffee drinks in Latte Land—from ultimate iced mochas laced with Bailey's and brandy to Canlis's ever-famous, tableside-prepared, flaming Café Diablo. And in what other city might you get a double-shot half-caf egg nog latte with a shot of Hennessy?

—KC

Honey Peach Julep

Sazerac

This cocktail goes well beyond the classic mint julep, which is little more than bourbon, mint, sugar, and ice. At Sazerac, they use Maker's Mark bourbon, but other bourbon can be used instead. You can simply combine the ingredients over ice and stir for an unshaken cocktail, but be sure to bruise the mint to help extract its flavor.

2 large mint leaves, plus a sprig for garnish | 1 fluid ounce soda water
1½ fluid ounces bourbon | Peach wedge, for garnish
1 fluid ounce sweet and sour mix |

PEACH PURÉE

1 pound ripe peaches, peeled and pitted | 3 tablespoons freshly squeezed lemon juice
⅔ cup honey | 3 tablespoons peach schnapps

FOR THE PEACH PURÉE, combine the peaches, honey, lemon juice, and peach schnapps in a blender and purée until very smooth. You should have about 4 cups or enough for about 8 cocktails. Refrigerate until ready to use.

HALF-FILL A COCKTAIL SHAKER WITH ICE, add the mint leaves, and muddle to crush the mint. Add ½ cup of the peach purée with the bourbon, sweet and sour mix, and soda. Cover the shaker and shake vigorously to mix. Pour the cocktail, ice included, into a tall glass (they use a hurricane-style glass at Sazerac). Garnish with the mint sprig and peach wedge.

Makes 1 serving

Zoë Cocktail

Restaurant Zoë

This vibrant blue cocktail was created by co-author Kathy Casey for chef-owner
Scott Staples as a signature drink for his Belltown restaurant. If you don't have a cocktail
shaker, you can stir the ingredients on ice before straining, but the force of shaking breaks up
the mint into tasty little flecks that add color and flavor to the drink. The lime sour mix
makes enough for four cocktails.

2 large sprigs mint
2 fluid ounces Bacardi Limón rum
¼ fluid ounce blue curaçao

LIME SOUR MIX

½ cup simple syrup (page 225)
½ cup freshly squeezed lime juice

FOR THE LIME SOUR MIX, combine the simple syrup and lime juice in a small pitcher or
bowl and stir to blend. Cover with plastic wrap and refrigerate until ready to use.

PLUCK ONE PRETTY MINT LEAF from the sprig and set it aside to garnish the cocktail. Put
the remaining whole mint sprig in a cocktail shaker and fill the shaker with ice. Add 2 fluid
ounces of the lime sour mix to the rum and curaçao. Cover the shaker and shake until very
cold, then strain the cocktail into a large chilled martini glass. Float the reserved mint leaf on
top and serve.

Makes 1 serving

Italian Caramel Apple

Salty's on Alki

Wintertime's warming drinks aren't limited to booze in coffee with whipped cream on top. This hot cocktail is a twist on hot apple cider, using Tuaca (an Italian brandy–based liqueur) for the spirited boost. The caramel syrup used at Salty's is the type you'd use in a coffee drink, the same type of syrup sold under Seattle's own Da Vinci label.

2 fluid ounces cranberry juice	1 tablespoon spiced cider mix
1¼ fluid ounces Tuaca	(about ½ envelope)
½ fluid ounce caramel syrup	1 cup very hot water
	1 cinnamon stick

POUR HOT WATER into a large coffee cup and let sit for a few minutes to preheat. Pour out the water, then add the cranberry juice, Tuaca, caramel syrup, and spiced cider mix. Stir in the hot water until the mix is dissolved and ingredients are well blended. Add the cinnamon stick to the hot drink and serve right away.

Makes 1 serving

Classic Martini

Oliver's

Over the years, Oliver's has become renowned for its outstanding martinis, which are shaken to order with your choice of gin or vodka. Longtime host of the city's Martini Challenge, Oliver's always manages to take the top prize for this classic cocktail. There's not much to the recipe, just great ingredients that need to be well chilled and some vigorous shaking. The glacial chill of a martini that has a few flecks of ice floating on top can't be beat!

¼ fluid ounce Cinzano dry vermouth
2½ fluid ounces Bombay Sapphire gin or Stolichnaya Cristall vodka

2 large vermouth-marinated Italian olives, skewered on a cocktail pick

ADD THE VERMOUTH to a cocktail shaker, twist and swirl it so that it evenly coats the inside, then discard the rest. Fill the shaker with ice and add the gin or vodka. Cover the shaker and shake vigorously until very cold. Put the skewered olives in a chilled large martini glass and strain the martini over the olives.

Makes 1 serving

Measuring Up

Bartenders traditionally use fluid-ounce measures when mixing drinks, so cocktail recipes are generally given in ounces rather than tablespoons or teaspoons. Here's a quick comparison, in case you don't have a jigger on hand.

⅛ ounce = ¾ teaspoon
¼ ounce = 1½ teaspoons
½ ounce = 1 tablespoon
⅔ ounce = 4 teaspoons
¾ ounce = 1½ tablespoons
1 ounce = 2 tablespoons
1¼ ounce = 2½ tablespoons
2 ounces = ¼ cup

—CN

Rain City Punch

Waterfront

This twist on rum punch is the creation of Waterfront beverage manager Jude Augustine, who has a particular passion for rums. You could multiply the quantities to make a pitcher for a party: combine the ingredients with a couple handfuls of ice and stir well to blend, then pour the punch into ice-filled glasses for serving.

1 fluid ounce pineapple juice	Splash Chambord
1 fluid ounce sweet and sour mix	Splash soda
⅔ fluid ounce dark rum	Lime slice, for garnish
⅔ fluid ounce amaretto	Maraschino cherry, for garnish

HALF-FILL A COCKTAIL SHAKER with ice and add the pineapple juice, sweet and sour mix, rum, amaretto, Chambord, and soda. Cover the shaker and shake until well chilled, then pour the contents, ice included, into a tall cocktail glass. Garnish the rim of the glass with the lime slice, float the cherry on top, and serve.

Makes 1 serving

Mojito

Fandango

Chef-owner Christine Keff did extensive research before opening Fandango,
her Latin American–inspired restaurant in Belltown. This included tracking down the most
authentic recipe for mojito, a specialty of Cuba. This version is based on the mojito
from the Hotel Inglaterra in Havana.

To make a batch of drinks for a party, blend the rum, lime juice,
and simple syrup in a big pitcher and keep chilled in the fridge, then pour the
mixture over the ice and mint just before serving.

1 ¼ fluid ounces white rum	1 fluid ounce simple syrup (page 225)
1 fluid ounce freshly squeezed lime juice	1 large sprig mint

HALF-FILL A COCKTAIL SHAKER with ice and add the rum, lime juice, and simple syrup.
Cover the shaker and shake well. Put the mint sprig in a tall glass and pour the mojito (ice
included) over the sprig. Serve with a swizzle stick for crushing the mint a bit to extract its
flavor.

Makes 1 serving

Rosemary Lemonade

Café Flora

"Rosemary lemonade is our most popular beverage, year-round,"
notes Cathy Geier from Café Flora. It is simple to put together: you're essentially making
rosemary "tea" and using this as part of the water in the lemonade. If you're in a hurry,
dissolve the sugar in the hot rosemary water and stir in ice cubes until the liquid
is chilled, then add the lemon juice with enough water to make 2 quarts.

2 quarts water	1 cup freshly squeezed lemon juice
1 bunch rosemary (about eight 6-inch sprigs)	Lemon slices, for garnish
1¼ cups sugar	

COMBINE 1 QUART OF THE WATER and the rosemary in a small saucepan. Bring the water to a boil over high heat, then reduce the heat to low and simmer, uncovered, for 20 minutes. Strain the rosemary water into a 2-quart heatproof pitcher. Add the sugar, stirring to dissolve, and let cool to room temperature. Refrigerate the lemonade base until fully chilled.

STIR IN THE LEMON JUICE and the remaining quart water. Serve in tall glasses over ice, garnished with lemon slices.

Makes 8 servings

Ultraviolet Martini

Four Seasons Olympic Hotel

Michael Vezzoni has been tending bar at the Four Seasons Olympic Hotel downtown for nearly 20 years. He's a regular contender in Seattle's annual Martini Challenge and stirred up this particular recipe one year for the "specialty martini" category. Vezzoni says, "The blueberries used to garnish the martini add flavor, look beautiful, and are fun to eat at the end." He gets them from his family's farm, Bybee Blueberry Farms, located just outside Seattle in North Bend, at the base of Mount Si.

The Jacopo Poli grappa used as a "wash" for the cocktail shaker is a luxurious flourish because it's quite expensive. You can use another brand in its place, but Vezzoni says the grappa plays an important role in giving the cocktail a clean, dry finish, so don't be tempted to leave it out of the recipe.

Splash Jacopo Poli grappa
2¼ fluid ounces Grey Goose vodka
½ fluid ounce Bombay Sapphire gin

⅙ fluid ounce (1 teaspoon) Chambord
6 drops crème de cassis
3 blueberries, for garnish

PUT THE GRAPPA in a cocktail shaker, twist and swirl to coat the insides of the shaker, then discard the rest. Fill the shaker with ice and add the vodka, gin, Chambord, and crème de cassis. Stir with a spoon (or cover and shake just once or twice) and strain into a chilled martini glass. Plop the blueberries into the cocktail and serve.

Makes 1 serving

Watermelon Kazi

Axis

This recipe is a long-loved signature at Axis. It is definitely seasonal,
since the starring ingredient is the sweet, red watermelon of summer. The watermelon needs
to be well crushed to release its color and flavor into the cocktail. Bartenders use a muddler,
a wooden tool that looks something like a mini baseball bat, to crush fruit in recipes like
this one. Use the end of a wooden spoon or something similar, preferably wooden,
if you don't have the traditional tool.

1 cup peeled, seeded, and diced watermelon	1¼ fluid ounces vodka
2 fluid ounces sweet and sour mix or	Dash (about ½ teaspoon) Triple Sec
lime sour mix (page 233)	Small wedge slice of watermelon, for garnish

PUT THE DICED WATERMELON in a cocktail shaker or sturdy pint glass with a handful of
ice cubes and muddle to crush the watermelon thoroughly, covering the glass with one hand as
much as you can while muddling. (It can be a messy technique, but muddling is a classic bar
method, and you'll get the hang of it.) Add the sweet and sour mix, vodka, and Triple Sec and
continue muddling to blend and chill the ingredients. (You could also shake the cocktail after
adding the remaining ingredients.) Strain the mixture into a chilled martini glass, garnish with
the watermelon slice, and serve.

Makes 1 serving

The Paradigm Shift

Oliver's

The bartenders at Oliver's shake up The Paradigm Shift with Rain vodka,
a superpremium domestic (and organic) label, and Bombay gin, although you're welcome to
use your preferred brands. This was a winner in the "specialty martini" category
at Seattle's Martini Challenge competition.

⅛ fluid ounce Campari
1 fluid ounce freshly squeezed Texas Ruby Red
grapefruit juice
2 fluid ounces Rain vodka

¾ fluid ounce Bombay gin
Grapefruit slice and raspberry, frozen,
for garnish

RASPBERRY LEMON-LIME SOUR MIX

5 tablespoons freshly squeezed lime juice
¼ cup freshly squeezed lemon juice

¼ cup simple syrup (page 225)
⅛ teaspoon raspberry purée

FOR THE SOUR MIX, combine the lime juice, lemon juice, simple syrup, and raspberry purée
in a small pitcher or bowl, stir to mix, and refrigerate until ready to use. You should have
about ¾ cup (enough for 6 drinks).

ADD THE CAMPARI to a cocktail shaker, twist and swirl it so that the Campari evenly coats
the inside, then discard the rest. Fill the shaker with ice, add the grapefruit juice and 1 fluid
ounce of the sour mix, followed by the vodka and gin. Cover the shaker and shake until very
cold, then strain the cocktail into a chilled large martini glass. Garnish with the frozen grapefruit slice and raspberry and serve.

Makes 1 serving

APPENDIX: RESTAURANTS & BARS

A P P E N D I X :
R E S T A U R A N T S   &   B A R S

AFRIKANDO

2904 First Avenue
Seattle, WA 98121
206/374-9714

ANDALUCA

407 Olive Way
Seattle, WA 98101
206/382-6999
www.andaluca.com

ANDRE'S EURASIAN BISTRO

14125 NE 20th Street
Bellevue, WA 98007
425/747-6551

ANTHONY'S HOMEPORT

6135 Seaview Avenue NW
Seattle, WA 98107
206/783-0780
www.anthonysrestaurants.com

ANTHONY'S PIER 66

2201 Alaskan Way
Seattle, WA 98121
206/448-6688
www.anthonysrestaurants.com

AVENUE ONE

1921 First Avenue
Seattle, WA 98101
206/441-6139

AXIS

2214 First Avenue
Seattle, WA 98121
206/441-9600
www.axisrestaurant.com

BAHN THAI

409 Roy Street
Seattle, WA 98109
206/283-0444

BANDOLEONE

2241 Eastlake Avenue E
Seattle, WA 98102
206/329-7559

BOAT STREET CAFÉ

909 NE Boat Street
Seattle, WA 98105
206/632-4602

BRASA

2107 Third Avenue
Seattle, WA 98121
206/728-4220
www.brasa.com

BRASSERIE MARGAUX

401 Lenora
Seattle, WA 98121
206/777-1990

CAFÉ FLORA

2901 E Madison Street
Seattle, WA 98112
206/325-9100
www.cafeflora.com

CAMPAGNE

86 Pine Street
Seattle, WA 98101
206/728-2800

CANLIS

2576 Aurora Avenue N
Seattle, WA 98109
206/283-3313
www.canlis.com

CARMELITA

7314 Greenwood Avenue N
Seattle, WA 98103
206/706-7703

CASSIS

2359 Tenth Avenue E
Seattle, WA 98102
206/329-0580
www.cassisbistro.com

CHEZ SHEA

94 Pike Street, 3rd Floor
Seattle, WA 98101
206/467-9990
www.chezshea.com

CHINOOK'S AT SALMON BAY

1900 W Nickerson
Seattle, WA 98119
206/283-4665

CUCINA! CUCINA!

901 Fairview Avenue N
Seattle, WA 98109
206/447-2782
www.cucinacucina.com

DAHLIA LOUNGE

2001 Fourth Avenue
Seattle, WA 98101
206/682-4142
www.tomdouglas.com

EARTH & OCEAN

1124 Fourth Avenue
Seattle, WA 98101
206/264-6060

EL CAMINO

607 N 35th Street
Seattle, WA 98103
206/632-7303
www.elcaminorestaurant.com

ELLIOTT'S OYSTER HOUSE

1201 Alaskan Way
Seattle, WA 98101
206/623-4340

ETTA'S SEAFOOD

2020 Western Avenue
Seattle, WA 98121
206/443-6000
www.tomdouglas.com

FANDANGO

2313 First Avenue
Seattle, WA 98121
206/441-1188

FLYING FISH

2234 First Avenue
Seattle, WA 98121
206/529-9483
www.flyingfishrestaurant.com

FOUR SEASONS OLYMPIC HOTEL

411 University Street
Seattle, WA 98101
206/621-1700
www.fshr.com

FULLERS

1400 Sixth Avenue
Seattle, WA 98101
206/447-5544
www.sheraton.com

THE GEORGIAN ROOM

411 University Street
Seattle, WA 98101
206/621-1700
www.fshr.com

HARVEST VINE

2701 E Madison Street
Seattle, WA 98112
206/320-9771

HATTIE'S HAT

5231 Ballard Avenue NW
Seattle, WA 98107
206/784-0175

THE HERBFARM

14590 NE 145th St
Woodinville, WA 98072
206/784-2222
www.herbfarm.com

THE HUNT CLUB

900 Madison Street
Seattle, WA 98104
206/343-6156

IVAR'S SALMON HOUSE

401 NE Northlake Way
Seattle, WA 98105
206/632-0767
www.ivarsrestaurants.com

KASPAR'S

19 W Harrison Street
Seattle, WA 98119
206/298-0123
www.kaspars.com

KINGFISH CAFÉ

602 19th Avenue E
Seattle, WA 98112
206/320-8757

LA MEDUSA

4857 Rainier Avenue S
Seattle, WA 98118
206/723-2192

LE GOURMAND

425 NW Market Street
Seattle, WA 98107
206/784-3463

LE PICHET

1933 First Avenue
Seattle, WA 98101
206/256-1499

LUAU POLYNESIAN LOUNGE

2253 N 56th Street
Seattle, WA 98103
206/633-5828

MACRINA BAKERY AND CAFÉ

2408 First Avenue
Seattle, WA 98121
206/448-4032

MADISON PARK CAFÉ

1807 42nd Avenue E
Seattle, WA 98112
206/324-2626

METROPOLITAN GRILL

820 Second Avenue
Seattle, WA 98104
206/624-3287

NELL'S

6804 E Green Lake Way N
Seattle, WA 98115
206/524-4044

NISHINO

3130 E Madison Street
Seattle, WA 98112
206/322-5800

OLIVER'S

405 Olive Way
Seattle, WA 98101
206/382-6995

THE PAINTED TABLE

94 Madison Street
Seattle, WA 98104
206/624-3646
www.alexishotel.com

PALACE KITCHEN

2030 Fifth Avenue
Seattle, WA 98121
206/448-2001
www.tomdouglas.com

PALISADE

2601 W Marina Place
Seattle, WA 98199
206/285-1000

RAGA CUISINE OF INDIA

212 Central Way
Kirkland, WA 98033
425/827-3300
www.ragarestaurant.com

RAY'S BOATHOUSE

6049 Seaview Avenue NW
Seattle, WA 98107
206/789-3770
www.rays.com

RESTAURANT ZOË

2137 Second Avenue
Seattle, WA 98121
206/256-2060

ROVER'S

2808 E Madison Street
Seattle, WA 98112
206/325-7442
www.rovers-seattle.com

ROY'S

1900 Fifth Avenue
Seattle, WA 98101
206/256-7697
www.roysrestaurants.com

SALTY'S ON ALKI

1936 Harbor Avenue SW
Seattle, WA 98126
206/937-1085
www.saltys.com

SANTA FE CAFÉ

5901 Phinney Avenue N
Seattle, WA 98103
206/783-9755

SAZERAC

1101 Fourth Avenue
Seattle, WA 98101
206/624-7755

SIX DEGREES

7900 E Green Lake Dr N
Seattle, WA 98103
206/523-1600
www.sixdegreesrestaurant.com

STILL LIFE IN FREMONT COFFEEHOUSE

709 N 35th
Seattle, WA 98103
206/547-9850

TULIO

1100 Fifth Avenue
Seattle, WA 98101
206/624-5500

UNION SQUARE GRILL

621 Union Street
Seattle, WA 98101
206/224-4321

WATERFRONT

2810 Alaskan Way
Seattle, WA 98121
206/956-9171

WILD GINGER ASIAN RESTAURANT & SATAY BAR

1403 Third Avenue
Seattle, WA 98101
206/623-4450

YAKIMA GRILL

612 Stewart Street
Seattle, WA 98101
206/956-0639
www.yakimagrill.com

YARROW BAY BEACH CAFÉ

1270 Carillon Point
Kirkland, WA 98033
206/889-9052

INDEX

INDEX

A

Afrikando
Thiebu Djen (Parsley-Stuffed Halibut with Vegetables and Rice), 138–39
Yassa au Poulet (Chicken in Onion-Mustard Sauce), 171

Ahi tuna
Ahi Tuna Tartare with Hazelnuts, Shaved Pear Salad, and Cilantro Hollandaise, 24–25
Grilled Ahi in Licorice Root "Tea" with Braised Red Cabbage, 120–21

Aïoli
for Pan-Fried Mussels on Rosemary Skewers, 32–33
See also Mayonnaise

Almonds
Almond Shortbread Crust, for Apricot, Rose, and Saffron Tart, 196–97
Pinchineta (Almond Tart), 216–17

Ancho chiles
Ancho Chile Mayonnaise, for Crab Cakes, 102–3
Ancho Chile Sauce, for Cumin-Seared Columbia River Sturgeon, 144–45

Andaluca
Paella, 156–57

Andre's Eurasian Bistro
Fall Pumpkin and Squash Bisque, 69

Anthony's HomePort
Baked Oysters with Beurre Blanc, 28–29
Fresh Roasted Corn with Lime and Chile, 93
Nectarine Blackberry Crisp, 204

Anthony's Pier 66
Seattle Cioppino, 60–61

Appetizers, 1–51
Ahi Tuna Tartare, 24
Artichoke Ramekins, 38
Asian Barbecue Beef Triangles with a Tropical Fruit Salsa, 10
Bahia Mussels, 17
Baked Oysters with Beurre Blanc, 28
Cataplana Mussels, 9

Cedar Plank–Roasted Crab-Stuffed Mushrooms, 18
Creole Shrimp with Two Salsas, 22
Four-Onion Tart, 20
Geoduck Batayaki, 36
Herb-Infused Olives, 3
Jalapeño Mussels, 49
Kippered Salmon and Asparagus Bread Pudding, 46
Muhammara, 26
Pan-Fried Mussels on Rosemary Skewers, 32
Pan-Seared Steelhead with Black Bean Vinaigrette, 14
Pâté de Campagne, 34
Razor Clams with Brown Butter and Salsify Chips, 6
Scallop and Shrimp Seviche with Cilantro Oil, 12
Spicy Vegetable Fritters, 16
Squid in Their Own Ink, 44
Steamed Clams, 39
Tequila-Cured Gravlax Salmon, 40
Tuscan White Bean and Rosemary Spread, 27
Vietnamese Spring Rolls, 50
Walla Walla Onion Pancakes with Smoked Trout Rémoulade, 4
Wild Mushroom Terrine with Goat Cheese Caillé and Berry Vinaigrette, 42

Apples
about, 183–84
Cameo Apple Salad with Treviso, Oregon Blue Cheese, and Cider Vinaigrette, 74
Dungeness Crab with Red Radishes and Braeburn Apples, 84
Granny Smith Apple Bread Pudding, 89

Apricots
Apricot, Rose, and Saffron Tart, 196–97

Artichokes
Artichoke Ramekins, 38

"Artisan-Baked Bread," 47–48

Arugula
Arugula Pesto, Lamb Chops with, 158

Asian influences, about, 51

Asian pears
  Local Garden Greens with Asian Pears and
    Five-Spice Glazed Walnuts, 72–73
Asparagus
  about, 83
  Kippered Salmon and Asparagus Bread
    Pudding, 46–47
  Roasted Pepper and Grilled Asparagus
    Salad, 82
"Asparagus—Herald of Spring," 83
Avenue One
  Ahi Tuna Tartare, 24–25
  Granny Smith Apple Bread Pudding, 89
Avocado
  Avocado Carpaccio with Radish and Herb
    Salad, 76
  Avocado Purée, for Scallop and Shrimp
    Seviche, 12–13
Axis
  Watermelon Kazi, 240

B

Bahn Thai
  Plig King Tofu, 107
  Tom Kah Gai, 55
Baked Hawaii, 214–15
Bananas
  Bananas Foster, 188–89
Bandoleone
  Creole Shrimp with Two Salsas, 22–23
  Red Kuri Squash and Pear Timbales, 9
Barbecue. *See* Grilled dishes
Barbecue sauce
  Asian Barbecue Sauce, for Asian Barbecue
    Beef Triangles with a Tropical Fruit Salsa,
    10–11
Basil
  Thai Basil-Seared Mahimahi with Red Curry
    Lobster Essence, 160–61
  Yakima Cherry, Walla Walla Sweet Onion,
    and Basil Salad with Balsamic Vinaigrette,
    85
Beans
  Tuscan White Bean and Rosemary Spread, 27
  See also Green beans
"Beautiful Berries," 211–12

Beef
  Asian Barbecue Beef Triangles with a Tropical
    Fruit Salsa, 10–11
  Bruschetta Steak Sandwiches, 108–9
  Lemongrass Rubbed Filet with Braised Short
    Ribs and Spicy Red Pepper Sauce, 146–47
  Steak Teriyaki, 134–35
Bell peppers
  Muhammara, 26
  Roasted Pepper and Grilled Asparagus
    Salad, 82
  Spicy Red Pepper Sauce, for Lemongrass
    Rubbed Filet with Braised Short Ribs,
    146–47
Berries
  about, 211–12
  Berry Vinaigrette, Wild Mushroom Terrine
    with, 42–43
  Blueberry-Port Sauce, Honey-Chèvre
    Cheesecake with, 198–99
  Chambord Berry Sauce, for Baked Hawaii,
    214–15
  Fresh Blackberry Tart, 180–81
  Nectarine Blackberry Crisp, 204
  Raspberry and Peach Shortcakes with Honey
    Whipped Cream, 210–11
  Strawberry Spice and Everything Nice, 225
Beurre blanc
  Alaskan Halibut with Tagliatelle of
    Vegetables, American Caviar, and, 166–67
  Baked Oysters with, 28–29
  for Orcas Rack of Lamb with Spring Pea Flan
    and Morels, 172–73
Beverages. *See* Drinks
Biscotti
  Lemon Rosemary Biscotti, 218–19
Bisque
  Fall Pumpkin and Squash Bisque, 69
  See also Soup
Blackberries
  Fresh Blackberry Tart, 180–81
  Nectarine Blackberry Crisp, 204
Black cod
  Kasu Black Cod, 174–75
  See also Cod; Lingcod
Bloody Mary, Elsie's, 226

Blueberries
    Blueberry-Port Sauce, Honey-Chèvre
        Cheesecake with, 198–99
Boat Street Café
    Herb-Infused Olives, 3
    Kale and Tomato Gratin, 97
Brasa
    Cataplana Mussels, 9
Brasserie Margaux
    Pan-Seared Duck Breast with Muscadet Wine
        Sauce, 116–17
Bread
    artisan, 47–48
    bruschetta, for Bruschetta Steak Sandwiches,
        108–9
    croutons, for Caesar for Two, 79
    See also Bread pudding; Bread salad
Bread pudding
    Granny Smith Apple Bread Pudding, 89
    Kippered Salmon and Asparagus Bread
        Pudding, 46–47
Bread salad
    Herb Roasted Chicken and, 70–71
Bruschetta, for Bruschetta Steak Sandwiches, 108–9
Butter
    Brown Butter Balsamic Vinaigrette, for
        Grilled Salmon with Lentils, 112–13
    See also Beurre blanc

C

Cabbage
    Braised Red Cabbage, Grilled Ahi in Licorice
        Root "Tea" with, 120–21
    in Thiebu Djen (Parsley-Stuffed Halibut with
        Vegetables and Rice), 138–39
Caesar for Two, 79
Café Flora
    Rosemary Lemonade, 238
    Spicy Polenta with Braised Fennel, Olives,
        and Goat Cheese, 136–37
Cake
    Bing Cherry Cake, 185
    Chocolate Chai Tea Soufflé Cake, 202–3
    Hawaiian-Style Coconut Cake, 194–95
    Macadamia Nut Cake, for Baked Hawaii,
        214–15
    See also Cheesecake

Cake filling
    Whipped Cream Filling, for Hawaiian-Style
        Coconut Cake, 194–95
Calamari
    Squid in Their Own Ink, 44–45
Caldillo Sauce, for Salmon con Tamarindo,
    130–31
Camembert cheese
    Old Chatham Camembert with Pear and
        Dried Cherry Chutney, 190–91
Campagne
    Heirloom Tomato Salad with Rode Esterling
        Potatoes and Tapenade, 86
    Pâté de Campagne, 34–35
Canlis
    Hawaiian-Style Coconut Cake, 194–95
    Steak Teriyaki, 134–35
Caramelo
    Flan with Caramelo Drizzle, 206–7
Carmelita
    Avocado Carpaccio with Radish and Herb
        Salad, 76
    Muhammara, 26
Cassava
    in Thiebu Djen (Parsley-Stuffed Halibut with
        Vegetables and Rice), 138–39
Cassis
    Honey-Chèvre Cheesecake with Blueberry-
        Port Sauce, 198–99
    Lavender-Honey Ice Cream, 193
    Pan-Seared Alaskan Cod with Green Beans,
        Niçoise Olives, and Smoked Paprika
        Vinaigrette, 154
    Yakima Cherry, Walla Walla Sweet Onion, and
        Basil Salad with Balsamic Vinaigrette, 85
Cauliflower
    Gratin de Chou-fleur (Cauliflower Gratin),
        90–91
    in Spicy Vegetable Fritters, 16
Chard
    Sautéed Greens, for Salmon con Tamarindo,
        130–31
Cheese
    Old Chatham Camembert with Pear and
        Dried Cherry Chutney, 190–91
    See also Cheesemakers; Goat cheese; Gratin
        dishes

Cheesecake
    Honey-Chèvre Cheesecake with Blueberry-
        Port Sauce, 198–99
    Spoon Cheesecake, 179
Cheesemakers, local, 191–92
"Chef's Secrets," 162–63
"Cherries," 123–24
Cherries
    about, 123–24
    Bing Cherry Cake, 185
    cherry vinegar, 123
    freezing, 123
    Pear and Dried Cherry Chutney, Old
        Chatham Camembert with, 190–91
    Pork Tenderloin with Bing Cherries and Mint,
        122–23
    Yakima Cherry, Walla Walla Sweet Onion,
        and Basil Salad with Balsamic Vinaigrette, 85
Chez Shea
    Fresh Blackberry Tart, 180–81
    Walla Walla Onion Pancakes with Smoked
        Trout Rémoulade, 4–5
Chicken
    Enchiladas en Salsa Suiza, 126–27
    Herb Roasted Chicken and Bread Salad, 70–71
    Malai Kebab, 104
    Roasted Chicken with Caramelized Garlic
        and Sage, 143
    Smothered Game Hens, 164–65
    Swiss Leek, Oat, and Smoked Chicken
        Soup, 58
    Yassa au Poulet (Chicken in Onion-Mustard
        Sauce), 171
Chicken liver
    Pâté de Campagne, 34–35
Chile peppers
    Ancho Chile Mayonnaise, for Crab Cakes,
        102–3
    Ancho Chile Sauce, for Cumin-Seared
        Columbia River Sturgeon, 144–45
    Fresh Roasted Corn with Lime and Chile, 93
    Green Chile Sauce, for Grilled Pork and
        Pumpkin Poblano Tamales, 168–69
    Jalapeño Mussels, 49
    Pumpkin Poblano Tamales, Grilled Pork and,
        168–69

Chinook's at Salmon Bay
    "Blue Plate Special" Lingcod with Sour
        Cream, Red Onion, and Fresh Dill, 159
Chocolate
Chocolate Chai Tea Soufflé Cake, 202–3
Chocolate Hazelnut Kisses, 186–87
Chowder
    Corn Chowder with Dungeness Crab, 56–57
    Seafood Chowder, 68
    See also Soup
Chutney
    Pear and Dried Cherry Chutney, Old
        Chatham Camembert with, 190–91
Cilantro
    Cilantro Hollandaise, for Ahi Tuna Tartare,
        24–25
    Cilantro Oil, for Scallop and Shrimp Seviche,
        12–13
    Spicy Cilantro Salsa, for Corn Chowder with
        Dungeness Crab, 56–57
Cinnamon Ice Cream, 205
Cioppino, 60–61
"City Grilling," 105–6
Clams
    about, 7–8
    Geoduck Batayaki, 36–37
    Razor Clams with Brown Butter and Salsify
        Chips, 6–7
    in Seattle Cioppino, 60–61
    Steamed Clams, 39
"Clams & Mussels," 7–8
"Cocktails," 230–31
    See also Drinks
Coconut
    Coconut Curried Lamb Shanks, 128–29
    Coconut Ginger Salsa, for Coconut Curried
        Lamb Shanks, 128–29
    Coconut Ice Cream, for Baked Hawaii,
        214–15
    Flan with Caramelo Drizzle, 206–7
    Hawaiian-Style Coconut Cake, 194–95
Cod
    Pan-Seared Alaskan Cod with Green Beans,
        Niçoise Olives, and Smoked Paprika
        Vinaigrette, 154–55
    See also Black cod; Lingcod

Collard greens
     Sautéed Greens, for Salmon con Tamarindo,
        130–31
"Comfort Foods and Sacred Cows," 142
Cookies
     Chocolate Hazelnut Kisses, 186–87
     Lemon Rosemary Biscotti, 218–19
Corn
     Corn Chowder with Dungeness Crab, 56–57
     Fresh Roasted Corn with Lime and Chile, 93
Cornish game hens
     Smothered Game Hens, 164–65
Cornmeal
     Spicy Polenta with Braised Fennel, Olives,
        and Goat Cheese, 136–37
Crab
     about, 57
     Cedar Plank–Roasted Crab-Stuffed
        Mushrooms, 18
     Corn Chowder with Dungeness Crab, 56–57
     Crab Cakes with Ancho Chile Mayonnaise,
        102–3
     Dungeness Crab with Red Radishes and
        Braeburn Apples, 84
     in Seafood Chowder, 68
     in Seattle Cioppino, 60–61
Crisp
     Nectarine Blackberry Crisp, 204
Croutons, for Caesar for Two, 79
Crust
     Almond Shortbread Crust, for Apricot, Rose,
        and Saffron Tart, 196–97
     for Four-Onion Tart, 20–21
     for Fresh Blackberry Tart, 180–81
Cucina! Cucina!
     Sausage and Lentil Soup, 63
Cucumber
     Chilled Cucumber Soup with Smoked
        Sturgeon and Curry Oil, 64–65
     Raita Salad, for Tequila-Cured Gravlax
        Salmon, 40–41
Curry
     Coconut Curried Lamb Shanks, 128–29
     Curry Oil, for Chilled Cucumber Soup,
        64–65
     Red Curry Lobster Essence, for Thai Basil-
        Seared Mahimahi, 160–61

Custard
     for Apricot, Rose, and Saffron Tart, 196–97
     for Pinchineta (Almond Tart), 216–17
     See also Pastry cream

D

Dahlia Lounge
     Orcas Rack of Lamb with Spring Pea Flan
        and Morels, 172–73
Desserts, 177–219
     Apricot, Rose, and Saffron Tart, 196
     Baked Hawaii, 214
     Bananas Foster, 188
     Bing Cherry Cake, 185
     Chocolate Chai Tea Soufflé Cake, 202
     Chocolate Hazelnut Kisses, 186
     Cinnamon Ice Cream, 205
     Earl Grey Sorbet, 213
     Flan with Caramelo Drizzle, 206
     Fresh Blackberry Tart, 180
     Gateau de Riz Façon Grand-Mère
        (Old-Fashioned Rice Pudding), 208
     Hawaiian-Style Coconut Cake, 194
     Honey-Chèvre Cheesecake with Blueberry-
        Port Sauce , 198
     Lavender-Honey Ice Cream, 193
     Lemon Rosemary Biscotti, 218
     Nectarine Blackberry Crisp, 204
     Old Chatham Camembert with Pear and
        Dried Cherry Chutney, 190
     Pear and Rose Hip Sorbet, 182
     Pinchineta (Almond Tart), 216
     Raspberry and Peach Shortcakes with Honey
        Whipped Cream, 210
     Spoon Cheesecake, 179
Dips and spreads
     Aïoli, for Pan-Fried Mussels on Rosemary
        Skewers, 32–33
     Muhammara, 26
     Tuscan White Bean and Rosemary Spread, 27
     See also Salsa; Sauces; Tapenade
Drinks, 221–41
     Absolut Mandarin Martini, 223
     Cadillac Margarita, 224
     Classic Martini, 235
     cocktails, 230–31
     Elsie's Bloody Mary, 226

Hawaiian Punch, 228
Honey Peach Julep, 232
Italian Caramel Apple, 234
measurements for, 235
Mojito, 237
Paradigm Shift, The, 241
Priestess, The, 227
Rain City Punch, 236
Rosemary Lemonade (nonalcoholic), 238
Silver Rocket, 229
Strawberry Spice and Everything Nice, 225
Ultraviolet Martini, 239
Watermelon Kazi, 240
Zoë Cocktail, 233
Duck
Pan-Seared Duck Breast with Muscadet Wine
Sauce, 116–17
"Dungeness Crab—Are You a Picker or a Piler?"
57

E

Earl Grey Sorbet, 213
Earth & Ocean
Old Chatham Camembert with Pear and
Dried Cherry Chutney, 190–91
"Eastern Washington," 114–15
Eggplant
in Orecchiette with Fall Vegetables, 118–19
in Thiebu Djen (Parsley-Stuffed Halibut with
Vegetables and Rice), 138–39
El Camino
Enchiladas en Salsa Suiza, 126–27
Flan with Caramelo Drizzle, 206–7
Salmon con Tamarindo, 130–31
Elliott's Oyster House
Jalapeño Mussels, 49
Pan-Fried Oysters with Jack Daniel's
Sauce, 125
Enchiladas en Salsa Suiza, 126–27
Entrées. *See* Main dishes
Etta's Seafood
Razor Clams with Brown Butter and
Salsify Chips, 6–7

F

Fandango
Bahia Mussels, 17
Mojito, 237
"Farmers Markets, P-Patches & Garden
Gourmets," 87–88
Fennel
Alder-Barbecued King Salmon with Fennel
and Mint, 101
Braised Fennel, Spicy Polenta with Olives,
Goat Cheese, and, 136–37
in Orecchiette with Fall Vegetables, 118–19
salad, with Old Chatham Camembert with
Pear and Dried Cherry Chutney, 190–91
Orange and Fennel Salad with Sicilian Olives
and Pecorino Romano Shavings, 75
Figs
Balsamic Roasted Figs, 137
Finishing in the oven, 162–63
Fish
"Blue Plate Special" Lingcod with Sour
Cream, Red Onion, and Fresh Dill, 159
Ahi Tuna Tartare with Hazelnuts, Shaved
Pear Salad, and Cilantro Hollandaise, 24–25
Alaskan Halibut with Tagliatelle of Vegeta-
bles, Beurre Blanc, and American Caviar,
166–67
Alder-Barbecued King Salmon with Fennel
and Mint, 101
Cumin-Seared Columbia River Sturgeon,
144–45
Grilled Ahi in Licorice Root "Tea" with
Braised Red Cabbage, 120–21
Grilled Salmon with Lentils and Brown Butter
Balsamic Vinaigrette, 112–13
Kasu Black Cod, 174–75
Kippered Salmon and Asparagus Bread
Pudding, 46–47
Pan-Seared Alaskan Cod with Green Beans,
Niçoise Olives, and Smoked Paprika
Vinaigrette, 154–55
Pan-Seared Steelhead with Black Bean
Vinaigrette, 14–15
Salmon con Tamarindo, 130–31
in Seattle Cioppino, 60–61
Smoked Trout Rémoulade, Walla Walla
Onion Pancakes with, 4–5

Spaghetti con le Sarde (Spaghetti with
   Sardines), 110–11
Steamed King Salmon on Hungarian Paprika
   Sauerkraut, 153
Tequila-Cured Gravlax Salmon, 40–41
Thai Basil-Seared Mahimahi with Red Curry
   Lobster Essence, 160–61
Thiebu Djen (Parsley-Stuffed Halibut with
   Vegetables and Rice), 138–39
See also Seafood/shellfish
Flan
   Flan with Caramelo Drizzle, 206–7
   Spring Pea Flan, 172–73
Flying Fish
   Pan-Seared Steelhead with Black Bean
      Vinaigrette, 14–15
Four Seasons Olympic Hotel
   Silver Rocket, 229
   Ultraviolet Martini, 239
   See also Georgian Room, The
Fritters
   Spicy Vegetable Fritters, 16
Fruit
   Balsamic Roasted Figs, 137
   Bing Cherry Cake, 185
   eastern Washington, 114–15
   Fresh Blackberry Tart, 180–81
   grilling, 106
   Nectarine Blackberry Crisp, 204
   Pear and Herb Salad, Ahi Tuna Tartare with,
      24–25
   Plum Compote, for Gateau de Riz Façon
      Grand-Mère (Old-Fashioned Rice Pudding),
      208–9
   Raspberry and Peach Shortcakes with Honey
      Whipped Cream, 210–11
   Savory Nectarine and Shiso Soup, 59
   Tropical Fruit Salsa, for Asian Barbecue Beef
      Triangles, 10–11
Fullers
   Tequila-Cured Gravlax Salmon, 40–41

G

Gadgets, 163
Game hens
   Smothered Game Hens, 164–65
Garlic
   Caramelized Garlic, for Roasted Chicken
      with Sage and, 143
Garnishes
   Gremolata, for Baked Oysters with Beurre
      Blanc, 28–29
   leek garnish, for Pan-Seared Steelhead with
      Black Bean Vinaigrette, 15
Geoduck
   about, 7–8
   Geoduck Batayaki, 36–37
Georgian Room, The
   Morel Mushroom Ravioli with Chanterelle
      Mushroom Ragout, 148–50
   See also Four Seasons Olympic Hotel
Goat cheese
   Caillé, Wild Mushroom Terrine with, 42–43
   Honey-Chèvre Cheesecake with Blueberry-
      Port Sauce, 198–99
Gratin dishes
   Gratin de Chou-fleur (Cauliflower Gratin),
      90–91
   Kale and Tomato Gratin, 97
Gravlax
   Tequila-Cured Gravlax Salmon, 40–41
Green beans
   in Plig King Tofu, 107
   Sichuan Green Beans, 92
   in Spicy Vegetable Fritters, 16
Green Chile Sauce, for Grilled Pork with Pumpkin
   Poblano Tamales, 168–69
Green Onion Oil, for Salmon con Tamarindo,
   130–31
Greens
   Sautéed Greens, for Salmon con Tamarindo,
      130–31
Gremolata
   for Baked Oysters with Beurre Blanc, 28–29
Grilled dishes
   about, 105–6
   Alder-Barbecued King Salmon with Fennel
      and Mint, 101
   Bruschetta Steak Sandwiches, 108–9

Fresh Roasted Corn with Lime and Chile, 93

Grilled Ahi in Licorice Root "Tea" with
Braised Red Cabbage, 120–21

Grilled Pork with Pumpkin Poblano Tamales
and Green Chile Sauce, 168–69

Grilled Salmon with Lentils and Brown Butter
Balsamic Vinaigrette, 112–13

Malai Kebab, 104

marinades for, 105–6

Roasted Pepper and Grilled Asparagus
Salad, 82

H

Halibut

Alaskan Halibut with Tagliatelle of Vegetables, Beurre Blanc, and American Caviar,
166–67

in Seattle Cioppino, 60–61

Thiebu Djen (Parsley-Stuffed Halibut with
Vegetables and Rice), 138–39

Harvest Vine

Pinchineta, 216–17

Squid in Their Own Ink, 44–45

Hattie's Hat

Elsie's Bloody Mary, 226

Hawaiian Punch, 228

Hazelnuts

Chocolate Hazelnut Kisses, 186–87

Herbfarm, The

Apricot, Rose, and Saffron Tart, 196–97

Pan-Fried Mussels on Rosemary
Skewers, 32–33

Herbs

about, 77–78

Avocado Carpaccio with Radish and Herb
Salad, 76

grilling with, 106

Herb-Infused Olives, 3

Herb Roasted Chicken and Bread Salad,
70–71

See also Basil; Lavender; Rosemary; Shiso

"Herbs–From Back Yards to Menus," 77–78

Hollandaise sauce, cilantro, for Ahi Tuna Tartare,
24–25

Honey

Honey-Chèvre Cheesecake with Blueberry-
Port Sauce, 198–99

Honey Peach Julep, 232

Horseradish Cream, for Avocado Carpaccio with
Radish and Herb Salad, 76

Hunt Club, The

Alaskan Halibut with Tagliatelle of Vegetables, Beurre Blanc, and American Caviar,
166–67

Lamb Chops with Arugula Pesto, 158

Roasted Pepper and Grilled Asparagus
Salad, 82

I

Ice cream

Cinnamon Ice Cream, 205

Coconut Ice Cream, for Baked Hawaii,
214–15

Lavender-Honey Ice Cream, 193

See also Sorbet

Ivar's Salmon House

Alder-Barbecued King Salmon with Fennel
and Mint, 101

Steamed Clams, 39

J

Jack Daniel's Sauce, for Pan-Fried Oysters, 125

Jalapeño peppers

Jalapeño Mussels, 49

Julep, Honey Peach, 232

K

Kale

Kale and Tomato Gratin, 97

Kaspar's

Earl Grey Sorbet, 213

Steamed King Salmon on Hungarian Paprika
Sauerkraut, 153

Swiss Leek, Oat, and Smoked Chicken
Soup, 58

Kasu

about, 51

Kasu Black Cod, 174–75

Kebabs

Malai Kebab, 104

Kingfish Café

Smothered Game Hens, 164–65

L

La Medusa

Cinnamon Ice Cream, 205

Orange and Fennel Salad with Sicilian Olives and Pecorino Romano Shavings, 75

Spaghetti con le Sarde (Spaghetti with Sardines), 110

Lamb

Coconut Curried Lamb Shanks, 128–29

Lamb Chops with Arugula Pesto, 158

Orcas Rack of Lamb with Spring Pea Flan and Morels, 172–73

Lavender

Lavender-Honey Ice Cream, 193

Le Gourmand

Nettle Soup, 66

Pear and Rose Hip Sorbet, 182

Savory Nectarine and Shiso Soup, 59

Le Pichet

Gateau de Riz Façon Grand-Mère (Old-Fashioned Rice Pudding), 208–9

Gratin de Chou-fleur (Cauliflower Gratin), 90–91

Saucisse de Toulouse, 140–41

Leeks

leek garnish, for Pan-Seared Steelhead with Black Bean Vinaigrette, 15

Swiss Leek, Oat, and Smoked Chicken Soup, 58

Lemon

Lemon Mix, for Cadillac Margarita, 224

Lemon Rosemary Biscotti, 218–19

Rosemary Lemonade, 238

Lemongrass

Lemongrass Rubbed Filet with Braised Short Ribs and Spicy Red Pepper Sauce, 146–47

Lentils

about, 115

Grilled Salmon with Lentils and Brown Butter Balsamic Vinaigrette, 112–13

Sausage and Lentil Soup, 63

Licorice root

Grilled Ahi in Licorice Root "Tea" with Braised Red Cabbage, 120–21

Lime Sour Mix, for Zoë Cocktail, 233

Lingcod

"Blue Plate Special" Lingcod with Sour Cream, Red Onion, and Fresh Dill, 159

See also Black cod; Cod

Liver, chicken

Pâté de Campagne, 34–35

Lobster

Red Curry Lobster Essence, for Thai Basil-Seared Mahimahi, 160–61

"Local Cheesemakers," 191–92

Luau Polynesian Lounge

Bananas Foster, 188–89

Coconut Curried Lamb Shanks, 128–29

Hawaiian Punch, 228

M

Macadamia Nut Cake, for Baked Hawaii, 214–15

Macrina Bakery and Café

Corn Chowder with Dungeness Crab, 56–57

Kippered Salmon and Asparagus Bread Pudding, 46–47

Tuscan White Bean and Rosemary Spread, 27

Madison Park Café

Four-Onion Tart, 20–21

Pork Tenderloin with Bing Cherries and Mint, 122–23

Mahimahi

Thai Basil-Seared Mahimahi with Red Curry Lobster Essence, 160–61

Main dishes, 99–175

Alaskan Halibut with Tagliatelle of Vegetables, Beurre Blanc, and American Caviar, 166

Alder-Barbecued King Salmon with Fennel and Mint, 101

"Blue Plate Special" Lingcod with Sour Cream, Red Onions, and Fresh Dill, 159

Bruschetta Steak Sandwiches, 108

Coconut Curried Lamb Shanks, 128

Crab Cakes with Ancho Chile Mayonnaise, 102

Cumin-Seared Columbia River Sturgeon, 144

Enchiladas en Salsa Suiza, 126

Grilled Ahi in Licorice Root "Tea" with Braised Red Cabbage, 120

Grilled Pork with Pumpkin Poblano Tamales and Green Chile Sauce, 168

Grilled Salmon with Lentils and Brown Butter
Balsamic Vinaigrette, 112
Kasu Black Cod, 174
Lamb Chops with Arugula Pesto, 158
Lemongrass Rubbed Filet with Braised Short
Ribs and Spicy Red Pepper Sauce, 146
Malai Kebab, 104
Morel Mushroom Ravioli with Chanterelle
Mushroom Ragout, 148
Orcas Rack of Lamb with Spring Pea Flan
and Morels, 172
Orecchiette with Fall Vegetables, 118
Paella, 156
Pan-Fried Oysters with Jack Daniel's Sauce,
125
Pan-Seared Alaskan Cod with Green Beans,
Niçoise Olives, and Smoked Paprika, 154
Pan-Seared Duck Breast with Muscadet Wine
Sauce, 116
Plig King Tofu, 107
Pork Tenderloin with Bing Cherries and
Mint, 122
Roasted Chicken with Caramelized Garlic
and Sage, 143
Salmon con Tamarindo, 130
Saucisse de Toulouse, 140
Smothered Game Hens, 164
Spaghetti con le Sarde (Spaghetti with
Sardines), 110
Spicy Polenta with Braised Fennel, Olives,
and Goat Cheese, 136
Steak Teriyaki, 134
Steamed King Salmon on Hungarian Paprika
Sauerkraut, 153
Thai Basil–Seared Mahimahi with Red Curry
Lobster Essence, 160
Thiebu Djen (Parsley-Stuffed Halibut with
Vegetables and Rice), 138
Yassa au Poulet (Chicken in Onion-Mustard
Sauce), 171
Mandolines, 163
Mango
in Tropical Fruit Salsa, for Asian Barbecue
Beef Triangles, 10–11
Margarita, Cadillac, 224
Marinades
Five-Spice Marinade, for Pan-Seared
Steelhead, 14–15

for grilled dishes, 105–6
Herb Marinade, for Herb Roasted Chicken,
70–71
Kasu Marinade, for Kasu Black Cod, 174–75
for Pâte de Campagne, 34–35
Martinis
Absolut Mandarin Martini, 223
Classic Martini, 235
Ultraviolet Martini, 239
Mayonnaise
Ancho Chile Mayonnaise, for Crab Cakes,
102–3
See also Aïoli
"Measuring Up," 235
Meringue, for Baked Hawaii, 214–15
Metropolitan Grill
Bruschetta Steak Sandwiches, 108–9
Mise en place, 162
Mojito, 237
Muhammara, 26
"Mushrooms," 150–52
Mushrooms
Cedar Plank–Roasted Crab-Stuffed
Mushrooms, 18
Hungarian Mushroom Soup, 62
Morel Mushroom Ravioli with Chanterelle
Mushroom Ragout, 148–50
Roasted Morels, with Orcas Rack of Lamb,
172–73
in Spicy Vegetable Fritters, 16
wild, 150–52
Wild Mushroom Terrine with Goat Cheese
Caillé and Berry Vinaigrette, 42–43
Mussels
about, 7–8
Bahia Mussels, 17
Cataplana Mussels, 9
Jalapeño Mussels, 49
Pan-Fried Mussels on Rosemary Skewers,
32–33
in Seattle Cioppino, 60–61
Mustard greens
Sautéed Greens, for Salmon con Tamarindo,
130–31

N

Nectarines
  Nectarine Blackberry Crisp, 204
  Savory Nectarine and Shiso Soup, 59
Nell's
  Bing Cherry Cake, 185
  Dungeness Crab with Red Radishes and
    Braeburn Apples, 84
Nettles
  about, 67
  Nettle Soup, 66
Nishino
  Geoduck Batayaki, 36–37
"Northwest Fall Fruits: Pears & Apples," 183–84
Nuts
  Chocolate Hazelnut Kisses, 186–87
  Five-Spice Glazed Walnuts, Local Garden
    Greens with Asian Pears and, 72–73
  Macadamia Nut Cake, for Baked Hawaii, 214–15
  Pinchineta (Almond Tart), 216–17

O

Oats
  Swiss Leek, Oat, and Smoked Chicken
    Soup, 58
Oils, flavored
  Cilantro Oil, for Scallop and Shrimp Seviche,
    12–13
  Curry Oil, for Chilled Cucumber Soup with
    Smoked Sturgeon, 64–65
  Green Onion Oil, for Salmon con Tamarindo,
    130–31
Oliver's
  Classic Martini, 235
  Paradigm Shift, The, 241
Olives
  Herb-Infused Olives, 3
  Tomato and Olive Salsa, for Bruschetta Steak
    Sandwiches, 108–9
Onions
  Four-Onion Tart, 20–21
  Green Onion Oil, for Salmon con Tamarindo,
    130–31
  in Orecchiette with Fall Vegetables, 118–19
  in Spicy Vegetable Fritters, 16

  in Thiebu Djen (Parsley-Stuffed Halibut with
    Vegetables and Rice), 138–39
  Walla Walla Onion Pancakes with Smoked
    Trout Rémoulade, 4–5
  Walla Walla Sweets, about, 114
  Yakima Cherry, Walla Walla Sweet Onion,
    and Basil Salad with Balsamic Vinaigrette,
    85
Oranges
  Orange and Fennel Salad with Sicilian Olives
    and Pecorino Romano Shavings, 75
Orecchiette with Fall Vegetables, 118–19
"Oysters," 30–31
Oysters
  about, 30–31
  Baked Oysters with Beurre Blanc, 28–29
  Oyster Olympics, 31
  Pan-Fried Oysters with Jack Daniel's
    Sauce, 125

P

"Pacific Rim and Asian Influences," 51
Paella, 156–57
Painted Table, The
  Chocolate Hazelnut Kisses, 186–87
  Lemongrass Rubbed Filet with Braised Short
    Ribs and Spicy Red Pepper Sauce, 146–47
  Local Garden Greens with Asian Pears and
    Five-Spice Glazed Walnuts, 72–73
Palace Kitchen
  Cameo Apple Salad with Treviso, Arugula,
    Oregon Blue Cheese, and Cider
    Vinaigrette, 74
Palisade
  Cedar Plank–Roasted Crab-Stuffed
    Mushrooms, 18
  Seafood Chowder, 68
Pancakes
  Walla Walla Onion Pancakes with Smoked
    Trout Rémoulade, 4–5
Papaya
  in Tropical Fruit Salsa, for Asian Barbecue
    Beef Triangles, 10–11
Paprika
  Smoked Paprika Vinaigrette, for Pan-Seared
    Alaskan Cod, 154–55
Paradigm Shift, The, 241

Pasta dishes
    Morel Mushroom Ravioli with Chanterelle
      Mushroom Ragout, 148–50
    Orecchiette with Fall Vegetables, 118–19
    Spaghetti con le Sarde (Spaghetti with
      Sardines), 110–11
Pasta dough
    for Morel Mushroom Ravioli with
      Chanterelle Mushroom Ragout, 148–50
Pastry cream
    for Fresh Blackberry Tart, 180–81
    See also Custard
Pâté
    Pâté de Campagne, 34–35
    See also Terrine
Peaches
    Honey Peach Julep, 232
    peeling, 114
    Raspberry and Peach Shortcakes with Honey
      Whipped Cream, 210–11
Pears
    about, 183–84
    Anjou Pear Dressing, for Local Garden
      Greens with Asian Pears and Five-Spice
      Glazed
      Walnuts, 72–73
    juicing, 73
    Local Garden Greens with Asian Pears and
      Five-Spice Glazed Walnuts, 72–73
    Pear and Dried Cherry Chutney, Old
      Chatham Camembert with, 190–91
    Pear and Herb Salad, Ahi Tuna Tartare with,
      24–25
    Pear and Rose Hip Sorbet, 182
    Red Kuri Squash and Pear Timbales, 94–95
Peas
    Spring Pea Flan, with Orcas Rack of Lamb,
      172–73
"Peppers," 170
    See also Bell peppers; Chile peppers
Pesto
    Arugula Pesto, for Lamb Chops, 158
Pinchineta (Almond Tart), 216–17
Plank roasting, 19
    Cedar Plank–Roasted Crab-Stuffed
      Mushrooms, 18
Plating, 163

Plums
    Plum Compote, for Gateau de Riz Façon
      Grand-Mère (Old-Fashioned Rice Pudding),
      208–9
Poblano chiles
    Green Chile Sauce, Grilled Pork with
      Pumpkin Poblano Tamales and, 168–69
    Pumpkin Poblano Tamales, Grilled Pork with,
      168–69
Polenta
    Spicy Polenta with Braised Fennel, Olives,
      and Goat Cheese, 136–37
Pork
    Grilled Pork with Pumpkin Poblano Tamales
      and Green Chile Sauce, 168–69
    in Pâté de Campagne, 34–35
    Pork Tenderloin with Bing Cherries and Mint,
      122–23
    Saucisse de Toulouse, 140–41
Potatoes
    Rode Esterling Potatoes, Heirloom Tomato
      Salad and Tapenade with, 86–87
P-Patches, 87–88
Prawns
    in Seattle Cioppino, 60–61
    See also Shrimp
Preserving, 200–1
Priestess, The, 227
Pudding
    Gateau de Riz Façon Grand-Mère
      (Old-Fashioned Rice Pudding), 208–9
    See also Bread pudding
Pumpkin
    Fall Pumpkin and Squash Bisque, 69
    Pumpkin Poblano Tamales, Grilled Pork with,
      168–69
Punch
    Hawaiian Punch, 228
    Rain City Punch, 236
"Putting Foods Up," 200–1

R

Raga Cuisine of India
    Malai Kebab, 104
    Rice Pulao, 98
    Spicy Vegetable Fritters, 16
Rain City Punch, 236

Raita Salad, for Tequila-Cured Gravlax Salmon, 40–41

Raspberries

Raspberry and Peach Shortcakes with Honey Whipped Cream, 210–11

Ray's Boathouse

Crab Cakes with Ancho Chile Mayonnaise, 102–3

Cumin-Seared Columbia River Sturgeon, 144

Razor clams

about, 8

Razor Clams with Brown Butter and Salsify Chips, 6–7

Reducing liquids, 163

Rémoulade

Smoked Trout Rémoulade, 4–5

Restaurant Zoë

Grilled Salmon with Lentils and Brown Butter Balsamic Vinaigrette, 112

Priestess. The, 227

Scallop and Shrimp Seviche with Cilantro Oil, 12–13

Zoë Cocktail, 233

Rice

Gateau de Riz Façon Grand-Mère (Old-Fashioned Rice Pudding), 208–9

Paella, 156–57

Rice Pulao, 98

Smoked Turkey, Brown Rice, and Vegetable Salad in Creamy Soy-Balsamic Dressing, 80–81

Rose hips

Pear and Rose Hip Sorbet, 182

Rosemary

Lemon Rosemary Biscotti, 218–19

Pan-Fried Mussels on Rosemary Skewers, 32–33

Rosemary Lemonade, 238

Rover's

Chilled Cucumber Soup, 64–65

Wild Mushroom Terrine with Goat Cheese Caillé and Berry Vinaigrette, 42–43

Roy's

Asian Barbecue Beef Triangles with a Tropical Fruit Salsa, 10–11

Baked Hawaii, 214–15

Thai Basil–Seared Mahimahi with Red Curry Lobster Essence, 160–61

S

Salad, 70–87

Bread Salad, Herb Roasted Chicken and, 70–71

Caesar for Two, 79

Cameo Apple Salad with Treviso, Oregon Blue Cheese, and Cider Vinaigrette, 74

Dungeness Crab with Red Radishes and Braeburn Apples, 84

fennel salad, with Old Chatham Camembert with Pear and Dried Cherry Chutney, 190–91

Heirloom Tomato Salad with Rode Esterling Potatoes and Tapenade, 86–87

herb salads, 77–78

Local Garden Greens with Asian Pears and Five-Spice Glazed Walnuts, 72–73

Orange and Fennel Salad with Sicilian Olives and Pecorino Romano Shavings, 75

Pear and Herb Salad, Ahi Tuna Tartare with, 24–25

Raita Salad, for Tequila-Cured Gravlax Salmon, 40–41

Roasted Pepper and Grilled Asparagus Salad, 82

Smoked Turkey, Brown Rice, and Vegetable Salad in Creamy Soy-Balsamic Dressing, 80–81

Yakima Cherry, Walla Walla Sweet Onion, and Basil Salad with Balsamic Vinaigrette, 85

Salad dressing

Anjou Pear Dressing, for Local Garden Greens with Asian Pears and Five-Spice Glazed Walnuts, 72–73

for Caesar for Two, 79

Creamy Soy-Balsamic Dressing, for Smoked Turkey, Brown Rice, and Vegetable Salad, 80–81

Horseradish Cream, for Avocado Carpaccio with Radish and Herb Salad, 76

See also Vinaigrette

"Salmon," 132–33

Salmon

about, 132–33

Alder-Barbecued King Salmon with Fennel and Mint, 101

Grilled Salmon with Lentils and Brown Butter
Balsamic Vinaigrette, 112–13
Kippered Salmon and Asparagus Bread
Pudding, 46–47
Salmon con Tamarindo, 130–31
in Seattle Cioppino, 60–61
Steamed King Salmon on Hungarian Paprika
Sauerkraut, 153
Tequila-Cured Gravlax Salmon, 40–41
Salsa
Coconut Ginger Salsa, for Coconut Curried
Lamb Shanks, 128–29
Salsa Amarilla, 22–23
Salsa Roja, 22–23
Spicy Cilantro Salsa, for Corn Chowder with
Dungeness Crab, 56–57
Tomato and Olive Salsa, for Bruschetta Steak
Sandwiches, 108–9
Tropical Fruit Salsa, for Asian Barbecue Beef
Triangles, 10–11
Salsify Chips, 6–7
Salty's on Alki
Absolut Mandarin Martini, 223
Grilled Ahi in Licorice Root "Tea" with
Braised Red Cabbage, 120–21
Italian Caramel Apple, 234
Sandwiches
Bruschetta Steak Sandwiches, 108–9
Santa Fe Café
Artichoke Ramekins, 38
Cadillac Margarita, 224
Sardines
Spaghetti con le Sarde (Spaghetti with
Sardines), 110–11
Sauces
Ancho Chile Sauce, for Cumin-Seared
Columbia River Sturgeon, 144–45
Asian Barbecue Sauce, for Asian Barbecue
Beef Triangles with a Tropical Fruit Salsa, 10–11
for Bananas Foster, 188–89
Blueberry-Port Sauce, Honey-Chèvre
Cheesecake with, 198–99
Caldillo Sauce, for Salmon con Tamarindo,
130–31
Chambord Berry Sauce, for Baked Hawaii,
214–15
Cilantro Hollandaise, for Ahi Tuna, 24–25

Green Chile Sauce, Grilled Pork with
Pumpkin Poblano Tamales and, 168–69
Jack Daniel's Sauce, for Pan-Fried Oysters, 125
Muscadet Wine Sauce, for Pan-Seared Duck
Breast, 116–17
Red Curry Lobster Essence, for Thai Basil-
Seared Mahimahi, 160–61
Sardine Sauce, for Spaghetti con le Sarde
(Spaghetti with Sardines), 110–11
Smoked Trout Rémoulade, 4–5
Spicy Red Pepper Sauce, Lemongrass Rubbed
Filet with Braised Short Ribs and, 146–47
Teriyaki Sauce, for Steak Teriyaki, 134–35
See also Beurre blanc; Chutney; Dips and
spreads; Mayonnaise; Salsa; Tapenade
Sausage
in Paella, 156–57
Saucisse de Toulouse, 140–41
Sausage and Lentil Soup, 63
Sazerac
Honey Peach Julep, 232
Strawberry Spice and Everything Nice, 225
Scallops
Scallop and Shrimp Seviche with Cilantro Oil,
12–13
Seafood/shellfish
Bahia Mussels, 17
Cataplana Mussels, 9
clams, about, 7–8
Corn Chowder with Dungeness Crab, 56–57
Crab Cakes with Ancho Chile Mayonnaise,
102–3
Creole Shrimp with Two Salsas, 22–23
Dungeness crab, about, 57
Dungeness Crab with Red Radishes and
Braeburn Apples, 84
Geoduck Batayaki, 36–37
Jalapeño Mussels, 49
mussels, about, 7–8
in Paella, 156–57
Pan-Fried Mussels on Rosemary Skewers, 32–33
Pan-Fried Oysters with Jack Daniel's
Sauce, 125
Razor Clams with Brown Butter and Salsify
Chips, 6–7
Scallop and Shrimp Seviche with Cilantro Oil,
12–13
Seafood Chowder, 68

Seattle Cioppino, 60–61
Steamed Clams, 39
See also Fish
Seattle Tilth, 87
Seviche
Scallop and Shrimp Seviche with Cilantro Oil, 12–13
Shellfish. *See* Seafood/shellfish
Shiso
Savory Nectarine and Shiso Soup, 59
Shortcake
Raspberry and Peach Shortcakes with Honey Whipped Cream, 210–11
Shrimp
Creole Shrimp with Two Salsas, 22–23
Scallop and Shrimp Seviche with Cilantro Oil, 12–13
in Seafood Chowder, 68
in Seattle Cioppino, 60–61
Side dishes, 89–98
Balsamic Roasted Figs, 137
Fresh Roasted Corn with Lime and Chile, 93
Granny Smith Apple Bread Pudding, 89
Gratin de Chou-fleur (Cauliflower Gratin), 90–91
Kale and Tomato Gratin, 97
Red Kuri Squash and Pear Timbales, 94–95
Rice Pulao, 98
Sichuan Green Beans, 92
Silver Rocket, 229
Simple syrup, 225
Six Degrees
Raspberry and Peach Shortcakes with Honey Whipped Cream, 210–11
Smoked foods, 19
Sorbet
Earl Grey Sorbet, 213
Pear and Rose Hip Sorbet, 182
See also Ice cream
Soufflé cake
Chocolate Chai Tea Soufflé Cake, 202–3
Soup, 55–69
Chilled Cucumber Soup with Smoked Sturgeon and Curry Oil, 64–65
Corn Chowder with Dungeness Crab, 56–57
Fall Pumpkin and Squash Bisque, 69
Hungarian Mushroom Soup, 62

Nettle Soup, 66
Sausage and Lentil Soup, 63
Savory Nectarine and Shiso Soup, 59
Seafood Chowder, 68
Seattle Cioppino, 60–61
Swiss Leek, Oat, and Smoked Chicken Soup, 58
Tom Kah Gai, 55
Soy-Balsamic Dressing, for Smoked Turkey, Brown Rice, and Vegetable Salad, 80–81
Spaghetti con le Sarde (Spaghetti with Sardines), 110–11
Spinach
Spinach Sauté, for Baked Oysters with Beurre Blanc, 28–29
Spiral cutter, 163
Sponge cake, for Hawaiian-Style Coconut Cake, 194–95
Spoon Cheesecake, 179
Spreads. *See* Dips and spreads; Tapenade
Spring rolls, Vietnamese, 50–51
Squash
cooking, 96
Fall Pumpkin and Squash Bisque, 69
in Orecchiette with Fall Vegetables, 118–19
Red Kuri Squash and Pear Timbales, 94–95
in Salsa Amarilla, for Creole Shrimp, 22–23
seeds, toasting, 96
winter, 95–96
Squid
Squid in Their Own Ink, 44–45
Steelhead
Pan-Seared Steelhead with Black Bean Vinaigrette, 14–15
Still Life in Fremont Coffeehouse
Lemon Rosemary Biscotti, 218–19
Smoked Turkey, Brown Rice, and Vegetable Salad in Creamy-Soy Balsamic Dressing, 80–81
"Stinging Nettles," 67
Strawberries
Strawberry Spice and Everything Nice, 225
Sturgeon
Cumin-Seared Columbia River Sturgeon, 144–45
Chilled Cucumber Soup with Smoked Sturgeon and Curry Oil, 64–65

T

Tamales
  Pumpkin Poblano Tamales, Grilled Pork with, 168–69
Tapenade
  Heirloom Tomato Salad with Rode Esterling Potatoes and, 86–87
Tarts
  Apricot, Rose, and Saffron Tart, 196–97
  Four-Onion Tart, 20–21
  Pinchineta (Almond Tart), 216–17
Tea
  Chocolate Chai Tea Soufflé Cake, 202–3
  Earl Grey Sorbet, 213
Teriyaki Sauce, for Steak Teriyaki, 134–35
Terrine
  Wild Mushroom Terrine with Goat Cheese Caillé and Berry Vinaigrette, 42–43
  See also Pâté
Thiebu Djen (Parsley-Stuffed Halibut with Vegetables and Rice), 138–39
Timbales
  Red Kuri Squash and Pear Timbales, 94–95
Tofu
  Plig King Tofu, 107
Tom Kah Gai, 55
Tomatillos
  in Green Chile Sauce, Grilled Pork with Pumpkin Poblano Tamales and, 168–69
Tomatoes
  in Caldillo Sauce, for Salmon con Tamarindo, 130–31
  Heirloom Tomato Salad with Rode Esterling Potatoes and Tapenade, 86–87
  Heirloom Tomato Vinaigrette, for Cumin-Seared Columbia River Sturgeon, 144–45
  Kale and Tomato Gratin, 97
  Tomato and Olive Salsa, for Bruschetta Steak Sandwiches, 108–9
Trout
  Smoked Trout Rémoulade, Walla Walla Onion Pancakes with, 4–5
Tulio
  Orecchiette with Fall Vegetables, 118–19
  Roasted Chicken with Caramelized Garlic and Sage, 143
  Spoon Cheesecake, 179

Tuna
  Ahi Tuna Tartare with Hazelnuts, Shaved Pear Salad, and Cilantro Hollandaise, 24–25
  Grilled Ahi in Licorice Root "Tea" with Braised Red Cabbage, 120–21
Turkey
  Smoked Turkey, Brown Rice, and Vegetable Salad in Creamy Soy-Balsamic Dressing, 80–81
Turnips
  in Thiebu Djen (Parsley-Stuffed Halibut with Vegetables and Rice), 138–39

U

Ultraviolet Martini, 239
Union Square Grill
  Caesar for Two, 79
  Herb Roasted Chicken and Bread Salad, 70–71

V

Vegetables
  Fresh Roasted Corn with Lime and Chile, 93
  Gratin de Chou-fleur (Cauliflower Gratin), 90–91
  Kale and Tomato Gratin, 97
  Orecchiette with Fall Vegetables, 118–19
  Plig King Tofu, 107
  Sichuan Green Beans, 92
  Smoked Turkey, Brown Rice, and Vegetable Salad in Creamy Soy-Balsamic Dressing, 80–81
  Spicy Vegetable Fritters, 16
  Tagliatelle of Vegetables, Alaskan Halibut with, 166–67
  Thiebu Djen (Parsley-Stuffed Halibut with Vegetables and Rice), 138–39
  See also Vegetarian dishes; individual entries
Vegetarian dishes
  Artichoke Ramekins, 38
  Avocado Carpaccio with Radish and Herb Salad, 76
  Cameo Apple Salad with Treviso, Oregon Blue Cheese, and Cider Vinaigrette, 74
  Four-Onion Tart, 20–21
  Fresh Roasted Corn with Lime and Chile, 93
  Granny Smith Apple Bread Pudding, 89

Gratin de Chou-fleur (Cauliflower Gratin), 90–91

Kale and Tomato Gratin, 97

Local Garden Greens with Asian Pears and Five-Spice Glazed Walnuts, 72

Muhammara, 26

Orange and Fennel Salad with Sicilian Olives and Pecorino Romano Shavings, 75

Orecchiette with Fall Vegetables, 118–19

Plig King Tofu, 107

Pumpkin Poblano Tamales, 168–69

Red Kuri Squash and Pear Timbales, 94–95

Rice Pulao, 97

Roasted Pepper and Grilled Asparagus Salad, 82

Spicy Polenta with Braised Fennel, Olives, and Goat Cheese, 136–37

Spicy Vegetable Fritters, 16

Spring Pea Flan, 172–73

Tuscan White Bean and Rosemary Spread, 27

Wild Mushroom Terrine with Goat Cheese Caillé and Berry Vinaigrette, 42–43

Yakima Cherry, Walla Walla Sweet Onion, and Basil Salad with Balsamic Vinaigrette, 85

Vinaigrette

Balsamic Vinaigrette, for Yakima Cherry, Walla Walla Sweet Onion, and Basil Salad, 85

Berry Vinaigrette, Wild Mushroom Terrine with, 42–43

Black Bean Vinaigrette, Pan-Seared Steelhead with, 14–15

Brown Butter Balsamic Vinaigrette, Grilled Salmon with Lentils and, 112–13

Cider Vinaigrette, Cameo Apple Salad with Treviso, Oregon Blue Cheese, and, 74

Heirloom Tomato Vinaigrette, for Cumin-Seared Columbia River Sturgeon, 144–45

Smoked Paprika Vinaigrette, Pan-Seared Alaskan Cod with Green Beans, Niçoise Olives, and, 154–55

See also Salad dressing

Vinegar

cherry vinegar, 123

W

Walnuts

Five-Spice Glazed Walnuts, Local Garden Greens with Asian Pears and, 72–73

Waterfront

Chocolate Chai Tea Soufflé Cake, 202–3

Kasu Black Cod, 174–75

Rain City Punch, 236

Watermelon Kazi, 240

Wild Ginger

Sichuan Green Beans, 92

Wine

Blueberry-Port Sauce, Honey-Chèvre Cheesecake with, 198–99

Muscadet Wine Sauce, for Pan-Seared Duck Breast, 116–17

"Wonderful Winter Squash," 95–96

"Wood Cookery," 19

X–Y–Z

Yakima Grill

Grilled Pork with Pumpkin Poblano Tamales and Green Chile Sauce, 168–69

Yarrow Bay Beach Café

Hungarian Mushroom Soup, 62

Vietnamese Spring Rolls, 50–51

Yassa au Poulet (Chicken in Onion-Mustard Sauce), 171

Zoë Cocktail, 233

Zucchini

in Orecchiette with Fall Vegetables, 118–19

in Spicy Vegetable Fritters, 16

Savor the Flavors of the Northwest

The Northwest Best Places® Cookbook
Recipes from the Outstanding Restaurants and Inns of Washington, Oregon, and British Columbia
Cynthia Nims and Lori McKean
125 Recipes • $16.95

The Food Lover's Guide to Seattle
Katy Calcott
More than 200 establishments • $16.95

Northwest Berry Cookbook
Finding, Growing, and Cooking with Berries Year-Round
Kathleen Desmond Stang
More than 40 recipes • $14.95

Cooking with Artisan Bread
Using Rustic Loaves for Perfect Crostini, Panini, Bruschetta, Flavorful Stuffings, and Inventive Main Courses
Gwenyth Bassetti and Jean Galton
More than 40 recipes • $15.95

The Northwest Essentials Cookbook
Cooking with the Ingredients That Define a Regional Cuisine
Greg Atkinson
150 recipes • $19.95

West Coast Seafood
The Complete Cookbook
Jay Harlow
250 recipes • $23.95

SASQUATCH BOOKS
SEATTLE

Available wherever fine books are sold.
For a complete list of Sasquatch books, call 800-775-0817 for a copy of our catalog.

ABOUT THE AUTHORS

Cynthia C. Nims is a lifelong Northwesterner who reveled in growing up surrounded by great food—both in her mother's kitchen and exploring the region with her family. She holds the Grand Diplome d'Etudes Culinaires from La Varenne cooking school in France, where she worked on numerous cookbooks with the school's president, Anne Willan, including the Look & Cook series. After six years as the editor of *Simply Seafood* magazine, Nims is currently food editor of *Seattle Magazine,* a cookbook author and editor, and freelance food writer. She is the author of the bestselling *Northwest Best Places Cookbook* and the *Northern California Best Places Cookbook.*

Kathy Casey is celebrated for paving the way for the emergence of Northwest cuisine on a national level. She was hailed as an "inventor of dishes that dazzle the eye and the palate" by Craig Claiborne in the *New York Times.* Casey received her first acclaim as Executive Chef at Fullers, where *Food & Wine* magazine named her as one of the 25 "hot new American chefs." She now runs her own company, Kathy Casey Food Studios, which focuses on delicious concepts and menu development for restaurants nationally, and also has cooking classes open to the public. Casey also writes a feature column, "Dishing," which appears monthly in the *Seattle Times.* She is the author of *Pacific Northwest: The Beautiful Cookbook* and *Kathy Casey Cooks Volume I.*